FAMILIES IN THE CHURCH:
A PROTESTANT SURVEY

FAMILIES IN THE CHURCH: A PROTESTANT SURVEY

By ROY W. FAIRCHILD
and JOHN CHARLES WYNN

ASSOCIATION PRESS • NEW YORK

FAMILIES IN THE CHURCH: A PROTESTANT SURVEY

Association Press, 291 Broadway, New York 7, N.Y.

Library of Congress catalog card number: 61-7109

Printed in the United States of America
By American Book–Stratford Press, Inc.

Contents

APPENDICES

Preface

SOME CURIOSITY ALWAYS SEEMS to arise about how two authors can write one book. The process is not really complicated; it works out by a simple division of labor through the relationship between two colleagues. In this case we had been accustomed to working together over a period of years. When it came to writing this book, we sat down and discussed thoroughly the contents and purpose of the book and then shared in its responsibility. Each of us accepted the assignment of outlining in detail a number of chapters. These outlines we traded then for criticism and alteration. Next we divided responsibility for the first draft of each chapter based upon these outlines; and at the end of the draft we took each other's work, edited it, and altered it after conference and study. Subsequently, through revision and rewriting, our separate contributions became so intermixed that sometimes it is now impossible for us to know who has written a specific section.

This kind of working together had begun in 1956 at the Board of Christian Education of the now United Presbyterian Church in the United States of America. At that time we were the staff personnel of the Office of Family Education Research; and we were charged with learning as much as possible about American Protestant families and their church relations, with particular detail about Presbyterian households and how the denomination might best relate to them in Christian education. To that Board, our colleagues there, and for that assignment we are profoundly grateful. The rich experience of working through that research design under their auspices led us into new studies and findings that proved of real value.

But our obligations stretch wider yet. We are likewise grateful to the Russell Sage Foundation for supplying additional funds and personnel to refine some subsequently designated data concerning parents, their occupations, education, and problems. The staff of the biweekly journal, *Presbyterian Life,* have been most helpful in assisting us to correlate statistical information about church families. Our debt of gratitude must also be extended to Dr. Merton Strommen of Lutheran Youth Research, to Rev. Oscar E. Feucht of the Lutheran Church, Missouri Synod, to Dr. Lauris Whitman and Miss Helen Spaulding of the Bureau of Research and Survey of the National Council of the Churches of Christ in the United States of America. More than four thousand persons made this study possible through hours of work and co-operation. Most of them remain anonymous; but their experiences and opinions from questionnaires and interviews enrich these pages. Others who organized or conducted interviews, who advised us in our task, worked beside us, and discussed research matters with us are appreciatively identified in the Appendices. To Dr. Everett Perry and the staff of the Office of Field Survey in the United Presbyterian Board of National Missions go our thanks for information about the communities in which churches of the sample are located. For special services in tabulation and classification we are indebted to Marilyn Fitting and Marilyn Houston. Nor are we unmindful of the generous provision of our respective schools, the San Francisco Theological Seminary and Colgate Rochester Divinity School, which made possible the time for us to write the pages that follow. A portion of the manuscript was read by Professors Arnold B. Come and J. A. Sanders, representing each of our schools, in that order, and from them came many helpful suggestions. An acknowledgment, vastly different from any of these, is the loving thanks we express to Verna M. Fairchild and Rachel L. Wynn who prepared the Index and Appendices, and assisted in counsel in many a decision about the book.

Although our inquiry had begun with a specific denominational group, the United Presbyterians, it was destined in time to become broadly Protestant. Our secondary research had delved into material about middle-class families in American life, regardless of church affiliation. Later we found ourselves in active consultation and comparison with other research studies concerning Baptists, Congregationalists, Episcopalians, Lutherans, Methodists, and others. By the time we had come to conceive the details of the book, this interest had taken us into the course of Reformation theology, the changing American family, and the common concerns of parents and their churches across the entire nation. Portions of the research study have been reported to the United Presbyterian Board of Christian Education; and some data of specific and confidential nature only to the Presbyterian program in that report are not included here. *Families in the Church: A Protestant Survey* therefore draws heavily upon the studies made under the auspices of the United Presbyterian Board of Christian Education, but branches well beyond them too.

Research as we see it can be neatly defined in the words of one consultant, Dr. David Saunders, as "commitment to an inquiry made without any axe to grind and with an open-minded willingness to accept any result that may emerge within the limitations of the design used." The purpose of this sort of unprejudiced inquiry has been to lay open a comprehensive description of the contemporary Protestant family in America, ask into their relationships at home and in church, seeking to understand more fully something of the pattern of pastoral ministry to families, and the direction in which home-church relationships might be expected to move. We were mindful of the laconic word of another research consultant who had written:

> To those who do not take it entirely for granted, the notion of family research suggests a large measure of temerity. To imagine that principles new and worthwhile can be ascertained about phenomena so familiar and so exhaustively scrutinized for millennia is the epitome of ambition. Depending upon how seriously they are taken, aspirations so grand could afford material for tragedy or comedy.*

Everyone has come from a family. Everyone has enough experience with family life to qualify in some sense as an expert on the subject. But the "temerity" with which we approach the subject is founded upon the conviction that the very universality of the subject often obscures from us its dynamic meanings in depth. And the considerable puzzlement with which specialists in social psychology and kindred fields now regard the family, to say nothing of the confusion of the churches, illustrates that we know far less about this field than in our closeness to it we had supposed. Churches, as a matter of fact, are confessing that they are in a quandary about the family and its place in their parish life.

* Nelson N. Foote, "The Appraisal of Family Research," *Marriage and Family Living,* Vol. XIX, No. 1, Feb., 1957, p. 92.

What only a few years ago they were certain they knew about church-home relations often appears today to be unsure and confused.

We make no claims here to have exhausted the subject or even all the studies relevant to our own segment of the subject of the Christian family. We sample the most useful materials and findings for an audience we picture as clergymen, directors of religious education, church parents, and seminarians. However, a description of the research methodology is given in enough detail, we hope, to satisfy the curiosity of the social scientist. It is our prayer that the reader will discover, by means of this stimulus, channels for approaching and understanding the family and ways of communicating the gospel to them.

ROY W. FAIRCHILD and J. C. WYNN

PART ONE

PROTESTANT HERITAGE AND THE CHANGING FAMILY

- **The Church and the Family**
- **Churches Assess Family Influence**
- **The Family in Crisis**
- **Research as a New Church Tool**
- **Description of the Research Project**

1

Introduction

There is a widely accepted current canard that all families are pretty much alike. This prejudicial concept presupposes that the typical suburban household we meet in the pages of slick magazines (both church and secular) is the only one that matters. Invariably the parents are in their midthirties; they have two or three well-dressed children, a station wagon in the driveway, and a twenty-year mortgage on their house. Of the numerous other types of families within our churches this takes no account: Negro households living in the tension-fraught slum area of a large city; a large family from a ranch in South Dakota; an older couple whose youngest child, the last still at home, is about to graduate from high school. Too many fallacious and misguided denominational programs in family education have been written and distributed because the real family constituency of the churches had been misconceived. But when we begin to examine the facts objectively, when we consider the numerous families in inner-city churches that have no adult male living with them, or when we remind ourselves of childless couples still awaiting the birth of a first child, when we note the proportion of working mothers away from home, then the fallacy of this stereotyped family in the magazines is exposed.

Shattered with that illusion is its correlative fable that a church can treat all families alike. The time has long since passed (if indeed it ever did exist) when denominations could reach all their families with an identical program anywhere in the nation. Families differ widely, as do pastors, parishes, areas of the country, and sections of our cities. To be sure, the family may be a station wagon load of five from suburbia. In this research study, we very frequently encounter them just that way. But even they, we were to find, have notable distinctions that prevent us from assuming they are as alike as two houses in Levittown.

The Church and the Family

The family is to be understood here as persons in relationship through blood, marriage, or adoption who live under the same roof or who share a common name. This family can be an extension of the life of the church, a kind of *ecclesia domestica* or what the Scriptures call "the church in your house." In this sense, the family is part of the fellowship of believers; and the church of Jesus Christ is to be found in their midst.

Because of prevailing ambiguity in the understanding of what is meant by the church and what is meant by the family, we cannot go forward without a fresh look at these terms. It is incumbent upon us to describe the relationships between church and family; but these terms mean many things to many people. Not a few of our respondents, in this research study, for instance, saw the church primarily, sometimes exclusively, in terms of an institution—an organization to belong to, to support, to attend, and to promote. This concept shows through the replies that came from clergymen as well as from the parents. Likewise a sizable group—both in this research sampling and beyond—tend to regard the family with an almost idolizing stance, with a nearly reverent concern for "togetherness," and a primary commitment that places the family beyond any other claim upon their loyalty.

The church, as we understand it, is certainly represented as an institution. But it is far more than that. The church is not limited to an institution, to a building, to a congregation, or to a denomination; it has assets beyond those of "the church visible." Rather it is what the New Testament shows it to be: a body of believers brought together by the call of God. Their center and head is Christ; and the church is found wherever faith in Jesus Christ is preached, believed, and carried into action.

The family, as we understand it, is grossly caricatured when regarded as an idol; for the Bible plainly sets the kingdom of God squarely before us, and we are reminded that it takes rightful precedence before family and other relationships. If the church, as our people come to know it, can be for them only an institution, they will hardly comprehend its true meaning in such a context. The relationship between church and family is peculiarly reversed when the church seems to us to be just another institution; for in this guise it may very well have to depend upon families for *its* own salvation. Our respondents, as subsequent chapters show, sometimes suffered from this very misunderstanding.

Still and all, it was the church with all its problems and the family with all its misunderstandings that prompted our study. And it was the church in its institutional cloak that had authorized this investigation of that often unstable, yet wondrously warm and influential configuration we know as the family.

Churches Assess Family Influence

In today's world, the church which undertakes its parish program without reference to the family background and connections of its members finds itself irrelevant and necessarily limited. It must be admitted, however, that there are such churches, and that their ministry suffers for this omission. It could hardly be otherwise; for the family remains the primary nurturing group for many aspects of the individual's life. This nurturing influence is formative not just for his family of orientation from which he comes, but even for his family of procreation wherein he becomes a parent.

Family relationships play their powerful role in helping us to form images of the world about us, of other persons around us, and not least of ourselves. The precepts of the family coupled with their living example impress a child when he is as plastic as he ever will be. Both verbal and nonverbal communication (and the family specializes in the latter) contribute heavily to the impressions on any young life. Even fleeting references to values and prejudices are repeated so often that they are impressed upon young minds at an early age. Parents play a dominant role from the outset whether their communication be conscious or unconscious. Their influence is not alone, but is backed up by the matrix of numerous intrafamily relationships: brother, sister, grandparent, and others. As Willard Waller and Reuben Hill have put it:

> The family is important in the life of the individual because it gets him first, keeps him longest, is his major source of cultural imperatives, and prescribes them with emotional finality. It is im-

portant because it not only satisfies the wishes of the individual but it is instrumental in shaping those wishes into a form which only the family can satisfy. In our society the family furnishes the basic environment for personality, and in its larger social aspects.*[1]

In its own distinct way, the family serves as an educational institution without peer throughout our culture. It is indeed, as Martin Luther named it, "a school for living." But the educational process of the home is seldom instruction as such; it is nearly always in terms of nurture. The home specializes in informal education. The nurturing process is found in the ordinary daily life of the home. It begins with supplying the baby's physical needs, and continues as members of the family communicate their way of life, their bases for making decisions, and their interpretation of values. It is here, in fact, that the rudimentary beginnings of faith are to be located: an understanding of what love is, of forgiveness, of relationships with persons, and gradually a relationship with God. These grow out of home life. Though it is possible to overestimate the influence of the family (and exaggerated claims have been made for its impact particularly during the early years of life), churches whose programs of Christian nurture fail to take realistic account of the power in family relationships cannot speak relevantly to contemporary mankind.

Protestantism has become alert to empirical discoveries regarding the effect of the home upon persons who live within it. The "language of relationships" in this most fully engaged, most intimate, of all relationships begins to affect the character, structure and self-image of the child long before he can engage the culture outside the home through language and concepts. As the late Lewis J. Sherrill summarized the findings of the personality sciences for us: "The self is formed in relationship with others. If it becomes de-formed, it becomes so in its relationships. If it is re-formed or trans-formed, that too will be in relationships."[2] Sigmund Freud who initiated the systematic study of family dynamics, carried this proposition one step further when he claimed not only that early family relations deeply affect character, but that one's perception of his family life colors also reactions to community life as well. In a sense, all institutional relationships are the "family writ large"; and reactions to father and mother figures, and brother and sister "colleagues," reactivate for the adult the feeling tone of the biological family experience. The church, even with its tongue-in-cheek attitude toward psychoanalysis, has often demonstrated this in-

* All numbered notes appear at the end of the chapter.

sight in its appropriation of family appellations for its clergy and institutional life.

Carl Jung, at this particular point following Freud, affirms the present longing in the psyche for a home in a homeless world: "The further away and the more unreal the personal mother is, the deeper the . . . longing to awaken the eternal image of the mother, through which everything . . . sheltering, nourishing and helpful assumes for us the maternal figure, from the *alma mater* of the university to the personification of towns, countries, sciences, and ideals."[3] Consciously or unconsciously then, the church has focused on the home and has received (and solicited) both theological and psychological support to do so. Peter Berger contends that "the liaison of hearth and altar is accompanied by a full-blown ideology."[4]

By and large, the churches have not been prompt to appropriate the more dynamic interpretations of family life. In spite of scriptural leads,[5] the voices of prophetic churchmen as long ago as the nineteenth century's Horace Bushnell,[6] and current understanding of social psychology, numerous clergymen and not a few denominational bodies often ignore these leads. The result, evidence shows, can be unfortunate as when the institutional church views the individual *versus* his family or even exploits the family for ecclesiastical ends. Moreover, when churches misunderstand their own responsibilities in augmenting family nurture, the division of labor between church and home becomes confused; and this is detrimental to education. Though it is true that church and family are mutually dependent in the task of Christian education, and that the whole mission of the community of faith cannot be sliced into neat sections for apportionment to one or the other, there are areas in which each makes a major contribution. The parish church, to be sure, is at times a nurturing group; but generally it must concentrate on the more formal aspects of education because of its historical obligation to teach doctrine. The home, on the other hand, does not so much teach as it nurtures; its educational thrust is seldom obvious, often goes unnoticed.

The Family in Crisis

On every side we are reminded that the American family has moved into crisis. Seen most tragically in the current divorce rate, the crisis is also underlined by other factors: the sexual revolution with its alarming laxity of sexual mores publicized by Alfred Kinsey, Pitrim Sorokin, and others, the breakdown of family discipline and increased juvenile delinquency, the sharp rise in illegitimate births, and the indication (so difficult to authenticate) of increasing illegal abortion. This critical phase in American family development is all too easily demonstrated.

When eighteen prominent students of family life were invited to submit a list of the outstanding changes that had occurred in family life in recent times, the following were mentioned by half or more of them: the increasing divorce rate, wider diffusion of birth control and/or decline in family size, decline in the authority of husbands and fathers, increase in sexual intercourse apart from marriage, increase in the number of wives working for pay, increasing individualism and freedom of family members, increasing transfer of protective functions from family to state, decline of religious behavior in marriage and family.[7] The church is painfully aware of the crisis because every aspect of it has somewhere touched parish life and pastoral ministry. Clergy are the more aware of it because of their inability to help solve some of the amazingly complicated and deep problems suffered by parishioners' families. Concerned that canon laws in regard to divorce and remarriage are hard to enforce, that pronouncements against interfaith marriage are frequently ignored, that reiteration of standards in sexual ethics makes so little impact, the church is seeking new directions in family education. Frankly bewildered that many families no longer strive to fulfill Christian ideals as promulgated by the denominations, the churches' leadership has turned increasingly to research to ask why, and how deeply, the crisis reaches into church families, and what can be done about it.

Research as a New Church Tool

Churches have turned to the systematic uses of research study only in recent years. This they have done for a quite practical reason: answers are required for difficult questions that cannot be settled in the traditional style of executive decision and conference, and from the repository of ecclesiastical experience. New riddles for which the churches have no ready precedent keep turning up: quandaries about where to place new church buildings to meet mobile populations, about inner-city parish challenges, about rapid social change and its effect upon church work. Church programing has become too expensive to invest hundreds of thousands, even millions, of dollars in new developments without learning in advance what are the probabilities of their acceptance and feasibility. In the United Presbyterian Church, it was important for us to learn what our family constituency was really like, by what values they actually lived, what their needs were, how the church might address itself to those needs, what patterns existed in church-family relations, what readiness existed for new programs in family education. We were not alone.[8] There have been other research studies into the family situation of church members conducted by the Lutheran Church, Missouri Synod,[9] into the problems of marriage and divorce by the United Church of Canada,[10] into practices and standards of young people conducted by six Lutheran bodies: the American, Augustana, Evangelical, Missouri, United Evangelical, and the Free synods.[11] Likewise the National Council of Churches carries on continuous research investigations into such questions as the relationships between church school children and their parents,[12] and the leisure-time activities of children and their families.[13] In addition, the Methodist Church has conducted an informal study of adults concerning family life attitudes[14]; the Protestant Episcopal Church has held a series of recorded interviews with parents in parishes[15]; and the Presbyterian Church in the United States has tabulated a questionnaire from pastors on their family ministry.[16]

Each of these various groups had addressed itself to the family problem as they viewed it. Something of the same underlying perplexity prompts each such research project (and there are others in process) because the American family in its current crisis presents disparate problems to which the churches must address themselves anew. Unless they do, the historic link between church and family—wherein the church understands itself to live partly through the homes of the faithful, and the families in turn look to the community of faith for guidance—will have been weakened.

Description of the Research Project

The research design that culminated in the findings of this book was a complex of questionnaires, interviews, consultations, and secondary studies. At the beginning, our technique was to search out those relevant data already documented or just being discovered about family life in the contemporary American scene. Such material is available in dissertations, books, scholarly journals, unpublished papers recorded on microfilm, and so on. This secondary research provided a background of information on already extant data that need not be searched out anew. Thus was made possible a series of working papers that serve as background to the primary research subsequently developed.

Because new family education for churches would probably be introduced through the clergy, it being a *sine qua non* of Protestant practice that the pastor holds the key to parish program, it was imperative to know many things about the clergy themselves, their own family life, and their ministry to the families of their particular churches. This aspect is discussed more fully in Chapter 7.

In order to tap the family life attitudes of parents, group interviews were held in 66 different churches across the nation. And by this method 845 families were reached. Fifty-four professionally trained interviewers conducted these sessions with parents; and their work turned up a veritable mine of material on the major conflicts and problems of the families, their attitudes in parent-child relationships, their satisfactions and goals, and their participation patterns in church life. Chapters 5 and 6 open these findings and analyze the results.

Both at these group interviews and on a number of other occasions where parents were present, such as couples' clubs, a questionnaire consisting of 25 questions was administered. Through this we learned more about the identification of these church families, their occupational status, number of children, reading habits, attitudes toward the church and its educational efforts, what goes wrong in their relationships, and where they need additional help. One thousand such questionnaires were tabulated.

But the church measures its ministry by the biblical record of revelation, and not just in the empirical data of its contemporary life. A theological inquiry was also essential to set this research design, if possible, within the framework of biblical theology. To that end a consultative conference of twenty ranking theologians was called together to work at a Protestant theological understanding of family life.[17] The papers presented for discussion and the topics assigned for deliberation at that conference constituted the first step in a series of studies later set forth in working papers addressed to theological subjects. This concern is traced further in Chapters 3 and 4.

The church, of course, cannot assume that it is the only agency that relates to family life or that it has a clear and exclusive channel through which to address families. An interdisciplinary approach to family education and counseling that would involve not only pastors but also psychiatrists, psychologists, teachers, writers, social workers, and government officials was clearly called for. Some twenty-six of these persons were interviewed to sample opinion on how a division of labor could be worked out between church and community to dent this vast project of family education. Their valuable insights enrich Part Two of this study.[18]

In addition, pilot experiments in the training of pastors for family counseling, in leadership education for parents' groups, and in family camping techniques were inaugurated in order to point the way for other experiments in "action research."

Safeguards and checks had to be built into the research design to ensure its reliability and validity. Research consultants were retained in the beginning to countercheck the design, later to aid in the refinement of statistics and in the interpretation of data. Our findings were checked against other research data in the cognate fields of sociology and psychology. The questionnaires were designed for internal consistency with questions that supplemented each other, with basic variables that were cross-tabulated in the statistical analysis, and with a broad enough sampling to get a widely representative group of respondents. In addition, interviews were correlated with the questionnaires to augment answers and to supply dynamic interpretation that a questionnaire could not in itself produce. An independent testing service firm (Educational Testing Service, Princeton, New Jersey) was employed to tabulate the replies from pastors' questionnaires so as to deliver material as free as possible from bias. Further objectivity was obtained in the processes used: IBM punch card tabulation in the pastors' questionnaire, and Keysort punch card operations for the parents' instrument. Throughout the process, close contact was maintained with other research organizations and projects to provide correctives and criticism of our methods. The many safeguards taken resulted in what a team of disinterested experts characterized as a "highly reliable study" when they examined the summation and audited the data.[19]

The results of this study, together with some additional comparisons and interpretations, are discussed in Chapters 2 through 8.

NOTES

1. Willard Waller and Reuben Hill, *The Family: A Dynamic Interpretation,* p. 33. New York: The Dryden Press, Inc., 1951.
2. Lewis J. Sherrill, *The Gift of Power,* p. 45.*
3. Quoted in *Psychological Reflections—An Anthology from the Writings of C. G. Jung.* Edited by J. Jacobi, p. 88.
4. *The Christian Century,* Dec. 2, 1959. See "The Second Children's Crusade," pp. 1399–1400.
5. Deuteronomy, Ch. 6, for instance, is renowned for its understanding of the influence of family routine. It emphasizes how parents condition their children to spiritual values through conversation, ritual, and tradition all through the day—"when you sit in your house, when you

* Full documentation for all sources not supplied in the Notes is found under "List of Sources," which begins on page 283.

walk by the way, and when you lie down, and when you rise" (Deuteronomy 6:7b).

6. See Horace Bushnell, *Christian Nurture,* to trace his persuasive viewpoint against that of contemporary revivalists with their exaggerated stress on individual conversion. He noted that the child is so conditioned by family living in the Christian family that it ought never to be possible for him to recall a time when he was not a Christian.
7. W. F. Ogburn and M. F. Nimkoff, *Technology and the Changing Family,* pp. 5–7.
8. For an interesting and highly competent comparative study, see John L. Thomas, S.J., *The American Catholic Family.*
9. See Oscar E. Feucht *et al., Engagement and Marriage,* and *The Church and Sex Attitudes.* More volumes are in preparation.
10. The Commission on Christian Marriage and Divorce, United Church of Canada, has surveyed its clergy to ascertain their practices in premarriage guidance of couples. Rev. Frank P. Fidler is secretary of the Commission.
11. Merton Strommen *et al., Lutheran Youth Research,* has been published, 1960, in eight mimeographed volumes for limited circulation prior to book publication.
12. Helen F. Spaulding and David W. Will, "A Study of the Church Relationships of Parents of Children in the Elementary Division of the Church School," Bureau of Research and Survey, National Council of the Churches of Christ in the U.S.A., 1958.
13. Lauris B. Whitman and Helen F. Spaulding, "A Study of the Summertime Activities of Children in Relation to the Summer Program of the Churches," National Council of the Churches of Christ in the U.S.A., 1959.
14. Dr. Edward S. Staples headed up a survey soliciting opinion and experience from Methodist adult classes. These were tabulated and reported to the Methodist Family Life Conference of 1958, and published in "Faith, Freedom, and the Family," Methodist Board of Education.
15. Dr. David Hunter, National Council of the Protestant Episcopal Church directs the educational and curriculum work ("The Seabury Series") for which these depth interviews have been held.
16. A 1960 mail survey conducted by Dr. and Mrs. H. Kerr Taylor, codirectors of the Office of Family Education, Presbyterian Church in the United States.
17. See Appendix VI for listing of the members of this consultative theological conference.
18. Names of these interdisciplinary interviewees are listed in Appendix V.
19. See Appendix II for names of these research consultants.

- **Has Protestantism Overemphasized the Family?**
- **The Current Reaction to "Familism"**
- **Contemporary Iconoclasm Overstates Its Case**
- **Our Focus: the Protestant Middle-Class Family**
- **The Causes of Family Change Are Complex**
- **Shifts in Family Living Patterns of the American Middle Class**

2

The Changing Family: A Challenge to the Church

TOO MUCH CHURCH LITERATURE betrays a wish for today's families to remain just as they were in the 1890's, not so much for the sake of the families' health as for the convenience of ecclesiastical *modus operandi.* Having learned to address the home in traditional ways, churches may be reluctant to start anew and adapt their ministries to the ever-changing family, the nature of which they often scarcely grasp. Church bodies pronounce morbidly upon the "disintegration" of the modern home.[1] Is it possible that they reflect, in part, resentment that "family-oriented" materials and programs go unheeded in homes far removed from the sociologically uncomplicated farm home of a half century ago? Indeed, we cling nostalgically to that idealized family image and allow it to dominate both policies and program in many a Protestant denomination. The literature often assumes the patriarchal, one-job family in which children of all ages invariably find their deepest satisfactions and their most effective identifications. Yet currently in metropolitan areas the "member" of a family is frequently an individualized fragment rather than part of a unified team, especially if he is a teen-ager. James Peterson contends that in 1890 it might have been asked of a boy walking down the street, "Who's that boy?" And back the reply would come: "That's John Smith's son." Today his counterpart might be recognized as a star basketball player on the high school team, and a different query would be put: "What does his father do? I'm not sure I know him." Status today often derives from community and occupational groups rather than from family membership. (Indeed, these influences bear heavily upon life *within* the family with younger children, as will be noted later.) Yet the family retains a crucial place in the scheme of things which we ignore at our peril. We must seek to understand its important, though curtailed, contribution to our world.

Has Protestantism Overemphasized the Family?

If Protestantism still places its chief hope for religious nurture in the family, that veneration is understandable. For as the church studies her Bible, she discovers that we cannot understand the biblical message in its essence unless something is known existentially about marriage and family (analogies of which are used throughout the record). Nor can the nature of sex, marriage, and family be apprehended until we understand the nature of God's covenant with his people. Family and Bible being inseparable, the community of faith which relies upon the Bible for the clue to its life is plunged into family concerns. Even the doctrine of the Trinity finds the family metaphor indispensable. Further, as she practices infant baptism and dedication, Protestantism knows that in God's providence parents become an expression of the community of faith in the home to bring up their children in the "nurture and admonition of the Lord." The relationship of church and home is here affirmed clearly.

The Current Reaction to "Familism"

That the family can become (some would say *has* become) a new idolatry, is a hard accusation for the church to accept. Yet the evidence for this contention is available for all who would see. The protest of some modern churchmen is not unlike that of Jesus in his day when he castigated the kind of family loyalty that stood in opposition to concern for the Kingdom. Alert, socially informed clergymen, schooled in the Christian doctrine of man, have balked at an exaggerated familism both on ecclesiastical and scientific grounds. They have objected that family-centeredness has helped to confine the understanding of Christian ethics to personal relationships only, ignoring the great policy-making, social structures which influence so profoundly all institutions and persons within them. Admittedly, this has been a weakness of Protestantism.[2]

The effect of hyperfamilism in the church upon members of incomplete families has already been noted. What is not so apparent, however, is the effect of a family focus upon the form which the church takes in the world. The "local" church is still predominantly a parish in the nineteenth-century neighborhood sense. That parish may now be a locale where people play and sleep, but not where they work and not where the important social issues are decided. As Gayraud Wilmore has said, "The New Testament term 'ekklesia' did not restrict the structure of the early church nor should it predetermine the church today when the cultural situation is exceedingly more mobile and complex than it was in the time of Paul and Barnabas. . . . Certainly social and economic structures today are far distant, spatially as well as socially, from the typical neighborhood (family-centered) church."[3] It is possible, as critics contend, that the constriction of the pastor's interest to family living in the parish has led to an overdevelopment of his "priestly" and "pastoral" roles, wherein he becomes a "father" instead of a "prophet" in his ministry. Moreover, this kind of family-centeredness may have contributed to a "within the four walls" concept of the church which serves to restrict its relevance to a small part of the world where our laymen are to "be the church" in their daily living. This cry against the new idolatry of the family calls attention to the fact that the home is but *one* area, though a very essential one, of ministry to the world. It calls our attention to missing arenas of witness.

To correct this situation, discerning voices have fostered a concept of "vocational evangelism"[4] which is gaining increased momentum in Protestant circles. Whatever sentimentalism, individualism, and escapism have been fostered by the recently advertised "togetherness" of family living is being questioned from within the church itself. This is a sign of health.

Contemporary Iconoclasm Overstates Its Case

There are values in the critical onslaught on family-centeredness in church and society. But such critique, because of its reactive nature, is tempted to go too far; it may throw out the baby with the bath. A balanced recognition of the remaining power of the family as well as its curtailed influence is in order. In his otherwise brilliant critique of the church's family-centeredness, Peter Berger leaves the family the hopeless pawn of impersonal social forces:

> In looking at society's large institutional network we find the family everywhere in a *dependent* situation. If the family were the basic unit of society, we would expect that whatever happens within this institution would act upon all other institutions—but this is not the case. . . . The family is dependent upon other institutions—political, economic, class. It is not a particular family that produces certain political or economic developments, but the other way around. Looked at sociologically rather than psychologically, this is largely true in the life of the individual also. It is not a certain kind of family life that gives an individual a certain job; rather a certain kind of job allows an individual to live his family life as he does.[5]

Thus individuals and families are "empty," and are simply the subjective reflection of culture!

We need to recognize the *mutual* dependence of family and wider culture upon each other. The family both responds to what is going on in other institutions and also influences the relationships and structures of those institutions. For one thing, cultural values are screened through family filters and do not come to the young child directly. We are not influenced *directly* by so-called "social forces." They are purely metaphors which, if treated as more than abstractions, obscure the basic source of social life in actual relationships. Anthropologists have used the concept "*in*vironment," which is the part of the cultural *en*vironment that the individual internalizes (largely through his family at an early age) and which becomes his conception of the environment around him. The invironment selects or filters what they see and subsequently respond to in the outside environment. In this way the living entity of the family is for most of us the dynamic link between personality and the culture in which we live.

The church needs to understand that the role of the family is not confined to its inner life as though it were isolated from other influences. It is not "a man's castle" from which a drawbridge is lowered to the world whenever its occupants choose. The walls separating a family from its cultural matrix are tissue-paper thin; but they are there. "The family is in many respects more of a transmitting than a generating station. It is constantly contacting, bringing into the home, assessing, and evaluating the outside world. The home is a sort of crossroads, to which comes constantly the outside world."[6] Family change and education and reform are not everything; the influence of the home can be overestimated. Elegant simplicities about the effect of a mystical family solidarity must not blind us to the fact that "the family is but one institution, and it is dependent upon other institutions, as they are dependent upon it. And all the indications point to the conclusion that the family faces a period of declining relative power over members of society when we compare it with political and economic institutions. Most of our problems are incidental to this transition."[7] It is with this recognition that we now move into a description of those changes which have most deeply affected Protestant family living. In doing so we shall try to avoid an overly optimistic bias which sees the institution of the family (supposedly endowed with some kind of evolutionary tendency toward an ideal form) developing from "institution to companionship."[8] Already there is some evidence that we have moved in less than a decade from the "companionship" to the "colleague" family which is a training ground for the "organization man."[9] We can be alert to the signs of health and adaptability of this American family without surrendering to an evolutionistic bias. We shall also avoid the premature judgment that the cultural "attack" on the family is "a present danger, more fearsome than the atom bomb."[10] Though the signs of crisis alluded to in Chapter 1 cannot be ignored, change does not necessarily mean decay except to those committed to an institutional *status quo*. Ideologically if not practically, Protestantism is never shackled to such a commitment.

Our Focus: the Protestant Middle-Class Family

In this book we do not deal with all types of Protestant families living in America. Indeed, these cover the complete spectrum of social classes and a variety of ethnic groups, and would be far beyond the scope of one volume. The common notion that American Protestantism is solely a middle-class phenomenon is not supported by the facts; the class structure of Protestantism *as a whole* resembles closely the class structure of the nation as a whole. To be sure, there are social class differentiations among the denominations[11] and to these we shall allude in discussion of our parent respondents in Chapter 5. Middle-class parents will claim most of our attention; they are, in some sense, the "pace setters" of the culture.

The breadwinner's *education* and *occupation* are predominant in assigning social class in America.[12] But more than these objective factors (although integrally related with them) is a "characteristic mentality" which differentiates this social stratum from its lower- and upper-class counterparts. "It is a class which makes long-term plans, pays its bills, keeps up appearances, prizes respectability and status, and provides for and educates its children. It is a class that climbs, tries to get along in the world, and seeks economic power, social recognition and security."[13] Some features of this mentality seem to be undergoing change with the shift to suburbia and the addiction of postwar installment buying.[14]

The Causes of Family Change Are Complex

As indicated above, there is an indirect relationship between social change and the family changes. Many factors play upon any noticeable shift in the activities of families. For example, an increased desire of wives to work for wages, *by itself,* is not a very helpful explanation of increased employment of married women unless we know what conditions made possible this heightened motivation: for example, postwar employment opportunities, Madison Avenue-fed aspirations for a higher standard of living, changed attitudes toward working wives, the availability of child care centers, and so on.

Further, it must be noted that social changes are not the simple consequence of mechanical impact of events or inventions on passive institutions or groups. Through inventions people are exposed to new experiences which may become satisfying to them. Patterns of behavior involving these inventions are repeated again and again and soon evolve into a set of explicit values which can and do change the way of life in a family. (Consider the profound impact of the automobile and television on church life. What did families once do with the more than twenty hours a week now devoted to television?) Technological developments offer a major challenge to the church family because they may lead to new values, but their effect is not automatic and direct; the impact is still open to educational influence. In a "world come of age" (to use an expression of Dietrich Bonhoeffer), it would be folly for the church to involve itself directly in the control of technological change, as has been the case in times past. It cannot stop the clock of history. The church is clearly committed, however, to influencing the impact of those innovations which may lead to depersonalization and to detrimental interpersonal relationships.

Along with two major world wars and a disastrous depression, four profound social innovations have had far-reaching effect upon the ideology and structure of family life in America from midnineteenth century to the present time. These are (a) the industrialization of the Western world, (b) the concentration of population in the great urban-metropolitan centers, (c) the rise of the centralized political state, and (d) the spread of mass education.

Industrialization and Urbanization

These two developments, though they are not identical, are so closely related that it is difficult to distinguish their separate effects upon the family. "Industrialization" refers to the transformation of a farm, household economy into a specialized, highly mechanized factory system. "Urbanization" depicts the sharp growth of cities and their surrounding suburbs; the concentration in a limited geographical area of large numbers of people whose livelihood comes from manufacture and trade. There has also mushroomed into existence a white-collar group: professional and office workers who manipulate not things but symbols and people through computation, advertising, and mass media.[15] The combined effect of urban growth and industrialization creates an atmosphere for the family which contrasts sharply with the rural social order that prevailed six decades ago. The family is no longer a productive business enterprise; it is a consuming unit. Family recreational life has changed since all activities tend to become commercialized and impersonal in the city. Heterogeneous populations are thrown closely together; family members are exposed to conflicting values. The ideological unity of the countryside is broken. Mass communications and better transportation shatter the islands of isolation which still remain, and the values of the city thus transform the entire culture. The city-suburban complex has become the "nerve center" of modern America.

Farm home life and its values, upon which the church relies even yet, is all but swallowed up as vast numbers of our people move from rural to urban areas, and the rural areas themselves are affected by an urbanism imported through education and mass media. Today's farmer is a new man; he often resembles the corporation executive and the commuter. How rapidly change is taking place is suggested by these figures: urban and rural nonfarm households increased by a million a year between 1950 and April 1957, and farm population decreased 4,700,000. The proportions of this shift are the more apparent when it is observed that during this same period of time the total population of the country increased by more than 19 million people. A few decades have transformed America from a rural to an essentially urban culture. In the 1800's, 64 per cent of our families lived on farms as compared with 12 per cent in 1960![16]

The Rise of the Centralized Political State

The Industrial Revolution and the growth of cities have indeed affected the functions, roles, and relationships within the modern family.

But perhaps another factor, historically considered, claims an even more formative influence. This is the political state, the "primary agent in the recent transmutation of social groups and communities."[17] In a penetrating analysis, Robert A. Nisbet argues that neither science and technology nor the city is "inherently incompatible with the existence of moral values and social relationships which will do for modern man what the extended family, the parish, and the village did for earlier man." It is the state, grown powerful during war (and the anticipation of future wars), which has absorbed or circumscribed the unique functions of economic, kinship, and ecclesiastical institutions. No home is immune from decisions made in Washington, D.C., and in city and state governments. Educational and protective functions of the family, relinquished with the exodus to the city, have been assumed by the state. Old age insurance and health plans; fire, police, and military protection; and the proliferation of schools and child-care centers—all remind us how much the family has given up of former tasks. It is obvious that there is both gain and loss in this transfer of functions.

An even more profound effect of the state is occasioned by its demand upon the individual for absolute loyalty to itself. There is "an increasing directness of relation between the sovereign authority of the state and the individual citizen."[18] Walter Lippman, in unequivocal terms, says that a state

> claims the right to a monopoly of all the force within the community, to make war, to make peace, to conscript life, to tax, to establish and disestablish property, to define crime, to punish disobedience, to control education, to supervise the family, to regulate personal habits, and to censor opinions. . . . There are lingering traces in the American constitutional system of the older theory of inalienable rights which government may not absorb. But these . . . can be taken away by constitutional amendment. . . . Ultimately and theoretically states can claim absolute authority as against all churches, associations, and persons within their jurisdiction.[19]

No thoughtful analysis by the church of its relationship to the family can overlook the potent effect of the state upon that family.

The Spread of Mass Education

Mass education not only contributed to the flow of population from rural to urban environs and provided a channel by which persons could move into a higher social class in America, but it also altered the status of women profoundly. The emancipation of the so-called "weaker sex" (so often regarded as inferior throughout church history) was instrumental in pushing the status of women toward a position more nearly equal to that of man. Certainly educational equality is related to the "sexual revolution" to be described later in this chapter.

These four massive influences upon the family seem to have pushed in the direction of its becoming more of an equalitarian, consuming group; toward heightened individualism in family patterns; toward further loss of family function; and toward increased family confusion of values and family conflict. We now look in detail at some of the changes which must be considered in our evaluation of church-family relations.

Shifts in Family Living Patterns of the American Middle Class

During the last two decades sociologists have spoken of the loss or "shrinking" of family functions,[20] as if each traditional service of the family, save reproduction and affection, had been transferred to another institution of society. To a certain extent research bears out the contention that such a transfer has occurred. It is also evident that in some areas of family life the trend is not irreversible; some functions are being reclaimed by the family. A description of the shifts in family functions since 1890 bears importantly upon the task of education in the church, and they are summarized below.

Changes in the Economic Life of the Family

The majority of our people have separated their work from their homes in the move from rural areas to city and suburb. As a consequence, family members find that they plot their days along entirely different lines that rarely intersect. The family is no longer a productive team working in the same enterprise; now the middle-class family organizes itself around the man's career and gains its status from it. In a sense, the most fundamental basis of the family's position in the community has become the job status of the husband and father. This occupational dominance of the middle-class family will influence deeply where they live, where and to what extent their children are educated, how they vote, what they read, who their friends are, and often the church to which they go.[21]

Family-centered living and concern for children are conspicuous in the suburbs to which middle-class Protestants flock. What is not so often discerned is the relationship between the father's occupation and his way of life in the family. For example, his expectations of his children and his discipline of them reflect in large part his occupational aspirations for them. He expects his sons to move in the same occupational world which he does (whatever he might say about their freedom of choice vocationally). Consequently, the middle-class father encourages initiative, scholastic achievement, emotional stability, and athletic prowess (the latter since it seems to connote the ability to be properly aggressive and competitive now and in the future).[22] Further, there is growing evidence that the *kind* of work the father does, within middle-class ranks, is associated with the mother's goals and methods in child care. Contrasting the mothers from homes in which the chief occupation was "entrepreneurial" (small business or sales) with families whose fathers worked in large, specialized, bureaucratic settings (typically corporations), Miller and Swanson uncovered some fascinating differences. "Children reared in individuated and entrepreneurial homes will be encouraged to be highly rational, to exercise great self-control, to be self-reliant, and to assume an active, manipulative stance toward the environment. . . . Children reared in welfare-bureaucratic homes will be encouraged to be accommodative, to allow their impulses some spontaneous expression, and to seek direction from the organized programs in which they participate."[23]

The middle class is socially as well as geographically mobile. Readiness to move from one's present residence seems to be associated with the advancement in job status which is so prized by middle-class Protestants. Corporations are now assuring a highly trained corps of managers for the organization by frequently requiring moving to a new location as a prerequisite for promotion.[24] Unless he has a very well-established community status (and another job of a commensurate level available to him), there are few bonds which would hold the junior executive at the promise of an advancement.[25] Thus, adaptability and the ability to make friends quickly is trained into children from the cradle. "Emotionally, they are gypsies," says one full documented study of middle-class suburbanites.[26]

The focus upon the husband's career as a basis for family importance and functioning puts a great strain upon the wife since it may deprive her of her role in the productive side of the economic enterprise. She does, of course, participate indirectly through her hospitality to guests, efficient domesticity, and community participation, all of which enhance the husband's effectiveness in his career if it be related to the public.[27] For a variety of reasons, however, an increasing number of middle-class wives are moving into employment outside the home. In 1890 only

13.9 per cent of the total female working force were married. And only a small number of those were mothers (widows and divorcées with children to support for the most part). By 1960 the number of married women in the working force exceeded the number of single women. Currently, about six and one-half million mothers of children under 18, living with their husbands—27.6 per cent of the total number of such mothers—are in the labor force. About twice as many mothers with children 6 to 17 years of age work, as compared with those who have preschoolers in the family. Between 1940 and 1950 the number of employed mothers in the U.S.A. increased by 350 per cent,[28] and this trend continues into the present decade. Ivan Nye, a sociologist who has studied intensively the phenomenon of the working mother predicts that barring a major depression, nonemployed mothers may soon be a minority rather than a majority group! Many implications are here for home-church co-operation in Christian education which leans so heavily on mothers both for voluntary leadership and the teaching task at home.

Why do married women work? Four main motivations have been discerned by students of the family: the first being by far the most compelling, the desire for more income; second, the need for interesting variation and personal contacts in daily activity; third, the prestige and status which derive from occupational competence; and fourth, a desire to escape from disagreeable domestic tasks and/or community demands. One of the working mothers interviewed for our study said:

> *Most mothers work to make money because there is a tendency for people to raise their standard of living (they would be better off if they didn't do this). But most everything you plan for, including the future education of your children, takes more money; and there are so many opportunities to do new things.*

Few wives work whose husband's income is adequate for the support of the family.[29] It is possible that the willingness of the wife to work and the possibility of her doing so in our postwar economy partially accounts for the reported increase in earlier marriage of young people. Relatively few mothers work when their children are young, although a small increase in the ranks of married women in their twenties and early thirties (the child-bearing years) has been noted by the Census Bureau. A wife is most likely to work up through the first year of her marriage and then again between thirty-five and forty-five years of age when her children are in school or have left home. The greatest increase in working wives in the past decade has been in the middle and older age groups, the "empty nest" stage when children have left home for marriage or work.[30] As women have gone from "scullery to salary," many alarmists have predicted dire results for the children in the family.

The church must not overlook the fact that the family has been radically transformed with its move to urban environs from a producing to a consuming group. One of the major activities of the family is planning and organizing for the purchase of goods and services. The family, much more than the individual, is the unit of consumption. However, in the middle-class home, wife and children have a much greater voice than formerly in determining expenditures.[31] The advertisers are alert to these new spending patterns and have exploited the mass media in their efforts to reach women and children principally on behalf of an increasing number of products.[32]

So that they may take part in the "art of consuming," our respondents frequently want their children to "learn the value of money." Token earning as an activity outside the home is encouraged for boys and tolerated for girls (the latter within a narrow range of jobs such as baby sitting and clerking). An allowance is commonly given and training is largely in terms of wise spending under the mother's supervision. Discipline for school-age children often involves the withholding or curtailing of the allowance. Middle-class parents now accept youth's use of the summer for earning and for accumulating adult work experience as constituting "economic realism" as well as "vocational guidance" of an important kind. The movement toward "summer jobs" and "summer school" is resulting in modification of the traditional youth conference program of Protestant denominations, and the long idle summer.

Family Organization Is in Transition

The change of the family from a producing to a consuming unit and the transfer of the father's work away from home has had repercussions on the traditional roles of parents and children in the home. With the disappearance of the need for the patriarchal foreman on the farm, father has lost both authority and functions in the family, and his wife and children have come into places of greater power in decision making.

As noted above, the middle-class woman is less dependent economically.[33] Even though one must admit of a fiction in these figures created by the husband's holding property in his wife's name for various economic reasons, the evidence of economic power of women as consumers is still impressive. She is well educated and, consequently, she is able to move into many more roles than formerly. Flexibility is the order of the day in many a middle-class home. "Home versus career tends to evaporate as a dilemma when each is seen as a desirable casting on occasion, lightly assumed and lightly doffed, rather than grimly restrictive and exclusive."[34] In contrast to this view, Mirra Komarovsky's studies of the lives of middle-class educated women reveal sharp changes in pattern as they pass from school to job, from work to homemaking and child rearing, into community activities, and return to employment or leisure after the children have left home. There is no smooth or consistent transition from one stage to the next. Early stages of child bearing and child rearing are characterized by overwork while the "empty nest" is accompanied by underwork.[35]

The emerging equality of women with men has enabled her to perform functions in the family which her 1890 counterpart could never have assumed. She shares more authority with her husband; decisions are often jointly made now. She has more companionship with her husband; sexually segregated amusements and fraternities are on the decline. The "extreme polarity of masculinity and femininity found in the past is diminishing somewhat as signified particularly in feminine sports dress and masculine beardlessness."[36] Sex in marriage is characterized more now by mutuality of desire and pleasure than by unilateral male demand and satisfaction.

With all these gains for the middle-class wife, one must also report an increase in her self-doubt, anxiety, guilt, and boredom. The very latitude of her possibilities has often caused frustration and a confusion of her identity. One of our respondents says, *"It's a rugged life being employed and married. You can't do justice to either. You're always cheating the other side of your life."* Another woman, grown restless within the four walls of her home opines: *"A family needs two incomes to live decently. . . . I feel I would be a more interesting person if I had more conversation than 'my children did this or that.' "* Max Lerner observes that the modern wife and mother

> finds it harder (than her husband or brother) to perform her variety of roles without feeling the full weight of cultural contradictions that bear down upon her. . . . She is bedeviled by too many functions. She leads simultaneously a multiplicity of lives, playing at once the role of sexual partner, mother, home manager, hostess, nurse, shopper, figure of glamour, supervisor of children's schooling and play and trips, culture audience and culture carrier, clubwoman, and often worker or careerist. Of the two sexes, it is the man who is specialized to making a living or money, or working at whatever productive job he is doing; the woman, remaining unspecialized, becomes the converging point for all the pressures of the culture.

> . . . The question "Are you happy?" is more often addressed to the woman than to the man and has come to have almost a technical meaning in the American cultural context, as if to say, "Are you content with your domestic arrangements, and are you getting along pretty well with your husband and children?"[37]

According to anthropologist Florence Kluckhohn, this variegated picture of the woman's position in the modern middle-class home leaves her with three persisting, interrelated, and always-to-be-solved problems: (1) the confused definition of the feminine role; (2) a faulty and far from satisfactory husband-wife relationship; and (3) a questionable parent-child, especially mother-child, relationship.[38]

But the *male* of the species has experienced a major shift in his own image of himself as the traditional "head" of the family. (Even if he clings to the image, in the middle-class home, the content of that picture has changed drastically.) It bears little resemblance to the classical theological positions to be reported in Chapters 3 and 4. In the nineteenth century the farm family father was sternly in command of the whole enterprise; wife and children knew their place. Male and female roles, culturally defined, have now moved closer together; and functions may shift as necessity demands. In fact, father seems now to have *more* responsibility within the home in traditional female spheres of operation but without commensurate authority.

To be sure, father is still regarded as "head" of the family; but headship has come to mean something quite unimposing in comparison with the views of both Protestant and Roman Catholic thinkers of a previous century. In that era, whether the differentiation of male and female found its basis in the Bible, in "natural law" or in functional necessity, the roles were kept quite distinct. In popular thought men are generally characterized by independence and initiative, physical courage, mechanical ability, sexual aggressiveness, and indifference to social graces. Their roles are directive, protective, and financially supporting. Women are seen as weak, dependent, proud of domestic skills, verbose, oversensitive to social approval and disapproval, and moody. They are followers, helpers, and emotional supporters primarily. This image, found even in women's magazines, presents a greater differentiation than actually exists (or probably ever has existed). Research in social psychology and cultural anthropology has shattered much of this stereotype.[39]

Gains in the rights of women are now generally approved by all; yet those rights are still curtailed by the mental picture of women's inferiority or by the male's fear of displacement or both. Until recently, then, the headship of the male was an expression of reciprocal female role—*subordination.*

Though the image of male "headship" in home and out still prevails, a number of factors have served to modify it deeply and to blur the roles of man and wife. The growing equality of women is one such influence. Equally potent, however, is the middle-class man's preoccupation with his work life. His job has become a major source of his identity; he tends to derive from it his deepest sense of worth (except when the struggle for status becomes predominant on the job).

The typical father in our study sees home and job as two separate foci for his life; they are for the most part "separate worlds." (The wife of the professional man senses this separateness even more than he does and is frequently threatened by his tendency to "outgrow" her intellectually while she stagnates in her routine.) It is apparent from our study, that difficulty in combining successfully his occupational and family roles is among the most common sources of guilt and anxiety for the middle-class male. It is a cause, or occasion, of profound conflict for the average Protestant clergyman who has growing children in his family. Yet the job is the "organizing role" for this modern husband and father; and he is ambivalent about it. One of our respondents, an engineer who attended a group interview, reveals this strain:

> *To me, attending this is important. I've been working 16 hours a day, seven days a week this last week. I've got work stacked up tonight I should have been working on. This is the first break, the first meeting of any kind that I've gone to and I thought it was worthwhile coming because I need a lot of answers. I'll get sympathy if nothing else. To me, my children and my family are the most important things there are.*

In much church and secular literature pressure is applied to make the middle-class male more of a family man than he is. It urges him to be a better companion to his wife and children, to become familiar with the newborn baby in his midst, and to share in the religious education of his children. This is an important contribution to the man who has become a vocational machine, forgetting about full personhood. Others warn, however, that once the male becomes thoroughly domesticated—through baby sitting, dishwashing, docilely answering every beck and call of wife and children—he will let atrophy any contribution he might make to the world. Margaret Mead, for example, warns that the emphasis on the "family man" is being overdone with the result that the development of men of adventure and daring, willing to give of themselves in the public good, is being inhibited by the culture. Already, she says, such "feminizing of the male" is evidenced by his increased occupation with security, high salaries, residence in a good suburb, prestige memberships in community organizations, and his affirmation of "home life as an end rather than a part of human life."[40]

Others, pointing up his job preoccupation from a psychiatric orientation, speak of the escape *from* intimacy by the modern male through his work. Yet in some sense he regards himself (and his wife regards him) as a thoroughgoing "family man." Movements in both directions, then, have been observed by today's family analysts.

In four-hour depth interviews of fifty upper middle-class Protestant church families, Robert W. Lynn discovered that the men rejected decisively the traditional patriarchal, authoritarian father role; they would neither own it for themselves, nor would they tolerate the associate who would try to reclaim this idea of headship for himself.

> The major trend is toward the ideal of both father and mother assuming *jointly* the headship of the family. The following fragment of conversation expresses the ideal of a majority of the families.
>
> The husband: "We split the job of disciplining fifty-fifty."
>
> The wife: "We *try* to split it fifty-fifty. Of course, I do it when he is on the road. When the father is away, the mother has to do it. But we have tried to stick together."[41]

The fathers in this study eschewed a *direct* disciplinary role; they served best as fathers, they thought, when they were companions to their children and shared their little leisure time with them. The authority of the father in his family comes through respect bestowed upon him by children who reward him for his participation in their activities.

In church-sponsored discussion groups, when suburban parents discuss "headship" in the many aspects of family life—provision for economic needs, discipline of children, hosting guests, citizenship, worship and religious education, housekeeping, purchasing, and recreation—it is only in the first item that the father clearly emerges as the undisputed leader. In all other functions he takes a collaborative or secondary role.

The actual state of affairs in the middle-class family has been adequately summarized by Ruesch and Bateson:

> . . . The division of function between the sexes is frequently blurred. . . . The parents act much more as checks and balances upon each other and constitute a sort of authority by combining their efforts. The child in turn is free to correct either parent. . . . Neither parent

> is in a position of recognized final authority. . . . It often happens that one parent is more active in making decisions than the other; or one parent may be more important than the other as the link between the family and the rest of the community. But a parent who takes over such special functions is still not a final authority or spearhead for the family unit. . . . The outstanding parent must act overtly as though he or she were orchestrating a diversity of opinions—and must perform this function not with a silent baton, but playing actually in the orchestra, exerting an integrating influence only by his or her contribution to the total sequence of sound.[42]

According to modern sociology, every role in a group (such as the family) is visualized as being the center of a network of roles. A change in one part may influence, directly or indirectly, any other part and modify the whole system. We have reported important changes in the roles of men and women in middle-class families. As one would expect, children's roles are deeply affected by these shifts. As a consequence of the changes reported, the life of the American middle-class family is especially organized around the child and anything which promises benefit and help to the child is readily accepted by the public. As Whyte suggests, the modern family seems to be not so much a patriarchy or a matriarchy as a "filiarchy."[43] In the 1800's, our ancestors tended to see the child as a period full of idle deviltry and full of mischief. "The child survived it and the parents endured it as best they could, until late adolescence when life hesitatingly began. We, of later vintage, regard childhood as a period of great importance, a period of twig bending during which the shape of the future tree is determined."[44] The additional attention given to the child in these later years has enhanced the conflict in parental roles. Consequently, a great increase of interest in psychology and parent education is in evidence.

As long as the productive, educational, and protective functions were performed in the family, the child was ascribed status by identification with the family and family name. Now a great part of his recognition (especially at adolescence) is achieved through accomplishment in school, community, and peer groups which compete strongly with the home for the time and loyalty of the child. The child, caught between his small family with its intense emotional bonds and the strenuous socialization of school and friendship group, oscillates from one to the other throughout his early life. The conflicting requirements are often a source of anxiety to him. Even in adolescence, when the "peer culture" predominates in influence over the family, the requirements for peer acceptance are so rigid as to cause deep pain to most children. Male athletic prowess and this year's edition of female glamour are only for the well-endowed few. It is doubtful that academic ability by itself, even in this postsputnik age, is a key to popularity among teen-agers.

When the grown child is launched from home, he is expected to create new cultural and family patterns, independent of his family of orientation. If the child "succeeds," the middle-class parents, still on the upward march, will identify with him and his new achievements.

This analysis of changing roles in the family would not be complete without mention of the *kinship relations* of the modern home. Half a century ago in the middle class, the nuclear family was a part of an extended family system. There were present in the household grandparents and perhaps aunts, uncles, and cousins as well as a lodger or two. Now the nuclear family wants to live alone. If a couple shares a home with relatives they feel compelled to explain that the relationship is a temporary one, that they are waiting to "get on their feet" financially or to move to a suitable place of their own. There has been a constant decline in the number of persons per household from 1890 until the present time; it is no longer expected that two generations of adult persons will live under the same roof. Though double-up families are decreasing, a minority of parents do live with their grown children or vice versa.

Among middle-class Protestants who have lost their ethnic characteristics, the weakening of kinship ties is in evidence, especially in the suburbs. The geographical mobility of these families, separating kin from one another, is undoubtedly a major cause of their tenuous relationship. But separation from kin is likely to grow not only in a geographical, but in a psychological sense as well. Difference in taste, education, values, and habits brought about by the college experience of the upwardly mobile children can be more formidable than geographical distance. Since prestige no longer depends upon family name and association, the extended family is often perceived as an obstacle to middle-class aspirations. The increased freedom of nuclear family members from the past, with distance from relatives, is enjoyed; no tradition or reputation can strait-jacket the future. Little effective pressure can be brought to bear in the determination of one's choice of mate, or occupation, or religion. The possibility of a clash of the roles of mother and daughter-in-law as household manager has diminished. With government support for the aged and infirm, the extent of financial obligation of children for aging parents has lessened somewhat. But with this freedom for middle-class parents comes also a sense of guilt.[45]

On the other hand, the emphasis in our culture on husband and wife's establishing a new residence represents a sacrifice of solidarity, mutual protection, and a continuation of family experience. Each nuclear family must now be on its own with minimum assistance from the extended family group. The baby sitter is a dramatic symbol of its isolation. Loneliness often grips the young mother with her first child as she faces the crises of parenthood. It is not surprising that parents should almost desperately turn to the clinic, the school, and the church (especially in suburbia) as quasi-grandparents.

The intimate relationships of the compact family must now bear a heavier emotional load among its fewer members. In a former time relatives often "diluted" family tensions as well as contributed to them. When friction occurs now (in the context of the middle-class family's emphasis on "togetherness"), every quarrel can become a crisis; each misunderstanding an evil portent of isolation and failure.

When the older generations are not on hand to keep family memories alive, the content of family tradition is often broken. A history is lacking which is essential to the establishment of healthy identity in family as well as in individual life. The family may attempt to replace its lost identity with values derived from the occupation, the social set, or "anonymous authorities" in the mass media. It becomes, in Riesman's terms, "other directed."

The situation in the typical suburban, mobile family has been described above. However, in many *urban* groups (especially those still possessing ethnic characteristics), the extended family still plays a vital role. In the cities, relatives continue to be a source of companionship and mutual support, if we can judge from the frequent visiting patterns.[46] But the higher the income, status, and education of families, the more likely they are to replace relatives with friends and neighbors as sources of companionship, even though they may visit their kin frequently.[47]

Some of the changes in family organization which we have noted are accentuated by *geographical mobility*. The growth of cities and their suburbs, the development of military establishments, the swelling college population, and large, ever-expanding corporations have made us a people "on the move." Excluding travelers to foreign countries, twenty per cent of our population have moved their residence across county lines each year for the last decade and a half. With the exception of migrant farm labor, professional and managerial people are the most mobile (and move farther) than other segments of our population. Migration trends are generally from South to North, from Middle West to Far West, from rural to urban, and from urban to suburban areas.

In recent years, suburbia has grown seven times faster than central urban areas; almost 80 per cent of its people have come from the city. (Eight of the ten largest cities in the U.S.A. had population losses in the last ten years.)

Motives for suburban living are as variegated as the people who migrate to the fringe of the city. The belief that they will encounter less congestion, dirt, and noise, more building space, better conditions for rearing children (a belief not borne out in fact), and desire for "neighboring" all motivate this centrifugal movement. Nearness to employment seems to be less essential to the middle-class family than proximity of good schools, and services used for children or necessary to efficient home operation.

When a move is not occasioned by a change in occupation or position, it is the necessity of adjusting the family's housing to its needs which most often prompts a change of residence. In other words, migrants feel that new space requirements must be satisfied for a growing or contracting family.[48]

Surprisingly, it has been found that frequent moving by itself has little effect on the amount of social contact and participation in community organizations engaged in by a family. Middle- and upper-middle-class people, mobile or not, tend to have more friends and active memberships than even stable, long-term residents of the lower class.

The Family's Changing Educational Role

A striking shift is noticeable in the educational activities of the contemporary home, whether its efforts be channeled into general or religious education, or expressed in informal recreational activities. Most dramatically during the last century general education has been transferred from home to school with penalties imposed by the government for noncompliance. This is inevitable in any culture where specialized knowledge outstrips the funded wisdom of the average family. In addition to the fundamental areas of study, training in values, manners and mores (including sex education) have become an integral part of public education and nonfamily social agencies. Generally, Protestantism has affirmed its faith in the public schools of America. It sees them, with a constructively critical eye, as devoted to the intrinsic worth of the child, and to the proposition that the search for truth must be undertaken and unfettered by ecclesiastical or other controls.[49] Public schools have the advantage of giving children experience and knowledge of a heterogeneous culture. On the other hand, Protestant families have discovered, by and large, that the school cannot be depended upon or expected to foster *their* religious heritage. It is recognized that the public schools do foster a corpus of values, some of which are congruent with, and some contrary to, their religious convictions. Social analysts have discerned in the public school systems a promotion of a middle-class value system, an amalgam of health, happiness, and success with some deference to traditional values. Patriotic holidays continue to increase, and religious holidays decrease in importance. The school has become the central purveyor of the ideals of national life, informed largely by the business community, the psychiatric clinic, and the State.[50] Large numbers of Protestant parents, it will be seen in Chapter 6, sense no discrepancy in this "cultural faith" with their Protestant heritage. This identification of "Americanism" with Christianity has forced a re-examination of the Protestant religious education approaches. A growing number of Protestant theologians are alarmed at the permeation of the educational scene by a humanist philosophy in concealed form.[51] A minority would fall back upon a church-related elementary and secondary day school system to correct this situation. Others, seeing no conclusive research evidence that these schools alter the child's values or church-relatedness in any perceptible way, have cast their lot with family and church to carry the burden of distinctive church teaching. It remains to be seen whether these two agencies of nurture, by themselves, can educate effectively in distinctly Protestant values.

Along with sporadic outbursts of criticism toward schools and community organizations, middle-class Protestant parents rather consistently express confidence in these channels to do the work of educating their offspring. Increasing enrollment of small children in nursery schools and kindergartens is apparent. Fifteen years ago, about 45 per cent of five-year-old children were in such schools. At the present time, the figure for middle-class five-year-olds has reached 75 per cent. The tremendous growth of nursery schools, many of them in churches, is mute testimony to the middle-class parent's hope in education outside the home. National youth-serving agencies enroll other millions of Protestant youth in their programs, thus augmenting, by the use of volunteer parent leaders, the education which parents wish for their children.

In the midst of this transfer of educational functions to the school and other community groups, the middle-class family itself pushes forward on the home front. Most middle-class parents prepare their children for first grade by teaching them the alphabet, nursery rhymes, and printing.[52] Parents are increasing the educational potential of the home with the purchase of encyclopedias, and the provision for special lessons related to the talent of the child, and for travel.[53]

Sociologists of the family almost universally speak of a decline in the *religious function* of the home and the transfer of these functions to religious institutions. Studies made during the depression reported decline in at least three religious practices—the family going to church together, the reading of the Bible at home, and saying grace at meals.[54] The trend toward less prayer at mealtime was confirmed by research involving a cross section of the national population polled in 1946 and 1947.[55]

Other research seems to indicate that until 1950 at least, the home as a religious agency was gradually losing its religious influence. In 1948, a study of middle-class college students revealed that 70 per cent clearly felt the need for a religious philosophy of life. Most of the students stated that their relationship with their parents was a decisive factor in their desire for a religious orientation. They claimed, however, that their parents, especially their mothers, not only had "stronger" religious beliefs but were more orthodox than they; only one-quarter of these students were theistically oriented.[56] The families of these college students seem to have been effective in creating a *hunger for religion,* yet ineffective in terms of transmitting a specific theological heritage or denominational loyalty to the young person which would persist through college years. The alleged decline in the effective religious functioning of the family is thought to be supported also by other studies which show that approximately half of college students would cross interfaith barriers in marriage if other aspects of the relationship were satisfactory.[57]

The last decade in America has seen a sharp revival of religious interest; the peak of this incline was apparently reached in 1958. Whether judged by church membership and attendance, giving to the churches, the erection of buildings,[58] or the reading of religious literature, the conclusion was obvious: there was a turn to religion among the American people in the 1950's. Analysts have been studying both the motivations for this religious upsurge and the general effect on the contemporary religious situation in America.[59] The consensus seems to be that religious *institutionalism* has been greatly enhanced in the midst of a trend toward secularism in ideas. There is mounting evidence that "religion in general" has replaced authentic Christian or Jewish content of the faith of Americans. Meanwhile, church-institutional programs have proliferated—an observation that will be documented in Chapter 6. That this is a widespread cultural phenomenon is apparent also from the observations of Roman Catholic sociologists:

> . . . Catholic families have tended to entrust the entire formal religious training of their children to the (parochial) school. In a study of over 16,000 parochial school children entering first grade, we discovered that only a little over one-half knew how to make the Sign of the Cross, one-third could recite the "Hail Mary," and less than one-fourth could recite the "Our Father." Knowledge of religious dogma is likewise deficient. . . . Specifically the failure of Catholic families to give their children adequate knowledge of family standards is reflected in the widespread demand for and introduction of marriage preparation courses in Catholic colleges and high schools.[60]

Many Protestant denominations in the middle and late 1940's created curriculum materials designed for the use of the church school teacher and the parent, often in a co-operative teaching plan. Though the hoped-for result in home co-operation was not forthcoming in the 1950's, nevertheless a healthy minority of Protestant homes, previously without such resources, are now using these Bible-related materials.[61] Family devotional material has been made available to millions of Protestant homes, judging by the sales of denominational publishing houses. Two major denominations (the Protestant Episcopal and the United Presbyterian) have reported sharp increases during the last decade in family corporate worship in the church sanctuary. On all three counts cited earlier—the family going to church together, the reading of the Bible at home, and saying grace at meals—there seems to have been an advance in the 1950's over the 1940's, if we can generalize from the data now available. Whether this trend will continue remains to be seen.

Turning now to the *recreational life* of the family, regarded by many of our parents as one of the chief educational opportunities with their children, we find that whereas in the third and fourth decades of this century, the trend was clearly for recreation to be dissociated from family life,[62] recent studies have indicated a self-conscious recovery of this function. Especially in the suburban family we find recreation being reinstated as a staple in family life. Indeed, as Nelson Foote has said, "Family living in the residential suburb has come to consist almost entirely of play. . . . The seriousness with which homemaking is pursued should not conceal its playful nature, because work and play at their best are indistinguishable."[63] Even though schools and community organizations continue to promote age- and sex-stratified recreation (and thus segmentalize the family), middle-class people are more and more orienting themselves to week ends when family activities, such as shopping, lunch, home projects, games, travel and church going, predominate.[64]

A study made by home economists of the Department of Agriculture indicates that the most striking change in recreational habits from 1940 to 1955 has been the decline of movies and the rise of television. In 1940, movies took 20 per cent of the family recreational budget; by 1955 this had been pared to 10 per cent. But expenditures for radio, TV, records, and musical instruments (most of which are used at home), jumped from 14 per cent to 23 per cent. In terms of expenditures, spectator amusements—including movies, theater, opera, and spectator sports—dropped 19 per cent but participant amusements (such as bowling, skating, and golf) increased 34 per cent. Greater interest in types of recreation in which family participation is possible, is also indicated by the big increase in the amount spent for such items as boats, bicycles, aircraft, and home sporting goods.[65]

The Current Confusion in the Meaning of Sex, Marriage, and Family

In contrast to the double standard which existed up until the First World War, increased sexual freedom between men and women of the middle class led to a new conception of sex for both. No longer fearful of detection, infection, and conception, numerous women began to seek the premarital sexual relations long claimed by men. There has been a sharp increase in premarital petting and coitus for both men and women in the last five or six decades.[66] At the same time, we note that public attitudes toward sex relations before marriage have become less condemnatory. As one searches for causes of this change in behavior, he is reminded of the breakdown of small-community social controls; the weakening of religiously grounded sex ethics; the use of the automobile which puts youth beyond the surveillance of adults; the ready availability of contraceptives; and the sex stimulation from mass media. A single cause would be sought in vain.

Clinical studies indicate the wide variety of motives which underlie this new sex behavior. Students of personality are impressed with the degree to which promiscuity and extramarital affairs are motivated by the "anxiety of aloneness, by the wish to conquer or be conquered, by vanity, by the wish to be hurt, and even to destroy."[67]

The meaning of love seems to have undergone transformation as well. Romantic love, so dominant in our time, seems to be an amalgam of emotional excitement, idealization, and sex attraction. It combines naïve confidence in the future with a sense of certitude in mate selection. Romantic love may have had its counterpart in medieval and Elizabethan times, but this "cardiac-respiratory" variety seems to be the product of the urban, mobile culture, in which family background is unknown, and visual stimulation (especially clothes and car) furnishes clues to identity. In mate selection the personal sexual attractiveness and general appearance of the girl and the appearance and spending ability of the boy often take precedence over "familistic qualities" (such as mutual desire for home ownership, children, staying at home, and religious participation) known to be positively associated with marital success.[68] Parents in the suburbs, however, tend to exercise indirect influence in the selection of a spouse for their children through restriction of choice by their place of residence and often by selective schooling.

Along with a decrease in the median age of marriage from 1890 until the present[69] we note a more profound change. Religious and social concepts of marriage, with their affirmations of monogamy, fidelity, and indissolubility, have progressively given way to an outlook which is openly tentative, experimental, and individualistic. With particular reference to the middle class, Sirjamaki has summarized the value system of Americans regarding the family which prevailed in the 1940's:

1. Marriage is a dominating goal for men as well as women.
2. The giving and taking in marriage should be based on personal affection and choice.
3. The criterion of successful marriage is the personal happiness of husband and wife.
4. The best years of life are those of youth, and its qualities are most desirable.
5. Children should be reared in a child's world and shielded from too early participation in adult roles and tribulations.
6. The exercise of sex should be contained within wedlock.
7. Family roles of husband and wife should be based upon the sexual division of labor but with the male status being superior.
8. Individual not familial values are to be sought in family living.[70]

Our survey of changes in the middle-class family and data yet to be presented, would lead us to believe that in order for this to be a contemporary statement of the goals of the middle-class family, items six, seven, and eight would be modified somewhat. As reported, a greater latitude with regard to premarital and extramarital sex experience is in evidence; hence, item six may have to be qualified somewhat.[71] As noted above, the sexual division of labor and status of the male is no longer seen in terms as clear as statement number seven implies. And though it is true that individualism is pronounced in family life today, "togetherness" and familial concerns have been reinstated, especially in these professional, college-educated, suburban families which are often taken as models by working-class families in the cities. With the rise of suburbanism, one more value might be added: the family is regarded as a retreat from the complexities of community and business life and the onslaught of world crises.[72]

The *reproductive function* is still taken seriously in middle-class American families. The unprecedented number of babies born in recent years cannot compare proportionately with the last two centuries, but shows a substantial increase over the low birthrate of the 1930's. The average family size has decreased from 7.4 children per family in the 1700's to 2.3 in 1960. According to predictions, the average family size may go as high as 3.0 children per family in a few years. (College students now mention four or five children as the ideal family size.) The recent increase may be related to the growth of suburban areas peopled as they are with young professional and semiprofessional workers. There is no longer clear evidence that the lower the class standing of a family, the more children are found in the family. (Recall the old saying, "The rich get richer, and the poor get children.") As recently as 1949, it became evident that the upper classes and the upper fringe of the middle-class were surpassing the white-collar business groups in fertility. This trend is borne out in our study of Protestant parents.

In general, it is still true that Roman Catholics, at middle-class levels, surpass Protestants in the size of families; at lower socio-economic levels, there is little, if any, difference in the fertility rate.[73] Roman Catholic fertility is declining faster than that of non-Roman Catholics due largely to the increased use of conception control by the Catholics. Recent studies show that Roman Catholic married couples use contraceptives in about the same measure as their Protestant and Jewish neighbors, reports the National Catholic Life Bureau.[74]

From this survey there is no warrant to assume that the reproductive function has been minimized in the modern family. However, in the future there may be a decreased emphasis upon the reproductive aspects of life in another sense. We refer to the noticeable decrease in the period of child bearing and child rearing. The combination of smaller families and increased longevity means among other things that a smaller proportion of the total married life is centered on the reproductive task. In 1890, on the average, one parent (usually the father) died two years before the last child grew up and left home. Now husband and wife can look forward to almost one-third of their married life together when their youngest child leaves the hearth for marriage or work.

An Increase in Family Tension and Disruption

Although divorce is not the only evidence of conflict in family living today, it does tell a great deal about domestic discord. Along with separation, annulment, and desertion ("poor man's divorce"), divorce represents a major sign of disruption and disorganization of the family unit; something damaging and painful has occurred to the members of a once intact family group. The effect, however, goes far beyond parents and children. Brothers and sisters, employers, friends, neighbors, co-respondents ("the other woman") and their families are indirectly involved. The sum of all these persons together, Edmund Bergler has shown,[75] can conceivably amount to ten times the number of reported divorces! Even though the divorce rate has been declining from a peak in 1946 (when the dissatisfaction with war marriages reached its zenith), and is leveling off currently, it is still a major indication of family disruption. More research data are available concerning divorce than upon any other disruptive family experience.[76]

Up to now, family disorganization, as evidenced by divorce, separation, and desertion has been markedly associated with lower socio-economic status. Perhaps this relationship obtains because of the greater impact of the industrial order upon these families in the form of insecurity, anxiety, poverty, adverse housing, and rootlessness—but perhaps also because of the relatively vulnerable ideology with respect to family which they exhibit in their concepts of duty and responsibility, and in their short-term, unplanned view of life. Family stability, on the other hand, is associated with higher-than-average education, occupational status, and job stability. Professional and semiprofessional vocations are not only associated with marriage adjustment[77] but also with success in remarriage.[78] In William J. Goode's investigation of divorced women in the Detroit area he found that unskilled laborers' families represented more than twice as much divorce as professional workers.[79] This suggests to him that a revision of certain literary clichés is due. The stereotyped picture of the lower-class family as one of warmth, love, and stability, contrasted with the neurotic, psychically aggressive, divorce-prone middle-class family makes for simpler novels but is not an accurate picture of our social situation. The possibility exists, however, that the middle class (because of its striving, social mobility, and higher aspirations) might spawn more family troubles but at the same time have more resources in personality and community to weather the storms blown up by their own characteristic mentality. Earl L. Koos confirms this hypothesis in his study of family reactions to crisis and concluded that middle-class families appear to have a high degree of tension but they come through their problems more successfully than working-class families; they do not so often end in disruption.

Even within middle-class occupations, three occupational factors emerge as being important to marital adjustment. First is the degree of stress associated with vocation (highly competitive small business, for example), since such stress may be reflected in family tensions. A second is the requirements of the job in hours and mobility (the salesman on the road is a classic illustration). A third comes from attitudes associated with specific occupations which may seriously affect marital adjustment (such as a perfectionistic attitude in a clergyman, the manipulative stance of an engineer, or the "correcting" habit of a teacher).[80]

Certain well-attested factors that affect divorce seem applicable to lower, upper, and middle classes alike. It is possible, however, that even with some of these, indirect relationships could be found. Those marrying under 18 years of age (or at an unusually advanced age) tend toward marital instability. The greatest number of divorces occur in the third year of marriage. After the third year of marriage a rapid drop in the number of divorces occurs until the seventh year; then a more gradual decline. Three-fifths of all divorces are granted to childless couples. However, premarital pregnancy is also associated with a high divorce rate. Divorce is denser in the Western and Southern regions of the U.S.A. Divorced people tend to have come from more unhappy childhoods (and their own parents' marriages were more unhappy) than in the case of the happily married. The divorced tend to know each other for shorter periods of time and to have shorter engagements, more conflict and less affection during courtship, than those married happily.

Even though the various social classes are differentially associated with divorce, there are broad cultural and social conditions that are undoubtedly related to the high rate of family disruption in this country as a whole. Henry Bowman has delineated this list of contributory social influences: the higher standard of living, a reduction in the institutional functions of the family, the higher status of women, the newer standards of marital success and the newer emphasis on companionship as an ideal in marriage, the decline of religious authority, changing ideas of masculine supremacy, the growth of cities with the concomitant breakdown of primary control groups, the growing ease with which divorce can be obtained, the exploitation of divorce news in the press, and the decline in the death rate (more marriages now can end in split-ups before death would accomplish the same effect).[81] An interesting parallel exists between marriage-divorce rates and the business cycle, indicating that both marriage and divorce will increase in prosperous times; both will decrease in hard times.[82]

Underlying much of today's divorce rate is society's rather easy acceptance of broken marriage as a common and a justifiable situation. Margaret Mead writes that "the most serious thing that is happening in the United States is that people enter marriage with the idea it is terminable." Protestant denominations (excluding many of the smaller conservative sects) have strengthened this impression with their recent rulings on divorce and remarriage.[83] Actually, what has been relaxed recently is an intransigent standard that divorced persons may not remarry, or an indefensible requirement that the "innocent" party be distinguished from the "guilty" in the assessment of the couple considering remarriage in the church. Conditions of readiness for remarriage (informed by psychological insights and a deeper biblical understanding), currently are considered to be more pertinent considerations in pastoral counseling and church decisions in the matter of remarriage.

The new freedom and equality of woman in society remains a controversial subject in studies of the high divorce rate. Confusion in the midst of her new roles has been alluded to; self-doubt and often marital dissension follow this confusion. The improved status of women in society, whatever its effect upon a given marriage, has given the modern woman an improved position of financial and job security which her grandmother lacked; she no longer needs to be trapped within a poor marriage because of economic handicaps.

It is obvious that antiquated legal procedure and divorce courts, permitting if not encouraging the speedy disorganization of families in the process of procuring a divorce, are a contributing factor to family disruption in this country. (A survey of legal practices and problems regarding marriage and divorce is found in Morris Ploscowe's book, *The Truth About Divorce*. Protestantism's concern about this situation and relationship to it is briefly sketched out in *Pastoral Ministry to Families* by J. C. Wynn, pp. 150–151.) Reform of the divorce system is being recommended by numerous law colleges, public agencies and the churches. It is the embodiment of a therapeutic approach into court procedure, using all the helping professions, that has begun to show the most promise. But this approach is still infrequently found.

Sociological data cannot plumb the depths of human motivations which make so tremendous a contribution to our national divorce statistics. Rather than the legal grounds given in court, or even the social conditions cited by the sociologists, the heart of the problem of antagonisms leading to divorce must be found in the personal and psychological realm. There are, of course, immense individual differences in the families of divorce. Meyer Nimkoff, a family sociologist, holds that there are two big classes of unhappily married people. There are those who are unsuited to each other (in which divorce and remarriage might be a solution) and those who are psychologically not fit for marriage (for which divorce is no solution at all since the inner seeds of conflict are carried with them into each subsequent union). Oversimplified as this classification is, it does point an important diagnostic question for the pastoral counselor who works with couples in dissension.

Evidence is now mounting that some families are chronically troubled families showing maladjustment in many areas of life, susceptible to disorganization and unable to live long under any other condition. Generation after generation this pattern is repeated.[84] These are not middle-class families but they land in the pastor's office nonetheless. Interdisciplinary and interagency co-ordination is the only answer to these problem-prone families.

One personality factor which appears again and again in studies of unhappy marriage is "impulsiveness." This is expressed in hasty marriage as well as in a lack of long-range planning, frustration-tolerance, and the sense of responsibility required for adequate marital adjustment.[85] These missing characteristics are, it will be noted, those prized by middle-class people. Conflict in roles is a more likely contributing factor to divorce in middle-class families. Unrealistic expectations of the position and performance of oneself and the mate in married life are responsible for much dissension.[86] Studies also show that it is the mutual satisfaction with the roles assumed and not so much the content of the roles themselves that is related to good marital adjustment. Church couples, incidentally, appear to have a better understanding of each other's roles than do couples whose marriages are in need of repair.[87] Intensive studies are now going on in an attempt to learn what types of personality combinations in man and wife are most likely to lead to trouble and what can be done about trouble when it comes.[88]

Contrary to the moralistic opinion of many persons, sexual infidelity does not account for any huge number of broken marriages; most often it is a symptom of a sick marriage. Goode's findings bore out this conclusion; he found sexual infidelity to be the cause for a far smaller proportion of divorces than is commonly believed, and even where it is cited as a major cause, it had deeper wellsprings in problems that really rocked the marriage. Adultery is not always named in the divorce complaint when it actually is a factor; still, this is an exceedingly small percentage.[89]

Problems related to sex come in at another point, however. Premarital pregnancy, as might be expected, turns out to be related to divorce. Harold Christenson's study in Indiana not only verified this but also the fact that divorces are frequent among those couples who experience an early pregnancy following marriage.[90]

It will be important for us to review briefly a few facts about the relation of religion to divorce and marital unhappiness. Three large studies have been made to determine the divorce rate in mixed Roman Catholic-Protestant marriages. (These studies did not distinguish between "valid" Roman Catholic marriages and those without the sanction of that church.) One of these studies, observing data from 4,108 mixed and nonmixed marriages among the parents of college students in Michigan, revealed that where both parents were Catholic the divorce rate was lowest, only 4.4 per cent of the marriages ending in divorce; if both were Protestant,[91] 6.0 per cent ended in divorce. If the father was Protestant and the mother Catholic, the figure rose to 14.1 per cent. If neither was religious, 17.9 per cent ended in divorce. The highest divorce rate of all existed in marriages in which the husband was Catholic and the wife Protestant; in this case 20.6 per cent were divorced. The two other studies made in widely separated parts of the country show approximately the same results.[92]

Happiness in marriage seems generally to be positively correlated with fairly steady church attendance for both partners at the same church.[93] Very few studies indicate the relationship of membership in specific religious groups to marital adjustment, rather than to divorce. A major research effort in this area by James A. Peterson[94] reveals comparisons on marital adjustment for six groupings which he defines: the sect group; the conservative-orthodox group; the institutional-authoritarian group; the liberal churches; the Jewish denominations; and the agnostic or nonchurch groups. Men belonging to the liberal religious groups have the highest level of adjustment; men belonging to institutional-authoritarian groups have the lowest. Among the men, the high level of adjustment of the nonchurch group contradicts the commonly held belief that those who are not members of churches are, by that token, unhappy in marriage. The results for women are similar but in this case the liberal and Jewish groups vie for top honors; and the nonchurch women have the lowest adjustment scores of any of the six groupings. Regarding the sexual relationship in marriage, the liberal and nonchurch groups have the lowest degree of disagreement between husband and wife regarding sexual matters; they also experience less guilt than the other groups regarding sexual relations. Again the liberal group and nonchurch group show the lowest percentage of guilt feelings about the use of birth control in marriage.

In concluding this chapter, we note that momentous changes have taken place in the middle-class families of America. These must be considered seriously by the church as it surveys its present ways of relating to the home. We conclude that because of the interdependence of the wider society with the family, the church and pastor who focus their attention *only* upon the family in its attempts at Christian nurture, do not really know that family. Since, as John Oman reminds us, we must be "life understanders" before we can be "life changers" it behooves the church continually to assess the changes taking place in family life; the complexity of the issues requires Protestant agencies to make this job a continuing permanent part of their program.

NOTES

1. Frequently we encounter such loaded terms as disorientation, disorganization, deterioration, decline, instability, and the like.
2. See the working out of this limited understanding of power structures in the birth control controversy of a New England town as documented by Kenneth Underwood in *Protestant and Catholic.*
3. "The Church as a Redemptive Fellowship," by Gayraud Wilmore, an unpublished manuscript.
4. Vocational evangelism, a concept adopted by the American Baptist Division of Evangelism, connotes the penetration of the Christian ethic through lay ministry into all daily work and living.
5. Peter Berger, "The Second Children's Crusade," *The Christian Century,* Dec. 2, 1959, p. 1400.
6. Willard Waller and Reuben Hill, *The Family: A Dynamic Interpretation,* p. 15.
7. See Note 6.
8. See Ernest W. Burgess and Harvey J. Locke, *The Family: From Institution to Companionship.*
9. Daniel R. Miller and Guy E. Swanson, *The Changing American Parent.*
10. The American Catholic Hierarchy on "The Christian Family" from *The Catholic Mind,* Vol. 43 (Feb., 1950), pp. 121–125.
11. See Boisen, Anton T., *Religion in Crisis and Custom: A Sociological and Psychological Study;* Braden, Charles S., "Churches of the Dispossessed," *The Christian Century,* Jan. 26, 1944, pp. 108–110; Brown, James S., "Social Class, Intermarriage, and Church Membership in a Kentucky Community," *American Journal of Sociology,* LVII (Nov.,

1951), 232–242; Cantril, Hadley, *The Psychology of Social Movements;* Clark, Elmer T., *The Small Sects in America;* Goldschmidt, Walter, "Class Denominationalism in Rural California Churches," *American Journal of Sociology,* XLIX (Jan., 1944), 348–355; Herberg, Will, *Protestant-Catholic-Jew;* Niebuhr, H. Richard, *The Social Sources of Denominationalism;* Warner, W. Lloyd, *et al., Social Classes in America.*

12. A complex objective rating scheme known as the "Index of Status Characteristics" is described in W. Lloyd Warner and M. H. Warner, *What You Should Know About Social Class,* pp. 32 ff.
13. Willard Waller and Reuben Hill (see Note 6), p. 5.
14. See William H. Whyte's article "Budgetism: Opiate of the Middle Class" in *Fortune,* May, 1956 (carried subsequently in his book *The Organization Man*) for evidence that the gospel of thrift, so long an integral part of the so-called "Protestant ethic," is being traded for the rhythm of regular monthly payments and the conviction that there is no sense in self-denial.
15. According to U.S. Department of Labor estimates it is expected that those engaged in white-collar jobs will be the largest segment of the nation's working force by 1975. A 75 per cent increase is expected in the proprietor and managerial group alone.
16. Unless otherwise indicated, all figures are derived from latest U.S. Census reports, with special help from Dr. Paul C. Glick of the U.S. Census Bureau.
17. Robert A. Nisbet, *The Quest for Community,* p. 97. New York: Oxford University Press, Inc., 1953.
18. Nisbet (see Note 17), p. 104.
19. Nisbet (see Note 17), pp. 102–103.
20. W. F. Ogburn, "The Changing Functions of the Family," *The Family,* XIX (1938), 139–143.
21. That it is not the only influence or even the chief influence on the child as he reaches adolescence, is also apparent. Then his way of life is influenced more by the "peer culture" than the family of orientation, as illustrated earlier in this chapter.
22. D. F. Aberle and Kaspar E. Naegele, "Middle Class Father's Occupational Role and Attitudes Toward Children," *The American Journal of Orthopsychiatry,* XXII (1952), 366–378.
23. Daniel R. Miller and Guy E. Swanson, *The Changing American Parent,* pp. 57–58.
24. William H. Whyte, Jr., in *The Organization Man* refers to the desire of large corporations "to make men interchangeable."
25. Leonard Reissman, "Levels of Aspiration and Social Class," *American Sociological Review,* XVIII (June, 1953), 233–241.
26. John R. Seeley, R. Alexander Sim, and E. W. Loosley, *Crestwood Heights: A Study of the Culture of Suburban Life,* p. 124.
27. See William H. Whyte, Jr., "The Wife Problem," in *Life,* Jan. 7, 1952, pp. 32–48, and *The Organization Man.*
28. Part-time as well as full-time jobs are included in this figure. It should not be assumed that employment outside the home is a permanent

status for these mothers; married women are slipping in and out of the labor force at different times within marriage.

29. "Support of the family" always has both an objective and a subjective reference; its meaning may change, as suggested in the quotation, when the family sets new goals and raises its aspiration level.
30. At present the average mother sees her youngest child married when she herself is but forty-seven years of age; from that time on she is, as a mother, out of a job.
31. Perhaps one in four wives now handle all family accounts in the homes involved in this study. Working during the early years of marriage has, no doubt, trained them for this role.
32. If the American woman forgets for a moment about cosmetics, deodorants, clothes, and washday soaps, the advertisers make sure that memory is stimulated each time she turns on the television, or has her eye caught by the blandishments of the newsstand magazine. Yet many wives have developed a resistance to the new tyranny of "planned obsolescence"; canning, dressmaking, and home-permanents within her domicile still halt the relentless pressure of Madison Avenue upon the family's life.
33. Max Lerner reports, "While there are no hard figures, the usual estimates are that women control up to 70 per cent of America's wealth, that they have 60 per cent of the savings accounts and are beneficiaries of 70 per cent of the insurance policies, that they represent more than half the stockholders in the big, gilt-edge corporations, that they own close to half of the nation's homes, and that at least three quarters of the nation's purchasing power is funneled through them. The catch is that women hold their purchasing power largely as wives and have acquired their wealth mainly as widows; economically they are disbursing agents, not principals." "The Ordeal of American Women," *The Saturday Review*, Oct. 12, 1957, p. 14.
34. Nelson Foote, "Family Living as Play," *Marriage and Family Living*, XVII, No. 4 (Nov., 1955), 297. That the shifting of a modern woman's roles in her family occurs, one cannot doubt; but whether this doffing is done "lightly" one can safely question. She is often ambivalent around her roles of "mothering" and being a socially conscious, intelligent individual, especially if she is college educated.
35. Mirra Komarovsky, *Women in the Modern World: Their Education and Their Dilemmas*.
36. Nelson Foote, "Changes in American Marriage Patterns," *Eugenics Quarterly*, Dec., 1954, Vol. I, No. 4. This latter observation was made before the appearance of "beatnik beards" which, however, are apparently a temporary phenomenon, probably more definitely related to cultural nonconformity than to an assertion of masculinity.
37. Max Lerner, "The Ordeal of American Women," *The Saturday Review* (see Note 33), pp. 61–62.
38. Florence Kluckhohn, "What's Wrong with the American Family?", *The Journal of Social Hygiene*, June, 1950.
39. See Llewelyn Queener, *Introduction to Social Psychology*, Chapter VIII, and Margaret Mead, *Male and Female*, for a scientific appraisal

of male-female differences and the effect of culture upon our definitions of "masculine" and "feminine."

40. Margaret Mead, "American Man in a Woman's World," *The New York Times Magazine,* Feb. 10, 1957, p. 11.
41. Robert W. Lynn, "Fifty Church Families and Their Role Expectations," an unpublished paper presented to the Consultative Conference on Theology and Family, Atlantic City, Oct. 17–20, 1957. Used by permission.
42. Jurgen Ruesch, M.D., and Gregory Bateson, *Communication: The Social Matrix of Psychiatry,* pp. 126, 162. New York: W. W. Norton Co., Inc., 1951.
43. William H. Whyte, Jr., *The Organization Man.*
44. James H. S. Bossard and Eleanor S. Boll, *The Sociology of Child Development,* pp. 654–655.
45. Studies show that Roman Catholic college students possess a stronger sense of obligation for this filial support than do college students who classify themselves "Protestant." R. M. Dinkel, "Attitudes of Children Toward Supporting Aged Parents," *American Sociological Review,* IX (1944), 370–379. From this study it is hard to determine whether it is the religious or the ethnic group influence which is the more highly correlated with this difference.
46. Scott Greer, "Individual Participation in Mass Society," an unpublished paper prepared for the Conference on the Study of the Community, Northwestern University, March 15–17, 1956.
47. M. Axelrod, "Urban Structure and Social Participation," *American Sociological Review,* XXI (1956), 13–18.
48. P. H. Rossi, *Why Families Move.*
49. Representative statements of Protestant positions on this matter are found in *Information Service,* a biweekly publication of the Bureau of Research and Survey, National Council of the Churches of Christ in the U.S.A., 475 Riverside Drive, New York 27, N.Y. "Church-Related Elementary and Secondary Schools in Continental United States," Jan. 3, 1959.
50. John R. Seeley *et al., Crestwood Heights,* p. 243, and W. Lloyd Warner *et al., Who Shall Be Educated?,* pp. 56, 57. David Riesman reports "new ways of using the school as a kind of community center, as the chapel of a secular religion perhaps," in *Individualism Reconsidered,* p. 211.
51. James D. Smart, *The Teaching Ministry of the Church,* pp. 187–204.
52. C. N. Stendler, "Social Class Differences in Parental Attitude Toward School at Grade I Level," *Child Development,* XXII:1, March, 1951.
53. Studies show that when a middle-class family's income is doubled, significantly larger expenditures occur in the areas of housing (110% increase); clothing and personal care for appearance (110%); *educational activities and reading* (300%); *travel and transportation* (500%); and recreation (145%). W. F. Ogburn, "Implications of the Rising Standard of Living in the United States," *American Journal of Sociology,* LX:6 (May, 1955), 541–546.

54. John Dollard, *The Changing Functions of the American Family,* pp. 204–206.
55. *Public Opinion Quarterly,* X (1946), 638; and XI (1947), 303–304.
56. Gordon W. Allport, J. M. Gillespie, and J. Young, "The Religion of the Post-War College Student," *Journal of Psychology,* 1948, XXV, 3–33.
57. Ray E. Baber, *Marriage and the Family,* Second Edition, 1954, p. 119.
58. In the decade 1946–1956, six billion dollars were spent on the erection of 70,000 church sanctuaries and 12,500 religious education units. Someone has dubbed this predominant interest in church buildings "the edifice complex."
59. See especially Will Herberg, *Protestant-Catholic-Jew,* and Martin E. Marty, *The New Shape of American Religion.*
60. John L. Thomas, S.J., *The American Catholic Family,* pp. 334–335. Englewood, N.J.: Prentice-Hall, Inc., 1956.
61. Among the Protestant denominations which provide such home-related curriculum materials are the following: American Baptist, Church of God, Congregational-Christian, Disciples of Christ, Evangelical and Reformed, Lutheran Church—Missouri Synod, Methodist, Protestant Episcopal, Southern Baptist, United Lutheran, United Presbyterian. Collectively, these denominations report about 35 million members.
62. The trend toward sedentary types of recreation, and the shift of recreation to outside the home was summarized by Burgess and Locke, *The Family: From Institution to Companionship,* p. 468, and by R. Denney and David Riesman, "Leisure in Urbanized America," in *Reader in Urban Sociology,* P. K. Hatt and A. J. Reiss, Jr., eds., pp. 469–480.
63. Nelson Foote, "Family Living as Play," *Marriage and Family Living,* XVII:4 (Nov., 1955), 297.
64. Evelyn M. Duvall, *Family Development.*
65. Reported in the *New York Times,* April 24, 1957.
66. Terman reports that for men, virginity at the time of marriage was 50.6 per cent of his sample born before 1890 as compared with 13.6 per cent of the group born in 1910 or later. For women the corresponding figures are 86.5 and 31.7 per cent. According to Kinsey, there are less premarital sexual relations among college-educated (middle-class) males than among grade-school-educated males; college-educated females engage in *more* premarital coitus than their grade-school-educated counterparts. Religiously active people engage in less premarital coitus than those who are religiously indifferent *within the same educational level.* But even religiously inactive college-educated people are more restrained sexually than religiously *active* grade-school-educated respondents. Kinsey also reports decrease in "commercialized outlets" for men and an increase in coitus with friends of the opposite sex. The figures in both these studies are inexact because of sampling errors but the trend cannot be denied.
67. Erich Fromm, *The Art of Loving,* p. 54.
68. Purnell Benson, "Familism and Marital Success," *Social Forces,* XXXIII (March, 1955), 277–280.

69. In 1890 the average male was 26.1 years of age at the time of marriage; now he is but 22.8 years of age. The 1890 woman was, on the average, 22.0 years of age when married; but in 1960 she is 20.3 years, slightly *older* than her counterpart of 1950 (who, on the average, was married at 20.1 years of age).
70. J. Sirjamaki, "Culture Configurations in the American Family," *American Journal of Sociology,* LIII:1 (July, 1947), 464–470.
71. About half of the men and women in Burgess and Wallin's study of college students felt that extramarital relations were "justifiable for men under certain circumstances." Fewer had tolerance for extramarital relations among women; women are less tolerant than men at this point. Ernest Burgess and Paul Wallin, *Engagement and Marriage.*
72. See Gibson Winter, *Love and Conflict.*
73. P. K. Whelpton and C. V. Kiser, "Social and Psychological Factors Affecting Fertility," *The Milbank Memorial Fund Quarterly,* XXI (July, 1943), 221–280.
74. At the organization's 27th convention, meeting in San Antonio, Texas, June 21, 1960, as reported by the *New York Times Service.*
75. Edmund Bergler, *Divorce Won't Help,* p. 232.
76. Evelyn M. Duvall and Reuben Hill in *When You Marry* have produced a handy table (of use by the pastor and service groups in the church) of the most common disruptive breakdowns of family life, classifying them according to type: *Dismemberment:* Loss of Child, Loss of Spouse, Orphaned, Hospitalized, War Separation; *Demoralization Only:* Nonsupport, Progressive Dissension, Infidelity, Sense of Disgrace; Reputation Loss; *Accession Only:* Unwanted Pregnancy, Deserter Returns, Stepmother, Stepfather Additions, Some War Reunions, Some Adoptions; *Demoralization Plus Dismemberment or Accession:* Illegitimacy, Runaway Situations, Desertions, Divorce, Imprisonment, Suicide, or Homicide.
77. H. Ashley Weeks, "Differential Divorce Rates by Occupations," *Social Forces,* XXI, 332–337.
78. Jessie Bernard, *Remarriage: A Study of Marriage,* p. 291.
79. William J. Goode, *After Divorce,* 1956.
80. See the research reported by Clifford Adams in *Preparing for Marriage* and Robert Williamson, *Economic Factors in Marital Adjustment,* unpublished Doctoral Dissertation, University of Southern California Library, June, 1951.
81. Henry Bowman, *Marriage for Moderns,* 1954.
82. "The Marriage Rate and the Business Cycle," Metropolitan Life Insurance Company *Statistical Bulletin,* XIX (7), 1–3.
83. See the new book on *Sex Ways in Fact and Faith,* Evelyn and Sylvanus Duvall, eds.
84. Bradley Buell, Paul T. Beisser *et al.* in their report for the Community Research Associates, Inc., *Classification of Disorganized Families for Use in Family Oriented Diagnosis and Treatment* (1954), have discovered that a relatively small number of such families (in St. Paul, Minnesota, just 6 per cent of the total community) provide a startlingly high proportion of social and health problems of the area (about 33 per

cent of these problems) and receive a wholly disproportionate share of the total service and funds provided for social service.

85. The dynamics of "impulsiveness" are obviously too complicated to explore in this book. It is discussed in many volumes of marital dynamics and psychoanalytic approaches to personality.
86. Robert S. Ort, "A Study in Role-Conflicts as Related to Happiness in Marriage," *Journal of Abnormal and Social Psychology,* XLV:4 (Oct., 1950), 691–699.
87. John V. Buerkle and Robin F. Badgley, "A Study of Marital Interaction," an unpublished paper made available to the authors; and Alver H. Jacobsen, "Conflict of Attitudes Toward the Roles of the Husband and Wife in Marriage," *American Sociological Review,* XVII:2 (April, 1954), 146–150.
88. Buell, Beisser, *et al., Classification of Disorganized Families for Use in Family Oriented Diagnosis and Treatment,* p. 25.
89. Duvall and Hill, *When You Marry,* p. 466.
90. Harold T. Christenson and Hanna H. Meissner, "Studies in Child Spacing. III. Premarital Pregnancy as a Factor in Divorce," *American Sociological Review,* Dec., 1953.
91. One of the difficulties with all such studies is the catch-all nature of the term "Protestant"; it often connotes no organic relationship with a Protestant denomination but only "non-Catholic" leanings.
92. For a complete discussion of these studies, see Judson T. Landis and Mary G. Landis, *Building a Successful Marriage,* pp. 146–166.
93. Reported in James Peterson, *Education for Marriage,* pp. 317–318.
94. Peterson (see Note 93), pp. 319–331.

- Polemics Surround Family Teachings
- Theology as an Afterthought
- The Family and the Tribe
- Family Relationships: Parenthood, Marriage
- The Image of God
- From Old Testament to New—a Transition
- Order and Subordination
- Sexual Relation in Christian Thought
- The New Testament Challenge to the Family
- Jesus' Own Family Life

3

The Biblical Perspective

BOTH THE OLD TESTAMENT and the New Testament begin with families and the stories of their relationships. Literally every book of the Bible contains some family reference, for the Scriptures are rich with allusions and descriptions about home life.

Polemics Surround Family Teachings

However, most biblical teachings about family relationships are set into the context of specific problems or within polemical situations. Thus divorce is discussed by Jesus after a direct challenge from a group of Pharisees (Matthew 19:1–12, Mark 10:2–12, Luke 16:14, 18). Interfaith marriages come up for discussion by Ezra when he is insisting that Israel's heritage be protected from foreign entanglements,[1] and by Paul when he is dealing with questions from Corinthians about the impact of paganism upon the faith if Christian believers are wedded to non-Christians.[2] The Bible poses a problem for us if it is our intention to formulate an inclusive definition of Christian marriage or a systematic "theology of the family." Our task is to find the relevant word of God for today's families and to discover how Christian theology can speak in explicit terms to current family concerns, for theology is a valuable tool in this task not for the sake of academic curiosity, but only when its truth becomes applicable to specific families of the twentieth century. The biblical record sets the example; as Dietrich Bonhoeffer reminds us, it never speaks abstractly to general situations but only addresses specific words to particular men.

Urgent need for theological light on our family problems becomes increasingly apparent as the disorientation described in the preceding chapter besets homes of the world. It is within these untoward circumstances that we begin to ask questions about the nature of the family, and inquire where we can solicit the aid of theology. Biblical revelation provides us with immense enlightenment for this quest; yet we must be prepared also to look beyond the Bible for our insights. The Bible itself, in fact, places upon us an obligation to seek additional answers. This is not only because the changes in family life from the days of ancient Israel or first-century Christianity have brought us into a greatly different period necessitating reinterpretation, but also because we dare not treat the Bible as a talisman that would magically solve all our current problems for us. To us, as to the men of that day, God reveals himself in history; and this can well mean current history. To us, as to them, he can indicate: "Son of man, stand upon your feet and I will speak with you" (Ezekiel 2:1).*

Theology as an Afterthought

Theology is apparently often an afterthought to life. In many cases it has turned out to be a study awakened by the encounter of the church and the world at some crossroads of experience. Family life, of course, had been in existence for ages before there were any religious formulations about it. Thus the law of Moses with its many ordinances about family relationships may not so much have introduced new standards as to codify a number of them that were already taken for granted. Later, Christian ethics came to take up standards common to many civilized peoples and to hallow those of central importance.

This afterthought face of theology may account in part for the largely unco-ordinated nature of family teaching in religious history. Life itself precedes reflection about it. The church lived in and through its families, taking them much for granted, before churchmen began to theorize

* The scriptural quotations used in this book are from the Revised Standard Version of the Bible, copyrighted 1946 and 1952 by the Division of Christian Education of the National Council of the Churches of Christ in the U.S.A.

about the family, its being, and its purpose. It was not the community of faith that created family life; families had already been in existence for eons. Infidels had known home life prior to their conversion; and sometimes they found that their new faith even dealt a blow to family loyalties. Non-Christians, both in the times of the early church and now, could live a life not unlike that of many Christians. Many of them also respect chastity, fidelity, loyalty, and family stability. Our faith is unique neither in these principles nor in problems of how faithfully adherents observe them.

It must be squarely faced that modern society raises many complex problems for which the Bible has no direct answer, and that the family presents one of these. Yet a close examination of the Scriptures reveals what Suzanne de Dietrich has called "guiding lines" which can be of tremendous benefit in our quest.[3] There is a biblical view of man, of the major obligations in family and group responsibility, and of the worth of human personality. And these remain in force for our day. We need not throw in the sponge if we find that the New Testament church reflected many of the current cultural ideas of marriage and family relationships. This cultural conditioning affected its views of slavery, employment, and politics, to choose but a few examples. To ascertain through which biblical insights God is speaking directly to our day is no simple assignment. But this dare not prevent us from inquiring. The Bible speaks to us today; and the church measures its doctrine by the Scriptures.

Such inquiry is necessary because we can no longer assume that a family status that once was taken for granted is valid for now. Earlier concepts must be re-examined in the light of changing family structure, and the sociological complexities uncovered in research. Moreover, unless we ask the difficult, persistent questions that pertain to family life, and consider these theologically, the church runs the risk of proliferating inappropriate programs that do not further the gospel or the health of the church in Christian education or in pastoral work.[4]

Such an effort does not dream of an "ideal" Christian family of some yesteryear. Rather, it reminds us that institutions change and develop; and that the church believes that the gospel can speak to the family as well as to other institutions of society. Our day has to see the place of the family in the kingdom of God just as surely as did the people of New Testament times, and their experience will serve also to guide and instruct us. For them, too, a consideration of the stability of family life must have represented a quest for order in a disordered world.

The Family and the Tribe

To understand the multitudinous references to family life in the Old Testament, we must recall that for ancient Israel the family had been what Millar Burrows identifies as "the basic social unit."[5] Mere individuals did not become a fundamental unit in that society until later; and even today the nomadic peoples who populate the Mid-East area have far less regard for individualism than we of Western cultures have.[6] This basically unitary concept of family life underlies many of their practices that appear so foreign to our situation and viewpoint: for example, the patriarchal home, the prearranged marriage, the secondary status of women, and even wholesale punishment of an entire family for an offense of just one of its members.

The clan (*mishpachah*) in Hebrew culture was endowed with a fierce sense of loyalty. Theirs was a God-given relationship to one another; and they knew themselves as God's chosen people. Anything that threatened or violated this highly valued unity was condemned. Capital punishment could be exacted for a number of infractions that threatened the God-ordered oneness of marriage or upset the established relationships within the family. The death penalty might be invoked for striking one's father, for adultery, or for practices of sexual inversion.

The family unit itself was part and parcel of a still wider unity of the tribe, the people of the Covenant. Within this Covenant all persons were considered brothers or neighbors to one another. Mutual protection and loyalty demanded that the tribe act as a superfamily and significantly the same term, *mishpachah,* is applied to tribe and family alike. Any antisocial acts that destroy this principle of brotherhood or militate against neighborly trust and interdependence are severely punished. Murders, theft, blackmail, and covetousness, being injurious to the community family life, are explicitly proscribed.

So precious to Hebrew thinking is the centrality of the family that even after the nomadic economy was no longer their way of life, a romanticized ideal of the father's tent with the gathered clan remained their normative picture of a household as it ought to be. This ideal was regarded at its best in terms of parents, children, servants, flocks and herds. Years after they had given up the life of wandering Aramaeans, even after they had grown into a ranking nation, this concept of the inclusive family remained in the back of their thinking.

It was no narrow concept of togetherness that bound these people to one another. The family groupings through tribe and nation were evidently felt to extend as far as homology reached: throughout the kinship of the extended family and touching everyone who for various reasons of respect or dependency might look upon the head man (sheikh, judge, or king in different stages and circumstances) as father. Once it was securely founded with fecund heirs, a family line could live and grow through descendants stretching forward into the centuries, and be reckoned back into the past to all who contributed to it. Thus one man in Judah could relate himself to a complexity of lines, referring to Abraham as his father, identifying himself as of the house of David, designating his own personal status as the son of Simon.

From this family concept there gradually grew a set of moral values that were integrated with Jewish ethics and codified in the Torah. The nation which emerged from this culture was founded upon a covenant with Jahweh, and became known throughout the ancient world for its lofty sense of morality and its protection of the family by community law. Respect for parents was enjoined (Exodus 20:12), child welfare and prenatal protection were provided (Exodus 21:22), inheritance rights were arranged in orderly fashion (Deuteronomy 21:15 ff.), strangers were protected from victimization (Leviticus 19:33), and the approved treatment of neighbors and their property rights was plainly understood (Exodus 22:26). It was an astonishingly high understanding of ethical obligations in interpersonal relationships; and its *raison d'être* was the pattern of family life.[7]

It was but a simple step as Israel began to grow into a nation to consider herself as a confederation of families, indeed as a newer, inclusive national family. Eventually this principle was to be extended in the writings of Deutero-Isaiah to include all the peoples of the earth. Evidence of this family-of-families concept in the nation can be found in numerous Old Testament books, particularly in the prophets. Amos, for instance, prophesies against Israel as a family group, threatening: "You only have I known of all the families of the earth; therefore I will punish you for all your iniquities" (Amos 3:2). Micah, in turn, similarly cites the voice of the Lord to Israel: "Behold, against this family I am devising evil" (Micah 2:3).

The collective concept of family involvement in nation and clan had its important corollaries. They were a people of the Covenant, for example; and, as they understood this sacred type of contract, it involved not only the one who negotiated it but his entire family as well. It obligated not only a leader, but his entire people and even unborn descendants. A striking example is cited in Joshua's charge to the tribes in the formation of the Shechem covenant: "Choose this day whom you will serve . . . but as for me and my house, we will serve the Lord."[8]

Joshua supports his demands for their loyalty with a lesson from history that reminds them of the original covenant made with their father Abraham and of their family tradition of faithfulness to God and of what he had done for them in fulfilling his promises: "I took your father Abraham from beyond the (Euphrates) River and led him through all the land of Canaan, and made his offspring many" (Joshua 24:2, 3).

The family covenantal tradition with its concept of mutuality and loyalty carries down into New Testament times and is echoed today in the rites and sacraments of the church. Thus to this day, marriage is defined as a covenant made between man and wife, baptism is related to the covenant made in Christ and confirmed in the sacrament; and the Lord's Supper recalls the scriptural reference to the covenant in the liturgy of the cup: "This cup is the new covenant in my blood."[9]

Family Relationships: Parenthood, Marriage

Whatever uncertainty may have entered modern thinking about father, there was little doubt about his importance in Bible times. In that day he was not only the biological sire of his progeny, but also master and possessor of his family. He was the *ba'al* in the sense that his power included ownership and authority. (The very same word, it will be recalled, was used for certain pagan deities because of this definition that invested the term with authority and lordship.) The father's will was nearly absolute; and his power was seldom flaunted. Yet his was not a despotic position of unlimited dictatorship. He was also the source of strength and identity for his family and for the whole group that acknowledged him as their chief.[10]

Given these larger meanings to the word, father as the *pater familias* obviously had a position of rank and honor. To his family and/or tribe he could be judge, guardian, business executive, but a warm parental figure, too. It is small wonder that with so much power, some fathers were tempted to become autocratic, and that biblical allusions show a number to have been overly strict, even ruthless. That the tradition evidently developed men who could overdo their sternness is reflected in Paul's admonishment for men not to provoke their children to wrath. But, on the whole, father's parental authority enabled him to communicate a sense of affectionate security to the entire family.

He was therefore the object of honor and of unquestioning obedience. A son is expected to honor his father; and the Deuteronomic code gives specific and grim directions for the punishment of a rebellious son who will not obey his father.[11]

In a society so heavily patriarchal, mother's place is definable principally in relation to father. The commandment with promise, as Paul dubbed it, enjoins us to honor our father and mother so that longevity (of the national family, that is) will be the reward. In numerous points of the law, the mother is linked with father in such a way there can be no doubt that parents stand together. Though her position was subordinate to the man's, her place was both influential and revered. Many a biblical narrative illustrates the position of honor accorded to the wife and mother; tales of Sarah, Rebekah, and Rachel, the wives of patriarchs, spring to mind. And some women apparently reached positions of peculiar prominence in the society; among them would be Deborah the judge, Huldah the prophetess, and queenly Esther. It is significant, however, that in the patriarchal society of Hebrew culture, such women as attained positions of importance, did so by working with and through men who had the ranking power in the culture.

Sonship

To gain a still better concept of the meaning of family relations in the Bible, the factor of sonship must be introduced; for it plays an important part in the tradition. The strength and characteristics of the father, according to Hebrew thought, were transmitted to his sons, a principle with which geneticists need not quarrel, pre-scientific though it is. According to one tradition the forebears could eat grapes and set their children's teeth on edge; that is, the errors of ancestors are still being punished in their family line. But this view was strongly challenged by both Ezekiel and Jeremiah who insisted that the sinner himself is liable for his own retribution and can hardly pass his chastisement on to his heirs.[12]

But sonship had another cultural meaning: indicating a way of behavior, of kindred thinking, or emotion. Jesus uses this concept in figures of speech as when he accuses some of being the sons of them that slew the prophets (Matthew 23:31), or admonishes a crowd of listeners to love their enemies so that they may be sons of their Father who makes the sun to rise on the just and unjust alike (Matthew 5:44 f.). Or Semitic speech had a way of describing characteristics in terms of sonship. Thus Barnabas means son of encouragement; and we get references to sons of obedience, or of disobedience, or of peace, also (Acts 4:36, I Peter 1:14, Luke 10:6). Sonship tells much about the family line in this sense. The sons of this world and the sons of light are contrasted in the parable of the dishonest steward; the sons of the kingdom and the sons of the evil one are contrasted in the parable of the sower; the sons of this world and the sons of the resurrection are contrasted in a saying of Jesus about the differences in marriage between this world and the next (Luke 16:1–8, Matthew 13:38, Luke 20:35).

The concept of sonship is lifted to a new and different realm when it is seen theologically. But the experience of the Hebrew home is consistent even there. Obedience is again emphasized as the cardinal relationship between a son and the Father who is in heaven. In the book of Hebrews, it is re-emphasized that it is the work of the Father to discipline his sons, and we must endure such chastisement with humility (Hebrews 12:5–11). Sons of the kingdom have laid upon them heavy responsibilities—to forgive as their Father forgives them, to be peacemakers because they are sons of God, to love their enemies and pray for their persecutors because their Father does good to the evil and is kind even to the ungrateful (Mark 11:25, Matthew 5:9, Matthew 5:44, Luke 6:35). This sonship is seen in the New Testament to be a gift to those who have faith in Jesus Christ as Lord. Those who are invited into discipleship enter a brotherhood with Jesus and by this means are the adopted sons of God. The early church was considered to be a new family to its members. Had not Jesus turned to his disciples and indicated that they were his brethren and his mother in the new family relationship of the followers? Everyone in that fellowship became your brother or sister or mother because he was first of all a brother, or sister or mother in Christ. To those who had left goods and kindred, or who (more accurately) had been expelled from their homes for taking up the new life, the community of faith represented a family loyalty that could be deeper and more meaningful than any other earthly ties. It represented a family in which the Father was not only more loving than any earthly father, "For my father and my mother have forsaken me, but the Lord will take me up" (Psalm 27:10), but also more demanding in his expectation that this has priority over all other relationships. It was a highly disciplined company, that family of faith.

Brotherhood

The brotherliness of the new community in Christ had received notable impetus from Israel's heritage. Tribal mores had accepted the term neighbor as nearly equivalent to brother; and covenanted agreements bound men to each other in fraternity. This ideal was transmitted wholesale into the Christian community where the term brothers (*adelphoi*) became synonymous with Christians. The concept was an old one, but Jesus gave it a radically new interpretation. It had been said of old times that all men have one Father, and that they are *ipso facto* brothers. But now Jesus calls upon the brothers to treat each other in a way of love not even practiced in many families. It is clear that they are to love him more than members of their own family, and that by drawing close to him they also draw close to one another. Jesus, as Paul describes him in Romans 8:29, is the "first-born among many brethren"; and all Christians are joint heirs with Christ of the grace of God. As part of the household of God, the new brotherhood is to live by the standard of love.

As Paul Minear points out from his searching discussion of this topic,[13] it is impossible to have faith in Christ Jesus without also loving our brother (a review of I John 3:14–24 underscores this truth); for Christ "has made it impossible either to fix a limit outside which this love need no longer to be exercised, or to escape the immediate claim of every brother."[14] Such brotherhood reaches across class distinctions to include those whose company we might otherwise not choose unless we did see in them persons for whom Christ died. Thus the book of Philemon owes its position in the New Testament canon to Paul's insistence that the wealthy must accept in Christian brotherhood those whose status is that of slaves. This very inclusiveness appealed to the poor, the captives, the blind, and the oppressed. Such a fellowship reached out with love to any and to all. The new family of faith, in keeping with any other household, was to accept its members for themselves rather than for what they had achieved, to care for each other in mutual assistance, and to love one another, practicing forgiveness and sacrifice where these were needed.

Marriage

In biblical literature the marriage relationship is set deep within creation itself. The foundation for the doctrine of marriage is to be traced from the book of Genesis; and subsequent tradition draws attention to that first union of Adam and Eve as a prototype for the marital union. In the Jahvist thread (Genesis 2:4 ff.), a description of the world is set forth as formed by the Lord and climaxed by placing man at its center: ". . . then the Lord God formed man of dust from the ground, and breathed into his nostrils the breath of life; and man became a living being." Subsequently when the flora and fauna of the primitive world had been placed into creation, the Lord God said, "It is not good that the man should be alone; I will make him a helper fit for him."

In a warm and memorable story, the woman Eve is brought into life from the rib of an anesthetized Adam. And Adam gives a joyous cry that marks the end of his loneliness: "This at last is bone of my bones and flesh of my flesh; she shall be called Woman, because she was taken out of Man." *Therefore a man leaves his father and his mother and cleaves to his wife, and they become one flesh.*

This same one-flesh condition has characterized every true marriage since the beginning. This essential unitive relationship of man and woman in marriage is referred to by Jesus in his teaching[15] and echoed by the apostle Paul in his writings to the Corinthians.[16] The one-flesh relationship is described in the Bible as worthy in itself, as well as for the conception and bearing of children. The rabbinic term for marriage is *Kiddushin,* derived from the word meaning sanctification. In marriage, say the rabbis, is found the means of the love of God. The people were encouraged to be fruitful and to multiply, but this fertility was seen as a *result* and *blessing* of marriage rather than its sole purpose. The Hebrew wife was not to be regarded as a brood mare or plaything, as Richard M. Fagley writes.[17] But it would be mistaken to assume, by reading modern romantic ideals back into the biblical account, that Hebrew marriage could be considered as the simple, companionate existence of two loving persons. Marriage had far-reaching effects in family, tribe, and nation; in it the concept of covenant was written large. Indeed, these additional connections, wherein the value of a marriage to kin and clan were assessed, assumed paramount importance. The match was arranged by the heads of families, festival times being especially favored for this happy ritual. The Hebrew family was patrilocal: that is, the bride came to live in the clan of her husband. Gifts were exchanged on both sides. The father of the bride received a mohar of some fifty shekels, which was understood not so much to be a purchase price as a compensation for his loss of a daughter. Sometimes (and the case of Jacob is famous in this regard) the groom would work out his gift to the bride's father in bonded service that kept the couple in her father's tents for the first part of their marriage. Families necessarily wished to retain flocks and land within their own group; and they would go to considerable effort to arrange marriages that continued this policy.

Since the marriage concerned two families, each of them gave up something to this new home. The bride's family released their own flesh and blood in this daughter; the groom's family offered a mohar price. In such a bargain, both groups relinquished a value; and both gained in differing ways. From here on, it was the groom's task to support his wife and the children born to them. If she came from a wealthy clan, she might have some personal money supplied her by her own family; but it was now recognized that her possessions were the *de jure* property of her husband who was the *ba'al*. In the event of her husband's death, or if he wrote her the infamous "bill of divorcement" the woman might return to her father's family. If she was both widowed and childless, she might be taken into the home of her deceased husband's brother as his additional wife in order to raise up sons to the family name. This was the much discussed Levirate custom.

It was her duty in marriage to produce children for the family line; and, if she could not, there was a time when she might be driven to offer a concubine to her husband so at least to have children to adopt. This, of course, was the experience of Sarah who put forth her maid servant to Abraham. To preserve the family economy, and provide an unbroken line into posterity, sons and daughters (valued in just that order) were essential. It was a tremendous crisis for a marriage to be childless; and it was invariably assumed that if no children were born it must be the wife who was barren.[18]

An unfaithful wife could be put to death by lapidation. Adultery was never treated with lightness in Hebrew culture, but was strictly punished.

It is not a religious ceremony or state licensing that sealed a marriage (the Bible contains no record of these more modern inventions), but it was the consent of the families involved. The procedure seems rather simple. An agreement was made; a betrothal followed. After a while a feast was held, and the groom went to the tent of his betrothed and brought her back to his own. Sometimes this was the first that he had actually seen of her. Custom did play its part, often to an intimate degree unknown to our day;[19] but for the most part the procedure was simple in keeping with a stern desert life of few amenities. Still, the people of the Covenant saw in marriage something far beyond the mere utilitarianism characteristic of neighboring tribes. For them marriage was to fulfill a purpose, building a home of joy, of faith, and fruitfulness.

The New Testament carries on many of the same marital traditions; and, contrary to some ill-informed criticism, it is not inimical to marriage. In the early part of his ministry, Jesus took part in the marriage feast at Cana. He apparently enjoyed these festive occasions and gave to them his approval; for they come into frequent mention in parables.[20] But when he was accosted by the Pharisees and challenged on the subject of divorce he stated his position on marriage in the most affirmative words we have on record. He had been asked whether it is lawful for a man to divorce his wife. Everyone in the crowd knew of the current dispute between the schools of Hillel and Shammai, over what justifications constituted ground for divorce. They must have expected Jesus to comment on these legal problems, but he did not. Ever one to plunge beneath superficial tensions to ultimate causes, he recalled for them those lines from the creation story that Karl Barth has named "the Magna Carta of humanity"—namely, "From the beginning of creation, God made them male and female. For this reason a man shall leave his father and mother and be joined to his wife, and the two shall become one. . . . What therefore God has joined together, let not man put asunder" (Mark 10:6–9).

The Epistles underline the God-given sanctity of marriage in yet another way. Calling analogical relationship to mind, they often compare the marital union to that of Christ and his Church. Thus: ". . . I betrothed you to Christ to present you as a pure bride to her one husband" (II Corinthians 11:2). And "Nevertheless, in the Lord woman is not independent of man nor man of woman. . . . And all things are from God" (I Corinthians 11:11 f.). Ephesians 5 is famed for its oft-quoted passage on the subject:

> Husbands, love your wives, as Christ loved the church and gave himself up for her, that he might sanctify her. . . . For no man ever hates his own flesh, but nourishes and cherishes it, as Christ does the church, because we are members of his body. "For this reason a man shall leave his father and mother and be joined to his wife, and the two shall become one." This is a great mystery, and I take it to mean Christ and the church (Ephesians 5:25–32, in part).

Paul's letters, however, can be quoted on both sides of the marriage question, for he apparently at differing times had contradictory opinions about the subject. He held nothing against Christian marriage; but he sometimes did little to help it. He recognized the need for married persons to be loyal to their partners, and for them to enter into a permanent union (I Corinthians 7:10), but he had grudging praise for marriage in the uncertain times for which he wrote: "it is no sin"; "it is better to marry than to be aflame with passion"; or "because of the temptation to immorality, each man should have his own wife and each woman her own husband," all being quotations from his first letter to the Corinthians, Chapter 7. But Paul was writing in the firm expectation that "the form of this world is passing away"; and once again our interpretation of family life is colored by circumstances surrounding those who were teaching doctrine.

The Image of God

The profundity of Genesis 1:27 ("So God created man in his own image, in the image of God he created him; male and female he created them") offers some clues to the purpose behind the establishment of marriage and family life. If God made us in his own image, and we are male and female, then whatever else God may be (and he contains an infinite magnitude of characteristics beyond our reckoning) he must at least encompass maleness and femaleness. Man and woman were created for relationship with each other from the beginning.[21] The dialogue between them was set from the foundations of the world. It also provides in biblical literature the archetype for the relationship of God to his people Israel: ". . . I was their husband, says the Lord" (Jeremiah 31:32). Moreover it defines the relationship between Christ and his church as developed in Ephesians 5: "Husbands, love your wives, as Christ loved the church and gave himself up for her, that he might sanctify her, having cleansed her by the washing of water with the word."

From ancient times, the Hebrew people had such analogies held before them. The prophets reminded them of the wilderness period when they knew but one God who had put his mark upon them and claimed them as his own. The Covenant between them had once been marked with fidelity. But when Israel reached the Promised Land they played the wanton and coveted other gods. Here they were susceptible to new and strange deities of the various fertility cults of that time and area. Israel's most memorable phase of prostituting her faith can be dated from that time. The analogy is a daring one. We find it in the writings of Jeremiah and Hosea.

This close unity of a married couple is suggested in this hoped-for faithful unity between God and his chosen people. Jeremiah's opening prophecies, for instance, are a passionate plea for Jerusalem to return from her unfaithful conduct to her faithful and loving Lord. Jeremiah thunders of the doom to come if they continue in their infidelity with its syncretism of pagan fertility cults and Judaism. The day of destruction and exile is foretold.[22]

It is Hosea, of course, who is best known for this kind of writing. With him the man-wife analogy rises to heights of immortal poetry. Prophesying during the century previous to Jeremiah (about 745 B.C.), Hosea placed this analogy in its most dramatic terms by enacting its elements himself. He had learned from bitter experience something of the meaning of unfaithfulness, heartbreak, and desertion. God is represented by Hosea in pleading with Israel as a wronged, but still loving, husband might plead with an erring, headstrong wife. Using this metaphor of the most intimate personal relationship that humanity knows anything about, he speaks at first tenderly (Hosea 2:14 ff.) and then sternly in chastisement (3:3). Paul makes use of this same prophetic analogy in his writings. To the Romans he quoted Hosea for a purpose that the prophet could hardly have anticipated. About the entrance of Gentiles into the little Christian church, he writes: "Those who were not my people I will call 'my people,' and her who was not beloved I will call 'my beloved' " (Romans 9:25 from Hosea 2:23).

God's love is represented as a highly personal thing in this analogy. Unlike the deities of paganism, the Lord Jahweh was not considered to be "assigned" to his constituency by nature. He on his initiative claimed them as his own in a righteous, forgiving way[23] and from them he expected unwavering fidelity: "for I the Lord am a jealous God" (Exodus 20:5). This conviction that God himself has chosen us was later to be applied to still wider groups of people until the mystery of election and grace reaches its climax in the doctrine of salvation and becomes a capstone of Christianity.

From Old Testament to New—a Transition

Old Testament times had known a family-tribe connection in which these two were virtually inseparable and often indistinguishable from one another. But with the coming of the New Covenant this homogeneity was not destined long to continue. Hold-overs from the older order, of course, remained in many areas of life; and indeed some vestiges are still to be found in the church today. Yet the more person-centered emphasis of Christianity, coming as it did when Israel's tribal loyalties no longer meant what they had once in the days of wandering herdsmen, dealt a heavy blow to the old order. The Old Testament had affirmed and reaffirmed that God's promises were for Abraham's descendants; and for a while Christian Judaisers insisted that this condition still held and that new converts must come into the faith by way of Jewish circumcision. Still unable to see that salvation might apply to persons as individuals, they conceived of this privilege belonging to Abraham's seed forever, and mediated communally through the ancient people of God.[24]

The people of the Old Testament had considered Israel as God's people, his peculiar family. In blessing this chosen race, the Lord blesses his very own family. So cohesive were family and nation that the nation's welfare was advanced as a chief reason for which the family was to be held together. Progeny had been valued not only for themselves but particularly as a holy seed for the nation. Property was held in the family name, and in nomadic times only the tribe possessed wealth as a community; and, as we have seen, continuing the family name was important to retain the holdings, preserve the line in a social immortality, and insure the future. Such a conviction could only heighten the crucial issues of infertility, divorce, sexual aberrations, and family responsibility under the law.

The family, as a matter of fact, was necessary even for Israel to exist. It was for this reason that so many regulations were imposed upon family life. Standards that our day would think important to good family life were obviously less important to their theocratic times than was the welfare of the people of God. The family and their well-being were but instrumental toward this larger goal. It was for this reason that patriarchal values were so essential, that the rigorous code of tribal-family ethics was so strictly enforced.

The early New Testament church had at first also banded together much as a family-tribe, seeking mutual protection. They shared their meals, their material resources, and their funds with those Christians who were in need. It is almost as if they were attempting to carry on the best of Old Testament tribal tradition.[25] There was apparently a resolution, as Suzanne de Dietrich suggests,[26] that the new tribe should prove no less brotherly than the old. It was apparently the normal thing then to welcome the new brother in the faith to the family table.

These new Christians had no houses of worship as such; they met in homes.[27] Indeed, some of the earliest conversions were by households; so it was for Lydia, for the Philippian jailer, and for Stephanus (Acts 16:15, Acts 16:33, and I Corinthians 1:16). Quite understandably they carried over many family customs from their Jewish heritage. The role of father is not markedly different from Old Testament times. He still holds the dominating position, viewed as a source of strength and authority for the entire family.[28] Jesus put the weight of his teaching behind the traditional Old Testament estimate of the family, and used numerous family allusions to help his hearers understand what was for them so mysterious in his radical concept of the kingdom of God. His references to the responsibilities and the concern of fathers, to love and responsibility in the home, to loyalty and sacrifice among brothers all apply to this development.[29]

Relationships between parents and children had changed but little, as we can see in Mark 10, Colossians 3, and Ephesians 6. In fact, these "tables of duties" in the Epistles are recorded straight out of Jewish traditional mores but with one significant addendum: now these relationships are seen as existing "in the Lord." It is in this same context that Christian nurture is to be advanced, a continuation of the ancient ideal to instruct children in the faith; but now and especially, this admonition is set within faith in Jesus as Lord.

A change also is apparent in the concept of the New Israel as a chosen people. The existence of such an entity is no longer to perpetuate a political body (a point which the disciples had difficulty in absorbing) but more than ever before to express the realization of God's spiritual purpose for his creation. The church as the New Israel is to carry forth this goal of gathering God's family for his own.

Whereas the Old Testament had viewed the family as necessary to salvation, the New Testament puts a conspicuously greater emphasis on the person; and this notable difference emerges more clearly as the little community of faith begins to grow. The change may not be abrupt; for Israel now exists in a new realization: the promise is "to you and to your children . . . everyone whom the Lord our God calls to him" (Acts 2:39). The followers of the Way are also "a chosen race, a royal priesthood, a holy nation" (I Peter 2:9). We have the evidence already cited that entire families were received into the faith after the conversion of the father, as in the case of the Philippian jailer, but Timothy can be recalled as the signal of a different day; for he seems to have come from a religiously split Greek family in which father and grandfather are never mentioned as members of the church.

In a sense, memories of the Old Testament keep the community of Christian faith from straying. The early church recognized its continuity with the people of Israel; and, like that gathered people of the Old Covenant, the new *ecclesia* has a sense of God's directing and using them. Yet their sense of destiny also had its significant variation from the former days. Though the Hebrew had a sense of solidarity with corporate Israel, it was not so strong in the New Testament. The Israelite's link with his tribal family had been vital; and his genealogy was an important identification record. Without the tribe he is nameless and unrecognizable. He remained close to his family, avoided lonely places for the most part, and was terrified of ostracism. But Jesus breaks dramatically with this obligation of solidarity, voluntarily goes into solitary experiences, and repudiates the narrower ideas of family loyalty. He sets a new example of emancipation; and others then are able to find in him a new, reorganized family grouping.[30] The coming of Christ also calls into question some of the mores of the Old Covenant: the Levirate law, the unexamined obligation to fathers and their standards, and the narrower exclusiveness to be found in former tenets of faith.[31]

When it became possible for an individual to be a full-fledged member of God's people without first being part of an accepted family unit, a radical shift had taken place. The family is now seen to be a finite, semipermanent institution; but the community of faith is stable through all time, and the gates of hell shall not prevail against it. The early church de-emphasized all families except one—namely, the family of God—and all fatherhood but one.

In other respects, however, the place of family members is rather ambiguous throughout these New Testament references. We could wish for a great deal more clarity of specific material than we now have. As a matter of fact, the reader can infer that early churchmen were likewise puzzled about family relations in the new order of things. There is internal evidence that they were asking questions about whether it was wise to marry in such uncertain times, whether Christ's return is imminent, whether marriage is now permissible after divorce, and just what is to be the place of children in the community of faith.[32]

The transition between the Old and the New was not smooth; and misunderstandings were frequent. It was difficult for many to give up the hope that the kingdom of God might be a splendid and powerful replacement for the long-gone glories of the united kingdom under David and Solomon. Yet it was against this provincial yearning for their own political kingdom that the Jews best understood the family symbolism and references in the teachings of Jesus. Theirs after all was a police state. Able-bodied men could be pressed into service by Roman labor battalions. Tribute taxation was burdensome; and the civil liberties, so precious to Roman citizens, were virtually unknown to the Jews under military government. Of necessity they were circumspect about their words and appearances whenever they were in public. But when they returned home where they could be themselves, could speak candidly, and feel the sanctuary provided in normal family life, they experienced a feeling of security they must have valued highly. Is it not likely that this very appreciation of the sanctity of their homes conditioned those who heard the words of Jesus about his new type of kingdom where family love and acceptance are practiced, to comprehend it better?

Order and Subordination

The transition from Old Testament family philosophy to the New Testament is probably more confusing and opaque in regard to man-woman relationships than anywhere else. Holdovers from previous convictions that the wife is subject to the husband and must be submissive to him show up from time to time. The people of the period had before them in Holy Writ the word as spoken to Eve after the Fall: "Your desire shall be for your husband and he shall rule over you." The battle of the sexes in Old Testament literature depicts men and women as they attract and repel each other, as they seek to dominate one another, he by authority and she by feminine influence. No reader of that literature will miss how woman often mitigates her husband's authority in the patriarchal situation. Thus Rebecca deludes Isaac, Delilah hoodwinks Samson; Abigail influences her Nabal.

The New Testament reflects overtones of the male-dominated culture in which it is set. But the transition also brings new words that must have rung strangely on Semitic ears: In Christ "there is neither male nor female; for you are all one . . . heirs according to promise" (Galatians 3:28, 29). I Peter contains a passage in Chapter 3 that reminds men they and their wives are joint heirs of the grace of life; and Paul is explicit in pointing out that both husbands and wives have duties of consideration for each other in sexual intercourse because each "rules over" the other's body in the intimacy of marriage relations.

There are other passages, however, that have been called into question because of their conservative expectation that wives are to be subject to their husbands. Illustrative of these passages, and famous because of its comprehensive approach to the subject is the fifth chapter of the letter to the Ephesians. The disputed passage begins with verse 21 and continues through the end of the chapter. In it the entire matter of order of relationships is placed in Christological terms: "Wives, be subject to your husbands, as to the Lord. For the husband is the head of the wife as Christ is the head of the church, his body, and is himself its Savior." Only in a cursory and thoughtless reading will this be assumed to mean that man is superior and woman inferior in the relationship. The explicit reference to Christ's responsibility for his church should make this clear. Authority is involved; but this is a subject about which the Bible is never ambiguous. All authority, no matter who exercises it, derives from God and must be answerable to him.[33] Unless this passage is seen in the context of God's delegated authority, biblical references to subordination of family members can be objectionable and debatable. Derrick Sherwin Bailey clarifies the matter considerably when he writes:

> In the church, submission to spiritual authority must find its proper complement in the pastoral vigilance of those to whom over-

> sight of the flock has been committed. And so in marriage, the husband's rule and the wife's subjection must both be in love. As Christians they have already submitted to one another "in the fear of Christ," in whom sexual distinction possesses no ultimate meaning; as husband, however, the man is the "head" of his wife, and as wife, the woman is "in subjection" to her husband.[34]

If then, in this startling ratio, the wife is related to the husband as the church is to Christ, a new and unusual light is cast upon the matter. To be the head in this sense can mean, as Markus Barth reminds us, going on ahead in love. To rule after the analogy of Christ is not to become bossy but to act in a sacrificial, even servantlike way. In the New Testament, there is no less status in obedience and in submission than there is in commanding and directing. It is the Gentiles, Jesus prompts his disciples, who understand lordship to mean power and rule over others. A radical difference in the ministry of Christians is its service, not to be ministered unto, but to minister. We may consider it inferior to submit, but the Bible indicates it is our ministry. As Markus Barth goes on to say,

> The counsel given to husbands and wives does not include the sentence: "Husbands must be heads or bosses over their wives." In ancient times, as much as today, husbands always attempted to be chiefs. They have done so with little enough of success. No one needs . . . advice for the beginning or continuing that futile enterprise.[35]

Indeed, if each party of a marriage shares the one-flesh relationship, their true union transcends matters of who is boss or who is submissive. The husband and wife belong to one another, and each has responsibility for the other in a mutual subjugation. In their mutuality of love, husband and wife are to be subject to one another out of their common reverence to Christ.[36]

And another thing prompted the words of this passage and its parallel philosophies in the New Testament—the early church lived in expectation of the *parousia* and labored under an ardent desire to maintain their fellowship in the meantime. This meant that among other problems they had to withstand the marriage and sexual practices of surrounding Hellenistic cultures, no mean task for a young fellowship in the minority. Thus Emil Brunner contends that this passage "is part of the garment in which the message of the New Testament is clothed."[37] If the theme of man's superordination and woman's subordination is to be understood at all, it has to take account not only of the times in which it was written but also the patent intention of Paul that the note of ministering runs through it. Given the Christian idea of servanthood, and the perilous times in which these words were written, it would be astonishing if they reflected anything like the expression of twentieth-century equality of the sexes. Suzanne de Dietrich, bringing to the subject a feminine viewpoint, reminds us that behind the Testament's handling of this question must be seen the attitude of Jesus himself. He had dealt with women as persons, equally in need of salvation with men of the time. His freedom of association with women had puzzled not only the Pharisees but also the disciples (Luke 7:36–49, John 4:27). She recalls for us that it was a woman who had a foreboding of the crucifixion (she who anointed Christ's feet at Bethany); it was women who were heralds of the resurrection. Women exercised the ministry of prophecy, of hospitality, and of support. Generously, she notes "Paul is anxious for women to submit themselves to the accepted customs of their time. This is a matter of both dignity and decency. It seems to us that one should retain the spirit, not the letter of such advice. Customs change but every sensitive woman will feel, I believe, that what Paul wants to preserve is something of the essence of womanhood, her dignity and reserve."[38]

Sexual Relation in Christian Thought

The New Testament, as we have seen, subordinated every aspect of life under the demand of the kingdom of God. It was not unique for the family to be so subordinated; wealth, security, personal status and self-determination were likewise placed into an inferior position under the Kingdom. The New Testament also looks at sexual relationships in just this way. Sexual experience, contrary to much of our contemporary concern, is not considered for itself alone; but is invariably subsumed as one aspect of life under the rule of the Kingdom. One might become a eunuch for the Kingdom's sake (Matthew 19:12), or forsake his family because of the prior call to serve the Kingdom (Luke 14:26), but there is no indication that celibacy is of higher status. So too the criterion of sexual purity is set within the context of the Kingdom's ethos (Matthew 5:27–31).

As the teachings of Jesus were cast within the priority of the kingdom of God, all else was secondary. "Seek first his kingdom and his righteousness . . ." (Matthew 6:33) could only mean that marriage and divorce, family life and obligations, sexual experience and discipline were all to fit within this higher goal.

The apostle Paul, whose stand on sex relations is all too often cited as absolute in precisely those places where he was dealing with a temporary emergency, leaves us with a heritage of material on sexual conduct within Christianity. For instance, when he was writing his letter to the Corinthians, he was deeply concerned by the report that some minorities among them had apparently rejected sexual experience in marriage for some more allegedly "spiritual" relationship between the sexes (I Corinthians 7:5). Paul, with the worldly wisdom that ofttimes peeks through his writing, counsels that they should go right ahead and marry if the strain of continence becomes too great for the fragility of their flesh. But certainly they are not to presume that there is any sexual license permitted within the faith as it is in the pagan Corinthian culture. They should realize by now that their bodies have become one with Christ and that they are temples of the Holy Spirit (I Corinthians 6:19). God can be glorified in the body,[39] and Paul was likewise realistic enough to note that God can be blasphemed in the unchristian uses of the body.[40] There was also a special problem of incest within the Corinthian group (I Corinthians 5:1 ff.). One member of the church there had evidently married or cohabited with his own stepmother and was living in conjugal relationship with her. The church members are evidently not sufficiently scandalized at this dereliction. A shocked Paul directs that the church discipline the offenders. If they are unaware of normative sex standards, he will set them straight.

Paul was further worried about the attitude of married people who seemed to place more emphasis on the condition of their marriage than upon their faith (I Corinthians 7:32–35). Their chief attention, he believed, was given to pleasing each other rather than to pleasing God; and he comes very near to saying that those who are happily wedded cannot through their marriage strengthen one another in their faith, a highly debatable point. But Paul was anxious about the end of the age; and if time is drawing short, he reasoned, such loyalties and outward duties ought not to interfere with one's religious commitment.

Given his choice, Paul would prefer celibacy. In view of the impending distress that he anticipated he would advise that no one seek any kind of change in marital status. The single are to remain single, the married, married; but the latter who have wives should live as though they had none. Yet when he counsels his churchmen about marriage, he echoes the high regard for the institution to be found in the teachings of Jesus. He insists upon sexual purity, loyalty in marriage, and discourages divorce even in the controversial mixed marriages of the day, although in these cases certain exceptions might be made if the non-Christian spouse initiated the divorce.

On the subject of celibacy, Paul is confusing to our modern mind. It was a subject on which he blew hot and cold. Marriage, to be sure, was a God-given status ordained to be a permanent union. It was not sinful to enter into this estate; and yet it was a second-best condition as far as he personally was concerned. He would simply rather have persons remain unattached as he was. It presented fewer complications that way. It was a practical matter. If the unmarried could not contain their sexual desires, a problem that he took to be quite difficult for many, marriage would be preferable. The unmarried are to live blameless lives of self-control; and he puts this into ultimate terms: "Do you not know that your body is a temple of the Holy Spirit within you, which you have from God? You are not your own; you were bought with a price. So glorify God in your body" (I Corinthians 6:19, 20).

It is only fair to add that Paul's somewhat mixed counsel about marriage and celibacy supplied its own built-in correctives. He did regard celibacy as a better way of life for those who had a gift for it, as evidently he had. And his aim was clear; he wished to make sure that the Christians were able to give uncompromising attention to things of the spirit. But for most people, he realistically notes, marriage will be the choice, as evidently it had been for Peter and probably others of the disciples. And each of these estates, whether it be unmarried life or marriage, has its own gifts. To the married he advises that they do not refrain from conjugal relations overly long "except by agreement for a season, that you may devote yourselves to prayer" (I Corinthians 7:5), for temptation is active within such denial; and Paul would not want their regimen to encourage that. It is fascinating to observe the careful qualifications with which the apostle couches some of his words about sex and marriage. In speaking to the married about the permanence of their union, he emphasizes that it is not he but the Lord who gives this charge. But in speaking about the possibility of divorce, he points out that "not the Lord, but I say" these things. Paul's writings are sometimes criticized because of their different emphasis from the teachings of Jesus (a matter about which he was obviously mindful in these qualifications); yet it must be recalled that Jesus' listeners were mostly Jewish with a background these Hellenistic readers of Paul's letters did not share. The emphasis on the unmarried state in his epistles could be laid to this factor.

Sexual asceticism and celibacy became marks of piety in the early church, and in some branches have remained so to this day.[41] Scattered directives in the New Testament are aimed at correcting a false standard of holiness based upon such asceticism. The letter to the Colossians, for instance, contains a warning about bogus teachers who would promote a cult of celibacy among the faithful: "These have indeed an appearance of wisdom in promoting rigor of devotion and self-abasement and severity to the body, but they are of no value in checking the indulgence of the flesh" (Colossians 2:23). A similar concern finds expression in I Timothy, but here the language is more forceful. It speaks of "deceitful spirits," of the "doctrines of demons," and "the pretensions of liars whose consciences are seared." These disreputable propagandists have forbidden marriage and promoted abstinence. But everything created by God is good, argues the author of this pastoral epistle, and we can receive his gifts with thanksgiving and consecrate them to him in prayer (I Timothy 4:1–5). The letter of Titus takes umbrage at similar mountebanks, who by their evident promotion of celibacy, ". . . are upsetting whole families by teaching for base gain what they have no right to teach. . . . To the pure all things are pure, but to the corrupt and unbelieving nothing is pure" (Titus 1:11, 15).

In time the immediate expectation of the *parousia* dimmed as Christians grew reconciled to the idea that they would not see it in their lifetime; and the feeling of churchmen underwent a change. The writers of these pastoral epistles may reflect a different language from Paul partly because they lived in this later day of some disappointment; and their complicated pastoral task was to maintain the unity of the church. New problems now confronted the young church too. Young widows are advised to remarry; for there is some worry that otherwise they will crowd into the already large enrollment of that special class of church workers dependent upon the fellowship for their livelihood. The writer of the Timothy letters infers that this group is already well filled with widows, and no more are needed.

Nor is an unmarried clergy particularly appreciated. In no less than three places, the letter of I Timothy emphasizes the experience of one Christian marriage as a prerequisite for official church life.[42] Moreover, in Titus 1:6, the qualification for office of bishop, elder, or deacon is also prescribed that in each case he must be the "husband of one wife" or, if conversely a widow, "the wife of one husband."[43]

On the whole, much of the New Testament shows a clear suspicion of celibacy. It is broadly inferred that the promotion of celibacy is a false doctrine that in itself is seductive since it can lure new Christians away from the faith. But ensuing years found many churchmen unconvinced. Because of the predilection for asceticism on the part of some, and a false understanding of the believer's identification with his Lord, virginity came to be regarded as a splendid virtue in itself. Fondly the passage from Revelation 14:4 would be quoted, praising the 144,000 male virgins whose redemption is specifically connected with the fact that they had "not defiled themselves with women, for they are chaste." It is further averred that these spotless ones follow the Lamb wherever he goes.

Asceticism in the history of the church has too often been a substitute for faith; and therein lies its great danger. Rudolf Bultmann reminds us that the striving after perfection itself operates as a new temptation.[44] Certainly this danger was seen in the early church, judging from the number of passages that polemicize against it or advise against it or advise against glorying in this state. Those heretics who discourage marriage are given short shrift in the Timothy letters. As if to underline this thinking, the writer offers the interesting observation that salvation is to be found in family life. "Woman will be saved through bearing children, if she continues, in faith and love, and holiness, with modesty" (I Timothy 2:15), he writes.[45]

The New Testament Challenge to the Family

The grim divisiveness possible in family life is laid open by a hard saying of Jesus as recorded by Luke 12:52, 53: ". . . henceforth in one house there will be five divided, three against two and two against three; they will be divided, father against son and son against father, mother against daughter and daughter against her mother, mother-in-law against her daughter-in-law and daughter-in-law against her mother-in-law." For all its stark foreboding, the verse is consistent with a number of the more challenging references to the family found in the canon. The New Testament recounts among the teachings of Jesus several radical sayings that boldly affirm the new brotherhood in him, over and beyond any previous loyalties we have known in the home. Yet these notably negative sayings about the family must always be seen in tension with his warm, affirmative appreciation of the family lest they be entirely misunderstood. To review those teachings of Jesus that stabilize family values will serve us with a better vantage point from which to consider the gospel's alarming challenge to family life.

If they are read selectively, many of the teachings of Jesus go far in their affirmation of family life. Marriage is an indissoluble covenant in the Lord, uniting two beings in one flesh (Matthew 5:31, 32, 19:6,

Luke 16:18). (The Lord's teachings here replace the former basic family relationship from father and son with that between husband and wife.) Celibacy is not upheld as a superior way of life in the Gospels[46] but there are some whose devotion to the Kingdom, like that of Jesus, precludes marriage (Matthew 19:12). Such a choice, however, clearly involves a renunciation of something valued and good in itself, and might be compared to physical incapacity for marital life, which is more a misfortune than a blessing. Little children were singled out as models of the kingdom of Heaven; and loving care of them could be accounted as love toward the Lord himself (Matthew 19:14, Mark 10:15 f.). Jesus' own example of remaining with his carpentering family is often interpreted as a wordless approval of the family as the fundamental social group in Judaism. Some of his indirect references to the family are as instructive as any of his direct sayings. His allusions to the homemaker's vocation—leavening bread (Luke 13:21), sweeping the floor (Luke 15:8), even giving birth to a child (John 16:21)—provide cases in point. Frequent metaphors about the characteristics and duties of fatherhood, of course, appear in the Gospels (Matthew 21:31; Luke 11:11, 15:11–32).

And even when Jesus' sayings are negative in effect and militate against family solidarity for the sake of a higher loyalty of the Kingdom, it too was often interpreted in family terms. Perhaps the concept of the kingdom of God was too revolutionary, too hard to grasp unless couched in familiar terms; so again and again Jesus was to refer to family imagery in order to make clearer the picture of the Kingdom. Family love represented a useful point of beginning to conceive of the sacrificial love characteristic of the new order. Out of the home's experience of loyalty and mutual care, it was possible to make more intelligible the way a loving Father cares for his own (Matthew 7:9, Luke 11:11). As disciples and admirers increasingly tended to think of the Kingdom as a political movement (Luke 22:25, John 6:15, 12:15), the use of family analogies doubtless served as useful correctives.

In spite of the support that many New Testament references appear to give the family, such passages must be balanced against other material. It is sometimes difficult for the modern reader to realize how dramatic was much of the break between the Old and the New Testaments. Jesus' formula, "It has been said of old . . . but I say unto you," marks the breach between the old order and the new. The birth pangs of the new order, with the foreshortening of time so vividly felt by the early Christians, made old loyalties loom less urgent than the coming end of all things. A new personalism, as we have seen, began to supersede the sanctity of family ties. The road to faith became a solitary venture.[47]

The New Testament represents God as Father who is not only more loving than human parents can ever be, but also more demanding. To obey him involves a higher obedience than any other. Loyalty to him, though it might be compared in terms of family loyalty, involves a still greater devotion. Abraham had been called to leave his father's house and kindred and to go out to a new land to be shown him only after his journey of faith (Genesis 12:1, Hebrews 11:8). And although the blessing to accrue from this obedience will be a family inheritance, it is not commanded because it is an investment that promises rewards, but because it is integral with the will of God: "I will make of you a great nation . . . in you all the families of the earth will be blessed" (Genesis 12:2, 3). For God had a more inclusive cosmic plan into which Abraham's leadership was only a beginning, a plan which was to culminate in the Incarnation. Paul develops this argument in his letter to the Galatians (Chapter 3) and it is further expounded in Hebrews (Chapters 11 and 12): "And if you are Christ's, then you are Abraham's offspring, heirs according to promise" (Galatians 3:29).

Preoccupation with family loyalties involving the many evils of nepotism, cupidity for inheritance, and spheres of influence is ever capable of standing in the way of true surrender to God. It becomes an idolatrous religion all its own, a worshipful regard of the family for its own sake. Unless it is checked, the family, as Nicolas Berdyaev reminds us, "frequently enslaves personality and only the approximation of the family to the type of brotherhood can reduce this enslavement."[48] The more radical teachings of Jesus, boldly affirming a new brotherhood in himself, over and beyond any previous loyalties we have known in the home, works against such enslavement and saves us from some idolatry that would make of the family a new "graven image."

Jesus' Own Family Life

It is instructive to examine the biography of Jesus for the record of relationships with his own family; for they are a part of his teachings on the subject. Quite early in life, though the Gospels are regrettably sparse in their detail, we find evidence of his move toward independence when at the temple he separates himself from family and kin to pursue his own work. The anxiety expressed by his parents is of a kind with all parents everywhere and at all times. Uncertainty, reproach, pain, guilt can all be felt in the rather simple story of the twelve-year-old in his gathering maturity (Luke 2:41 ff.). Already Mary was beginning to feel something of the chilling prophecy of the prophet Simeon: "A sword shall pierce through your own soul" (Luke 2:35).

It is after he begins his public ministry, however, that the distance between Jesus and his family grows so painfully noticeable. All three synoptic Gospels record the uncomfortable episode of how his mother and brothers came to where Jesus was teaching, and sent to him a message that they wished to see him (with the implied intent of prevailing upon him to return home with them rather than to continue this strange, itinerant teaching ministry). His reply is memorable: " 'Who are my mother and my brothers?' And looking around on those who sat about with him, he said, 'Here are my mother and my brothers. Whoever does the will of God is my brother, and sister, and mother' " (Mark 3:34, 35).[49] In commenting upon this passage, Paul Tillich has observed:

> Jesus uses the family relations as symbols for a relation of a higher order, for the community of those who do the will of God. Something unconditional breaks into the conditional relations of the natural family and creates a community which is as intimate and as strong as the family relations, and at the same time infinitely superior to it. The depth of this gap is emphasized in the attempt of His family to seize Him and to bring Him home because of his extraordinary behavior which makes them believe that He is out of his mind. And the gap is strongly expressed in His saying that he who loves father and mother more than Him cannot be His disciple, words even sharpened in Luke's version, where everyone is rejected by Him who does not "hate" father and mother and wife and children and brothers and sisters and his own life.[50]

If distrust and misunderstanding were to meet him from his own relatives, then he was to open to all men the possibility of a newer family—a larger household of those who were within the fellowship of obedience. Disappointed as he may have been at the inability of his family to comprehend his mission, he was to face yet more and more rejection. Brothers and mother had sought to have him return home with them, but to what? To a village whose people were offended in him and who found his message so unacceptable that their unbelief prevented any possibility of his mighty works there. Indeed, their hostility led to the brink of mob violence, and they very nearly had lynched him once when he returned to Nazareth (Luke 4:16–30). These all had heard the message but had failed to accept it for themselves. In this they were like those men who had built a house upon a sand foundation which could not long stand the ravages of inclement weather (Matthew 7:26 f.).

That Jesus felt that he had enemies within his own family group may be indicated by inferences from his speech as when he quotes the prophet Micah, "A man's foes will be those of his own household" (Matthew 10:36, Micah 7:6), or even the more extreme, "Brother will deliver up brother to death, and the father his child, and children will rise against parents and have them put to death; and you will be hated by all for my name's sake" (Matthew 10:21, 22). And in the recorded tradition of how he split with his brothers to avoid attending the Feast of the Tabernacles in their company, we are told outright, "Even his own brothers did not believe in him" (John 7:5). Whether we can infer that the jealousy and rift between brothers as developed in the parable of the prodigal son was from experience, we cannot know. We can only say that the human emotions described in Luke 15 are accurately described from observation of life.

It was against such a background as this that Jesus described the costs of discipleship. Family ties, for all their compelling closeness, are not the closest. No earthly attachment, regardless how dear, dare stand between any follower and his commitment to discipleship. The gospel might have to bring division between a father and son, between a mother and daughter (Matthew 10:34–39, Luke 12:51–53, 21:16). His hard qualifications for discipleship called upon the candidate to be ready to renounce even home ties. And whether we cite the Matthean version with its claim that whoever loves his family more than Jesus is not worthy of him (Matthew 10:37 f.) or the harsher Lucan assertion that anyone who does not hate his own family members cannot be his disciple[51] (Luke 14:26), the demand is radical. And the call of Jesus transcends and splits the family and yet does not nullify a son's responsibilities (Mark 7:11). A would-be disciple is not permitted to return home to "bury" his father (Matthew 8:21) when the Kingdom is at hand, an astonishing reversal of Hebrew patriarchal values. The sons of Zebedee had understood this principle; when they were called they immediately left their half-mended nets and their thundering father standing in the boat to obey, according to the picture we are given in Mark 1:19 ff.

Peter expressed something of the human reaction to such drastic demands of discipleship in his plaint: "Lo, we have left everything and followed you." The reply of Jesus is curious: "Truly I say to you, there is no one who has left house or brothers or sisters or mother or father or children or lands, for my sake and for the gospel, who will not receive a hundredfold now in this time, houses and brothers and sisters and mothers and children and lands, with persecutions, and in the age to come eternal life" (Mark 10:28–30).[52] In this we note some interesting references. The description of rewards are in terms of the promise accorded to Abraham. These are the ancient tribal values—a large kin group, secure dwellings, ample lands. But a grim introduction, also reminiscent of Abraham's seed, is the expectation of persecution for this new and larger family. Then too, notice that word "now." In the growing family of the Kingdom, disciples were already finding new brothers, new kinship relations, and new though ever-changing dwelling places as they itinerated the Judean hills. In eternal life, God would recompense his own; but for the present they could expect hard discipline, difficult conditions, yet withal a community that held some riches no conventional home could offer.

Jesus had not hesitated to establish a category of duties that claimed a higher priority than even the closest of human associations. "To many people, even to many Christians, this demand has seemed excessive and repugnant," Paul Minear observes. "For many members of the church it has become a dead command. None of us finds it easy either to accept or to obey. Yet it is an inescapable part of the gospel."[53]

With all his high evaluation that he placed upon the family, upholding the permanency of the one-flesh relationship in marriage and honoring parenthood, Jesus refused to consider family ties as the most urgent or even the most intimate in his call. These could not be paramount for him; it would not be different for his disciples in such eventful days. It has been noted that his teachings did not depreciate marriage; indeed for him the marital union took definite precedence over the traditional father-son relationship of Old Testament times. But other loyalty was to rival their allegiance to the kingdom of God. He knew what he was asking, and assumed that the sacrifice of family ties was a costly one. Only if we concede this can we begin to comprehend the depth meaning of these expectations. Disciples had not been taught to hate their parents, as Minear observes, the better to love themselves. (No parody of the Corban principle was involved here.) They were expected to cut off these dearest of bonds because even these dare not impede them from the higher goal of kingdom discipleship.

What the disciples of Jesus lose in their family ties they replace by a more inclusive brotherhood. He had himself pointed the way when, stretching out his hand toward his disciples, he said, "Here are my mother and my brothers." So his followers also were now receiving new brothers for old, coming into a family whose bonds could be even stronger than those they had left behind for the Kingdom's sake. More inclusive, even more endearing than their previous family bonds, these made a differing sort of claim upon members: they are to love the Lord more than any earthly love. They were to share in the bonds of suffering an *esprit* that called many of them to martyrdom. They were to make available the resources of their common purse to the others. They were to forgive one another as God for Christ's sake had forgiven them.

Jesus' own example, let it be noted, had shown that the renunciation of family life for the Kingdom was not to lose touch with his kin or cease caring about them. But he had shown that an individual is justified in surrendering his family ties for the sake of the Kingdom. Anyone completely consecrated to his way could allow no impediments to deter him. It simply underlines what we in our day must also once in a while recall: that the family, as Paul Tillich observes, is not ultimate, precious and influential though it be.

> Family relations are not unconditional relations. The consecration of the family is not a consecration for the final aim of man's existence. . . . However in spite of its radicalism, the Christian message does not request the dissolution of the family. *It affirms the family and limits its significance*. . . . This is part of the profound ambiguity of the biblical teaching about the family.[54]

The tradition in which we stand is that of the New Testament church. Our community of faith is a continuation of that same household of faith. The call is to us as to them to understand ourselves as part of a larger family of God, to accept one another in the spirit of love and brotherhood. For us as for them (indeed as today it can be for Christians in non-Christian lands) the obligation can conceivably arise to subsume even the dearest of earthly ties and the strongest of human drives under the demands of the Kingdom. This is a necessary part of the tension in which we must view the family in our faith.

NOTES

1. See Ezra 10:44 for a case of radical surgery: "All these had married foreign women, and they put them away with their children."
2. I Corinthians 7:12–16 sets forth this question and its interpretation in the light of what has come to be dubbed "the Pauline privilege" to separate: "But if the unbelieving partner desires to separate, let it be so; for in such a case the brother or sister is not bound. For God has called us to peace."
3. Suzanne de Dietrich, *The Witnessing Community*, pp. 70 ff.
4. It is not enough, as John Casteel has pointed out, to follow the lead of one pastor whose goal was to get every member into some parish activity so that in this way "something will rub off on everybody." See John Casteel, *Spiritual Renewal Through Personal Groups.*

5. Millar Burrows, *An Outline of Biblical Theology,* pp. 146 ff.
6. Raphael Patai has shown a close connection between Old Testament family life and the practices of families in the Middle East of the present day in his readable *Sex and Family in the Bible and the Middle East.*
7. W. A. L. Elmslie writes, "The Hebrews employed the words People and Nation in reference to the large communities that shape history. But when we consider their use of those words, one fact of immense importance stands out, namely, the instinct and passion with which they held on to the root-conception that whenever any group of men—from the smallest to the largest numerically—lives and worships together, it is essentially a family; wherefore all its members, from the greatest to the least, must stand to one another in the intense social obligations proper to a family—as brethren, men of one flesh and blood—or else they would lose the sustaining Blessing. . . . The inspiring lovable obligations of family constitute for the Hebrew mind the sole basis on which human society can be successfully reconstructed. . . . Men must set themselves to treat one another not as things to be used, but as brethren whose welfare is their joy and their pride to advantage. That thought was the key to the concept of Justice, the discernment of Right from Wrong, in the relation of Israel. Western secular civilization, to its shame and misery, has fumbled the key or refused to employ it." W. A. L. Elmslie, *How Came Our Faith,* pp. 129 ff.
8. Cf. Joshua 24:15 as well as Genesis 31:43 ff. and I Samuel 20:42.
9. For a fuller explanation of the connection of family and Covenant, consult Frederick W. Dillistone, *The Structure of the Divine Society,* wherein he reminds us that the Covenant was sealed with a common meal, served family style. The eating of the meal brought together kinsmen and others and expressed their intimacy and mutuality in the Covenant. Holy Communion was later to become, through partaking of bread and wine, an expression of the tie binding together the church family.
10. The term *father* has a number of related meanings in biblical literature. It means, of course, the male parent, but also an ancestor—a man is buried with his fathers (II Kings 15:38); a patron as "Jabal the father of those that dwell in tents" (Genesis 4:20); or a patriarch, *e.g.,* "we have Abraham as our father" (Luke 3:8); a distinguished historical personality—*e.g.,* Noah or Elijah—and this is a frequent usage in the apocryphal Ecclesiasticus; as a distinguished teacher of the law in Talmudic references; as a benefactor such as "father to the poor" (Job 29:16); and climactically "the everlasting father" of the messianic hope (Isaiah 9:6). The reader is commended to the informative essay on the subject by Kenneth Grayston in *A Theological Wordbook of the Bible,* edited by Alan Richardson. See especially pages 77, 78.
11. Consult Malachi 1:6, Exodus 20:12, as well as Deuteronomy 21:18 ff.
12. Compare Ezekiel 18:4, 20 with Jeremiah 31:30 for their rebuttal on the traditional outlook concerning inherited guilt.
13. Paul S. Minear, *Jesus and His People,* pp. 52 ff.
14. We are compelled to see in the eyes of a brother "one for whom Christ died"; and our love may for him at times take the form of sacrifice, of

going the second mile, or of refraining from some act that could offend. Moreover, our mercy or our neglect of a brother is clearly mercy or neglect shown toward Christ: "As you did it to one of the least of these my brethren, you did it unto me" (Matthew 25:34–45).

15. Refer to Matthew 19 and Mark 10 for the fuller accounts of Jesus' teachings on marriage and divorce which are set within this reference to the one-flesh relationship established in the creation.
16. I Corinthians 6:12–20 offers a brief discourse on Christian ethics with special emphasis on godly discipline of the human body. In this passage, Paul makes a surprising application of the one-flesh principle in asserting that even in the illicit relationship of a man with a harlot "the two become one flesh." The apostle appears to be saying that in the sexual union we utilize a power we never fully understand, and we may therein find one-flesh where we least expect it. Numerous modern novels have developed this same realization in plots that involve a couple in a casual relationship that develops more deeply than had been expected, sometimes in what W. P. Wylie terms "one-flesh gone sour."
17. A careful and informative section of marriage and family in biblical times is included in Richard M. Fagley's *The Population Explosion and Christian Responsibility*, pp. 109 ff.
18. In the primitive Hebraic theory of genetics, the homuncular idea prevailed that male semen was practically a human being in liquid form, and that the woman's responsibility was chiefly to be an incubator.
19. Deuteronomy 22 sets forth the peculiar ritual of the "blood-stained garment."
20. John 2:1–12, Mark 2:18–20, Luke 5:34 f., Matthew 22:1–14, Matthew 25:1–13, Luke 12:35–40, Luke 14:7–11.
21. Derrick Sherwin Bailey's influential monograph on the one-flesh relationship as *henosis* develops this theme in *The Mystery of Love and Marriage*.
22. It is in the second and third chapters that the prophet tells how Israel has played the harlot with many lovers, and wherein the Lord is depicted as ready to cast her aside. See Jeremiah 3:1 for an explicit relational analogy between the indignation of a wronged husband and the wrath of the Lord.
23. Compare Hosea 2:20 and 11:8.
24. The evidences of this ideological debate are to be found primarily in the Epistles. See, *e.g.*, Romans 2, Philippians 3:3 ff., and Colossians 2:11 ff.
25. Consult The Acts of the Apostles, Chapter 2 for strains of this family-type collectivism.
26. Suzanne de Dietrich, *The Witnessing Community*, p. 151.
27. Evidences of the house church are indicated in Romans 16:5, I Corinthians 16:19, Colossians 4:15.
28. See Mark 7:10 ff. for teachings of Jesus based upon this commonly understood status.
29. To choose but several references among many, see Matthew 21:31, Luke 11:11, and 15:11–32.
30. Matthew 12:46–50, and 13:53–58 offer us interesting insight into this shocking independence of home and kindred.

31. Drastic criticism of reliance on fathers of the past is to be found in Luke 6:23 ff. and Matthew 23:9. See Alan Richardson's *A Theological Wordbook of the Bible,* p. 77, for other references concerning this dramatic change in thinking.
32. Portions of I Corinthians 7 and Ephesians 5 are evidently addressed to such questions as have arisen from the faithful. But the New Testament in its dynamic interpretation of the faith has less of the clear, consistent directives about specific intrafamily relationships than Old Testament law offers. It is part of the strength of the new faith that legalism is dead and the Spirit is alive in the midst of the congregation.
33. Refer, for instance, to John 19:11, Matthew 28:18, or Romans 13:1.
34. Derrick Sherwin Bailey, *The Mystery of Love and Marriage,* pp. 132 f. New York: Harper & Brothers, 1952.
35. Markus Barth, *The Broken Wall,* p. 232.
36. Gibson Winter has developed this point of view with cogency in his *Love and Conflict,* pp. 68 ff.
37. Brunner's *Man in Revolt,* contains noteworthy passages on marriage and the family, as does his *The Divine Imperative.*
38. Suzanne de Dietrich, *The Witnessing Community,* p. 177. It should also be remembered that for Paul, woman was the weaker sex and deeply dependent upon her husband.
39. William P. Wylie would add that God can be *worshiped* in sexual intercourse. See his *Human Nature and Christian Marriage,* pp. 120 ff.
40. Paul's startling reference to the one-flesh relationship existing even in the illicit union of a man with a harlot in I Corinthians 6:16 can be interpreted to mean that since God is present within the one-flesh relationship wherever it occurs, he is there blessing the marriage, but judging harlotry. See Note 15, above.
41. See Roland H. Bainton, *What Christianity Says About Sex, Love, and Marriage.*
42. See I Timothy 3:2, 3:12, and 5:9.
43. Kenneth Grayston's article on this subject in *A Theological Wordbook of the Bible,* p. 140, comments on this matter as follows: "This is commonly explained as referring to remarriage after the death of the first partner, but more probably it refers to Christians who had used the permission to separate from a nonbelieving partner (pagan epitaphs give the meaning of 'husband of one wife' as 'undivorced')."
44. See Rudolf Bultmann, *The Theology of the New Testament,* Volume II, pp. 223 f.
45. Richard M. Fagley develops this passage in an informative exegesis in his *The Population Explosion and Christian Responsibility,* pp. 141 f., and offers a possible alternate translation to mean "safe childbearing" for this verse.
46. Only in the Gospel of Luke is celibacy given much leeway. Fagley notes: "The Lucan version seems particularly concerned with establishing celibacy as a norm, and this puts a certain question mark over sayings bearing on this issue not found in other Gospels." Comparing the reply of Jesus to the Sadducees about the status of marriage in the resurrection in Matthew 22:30 with Luke 20:34–36, he draws attention to the strong

embellishment given by Luke to the same issue. *The Population Explosion and Christian Responsibility,* pp. 128 f.

47. "From its very beginning to the end of the road, the religious quest of the individual is solitary. Though he is socially interdependent with others in a thousand ways, yet no one else is able to provide him with the faith he evolves, nor even prescribe for him his part in the Cosmos." Gordon Allport, *The Individual and His Religion,* p. 141.
48. Nicolas Berdyaev, *Slavery and Freedom,* p. 233.
49. See also for comparison Matthew 12:46–50, Luke 8:19–21.
50. Paul Tillich, *The New Being,* p. 106. New York: Charles Scribner's Sons, 1955.
51. Interestingly the apochryphal *Gospel According to Thomas* translates this passage with three additional words curiously added: "Whoever does not hate his father and his mother *in My way* will not be able to be a disciple to me. And whoever does not love his father and his mother *in My way* will not be able to be a disciple to me." *Logia* 97:34, 35.
52. See also Luke 18:29 and Matthew 19:29.
53. Paul Minear, *Jesus and His People,* p. 45.
54. Paul Tillich, *The New Being,* pp. 106 f. New York: Charles Scribner's Sons, 1955. The italics are ours.

- **Protestant Diversity and Unity**
- **The Place of Marriage in the Christian Life**
- **The Relationship of the Family to the Church**
- **The Church Family's Place in Christian Nurture**
- **Protestant Insights into Family Government**

4

Reformation Perspectives on Family Issues

DIVERSITY OF BELIEF AND OUTLOOK is a conspicuous characteristic of Protestantism today just as it has always been.[1] The variety in thought and action can be attributed at one and the same time to human creativity, human pride, and human cussedness. It is the creative element in Protestantism which is often overlooked by its critics. Yet here, in this variegated pattern, are to be found signs of health as well as of sickness. It has been said that

> Protestantism is the story of individuals and groups who have taken their understanding of the gospel so seriously that they have been willing to create new forms of the church. In so doing they have not been unaware of tradition or of church history, but have insisted that they were reforming or changing the form of the church in the light of the demands of the gospel. Historically, of course, Protestantism begins with the Reformation in the sixteenth century. Although the reformers reluctantly broke with the medieval church, they did not think that they were starting a new church. On the contrary, they maintained that they were calling the church back to its genuine basis. Spurred to action originally because of the abuses in the medieval period, they soon became conscious that their understanding of the gospel was fundamentally different from that of the existing church. Since they were frustrated in every attempt to renew

the church from within, their only recourse was to bring Christians together in new forms of church life.[2]

The story of Protestantism must begin with (and, indeed, must continue to be) an understanding of this effort to recover the true nature of the community of faith in the light of the gospel. It carries within its diverse nature a corrective that makes it ever restless with the institutional forms with which the tradition clothes itself. Indeed, the "Protestant principle" holds that all historical forms stand under the judgment of God. Protestantism is not once and for all fixed in its understanding of the gospel, because it is related primarily to an historical event and not to propositions about it. Furthermore, Protestants have an openness to the culture to which they seek to witness. This is both a potential strength and a potential weakness: a strength in that it assumes the burden of making its message relevant to real men in specific historical circumstances; a weakness in that it is tempted to conform overmuch to the culture rather than speak prophetically the perspective of the gospel. Protestantism must always bear the tension of loyalty to the gospel and an openness which knows that "more light is to break forth from the Word." Knowing that God speaks not so much in principles and propositional absolutes as to particular men in particular situations, Protestants are involved in a continuing reformation because history is real and situations do change.

Protestant Diversity and Unity

We are to look at the family through the aperture which is Protestantism. In order to do so we must review for ourselves the several recurring themes which bestow upon the churches calling themselves "Protestant" a unity in spite of their diversity. It is neither necessary nor possible to elaborate every facet of the faith of Protestant Christians. Thorough expositions of this perspective are available elsewhere.[3] Protestantism cannot be understood apart from its Reformation beginnings; it is here in the atmosphere of conflict with the Roman Catholic church that the distinctive witness of its nature was hammered out. The issues clarified in those early days continue to meet us wherever the religious life is found. We have not outgrown them. So we return to that historical situation and to its chief spokesmen, Martin Luther and John Calvin, for any light they may shed upon the contemporary church's thinking about the families in her midst. Yet the reformers cannot be taken as an exclusive source of understanding. For one thing, it would not be true to their intention to fix upon their patterns of thought and life as absolutes. They sought to point not to themselves but to the God whose reality they had encountered afresh through the Scriptures. The snatches of Reformed thinking available to us about the family come clothed in ideological conflict, in an atmosphere of polemic. Consequently, because the family *per se* was not a problem to them (though the jurisdiction of the church over it was), we find little constructive thinking about family life in the sixteenth century. The reformers were more concerned at that period in history with correcting abuses than with a deep search into a theological understanding of marriage and family. For this reason and others, Protestantism comes armed with no "doctrine" of the family—if we mean by that term a framework of systematized, consistent beliefs which are integrally related to the pivotal doctrines of Protestant Christianity. In contrast to Roman Catholicism, there is, with regard to the family, no "unchanging, universal consensus in all basic doctrines."[4] We are left rather with guidelines springing from major assumptions. These will furnish the lenses through which to look at the family theologically. To a brief description of these distinctive Protestant themes we now proceed.

The *sovereignty of God* is one such central affirmation. It attests to the freedom of God to be himself, the freedom to be bound by nothing except his own identity. God can work outside established patterns and social forms. The sovereignty of God is a confession that God can and does make his truth known in new ways. He is not bound by human experience or human logic or even by the human systems of thought which theologians construct about him. Negatively, this means we are to reject every human claim to finality; all human reality is tentative and conditioned. Positively, this affirmation calls for a creative stance toward the social institutions and human realities with which we deal. With sobering self-criticism, then, Protestantism faces the fact that she, too, has deified the finite—even in her adulation of the family.

The *doctrine of the living Word* reminds us that we are guided by one crucial presupposition; the final adequacy of Jesus Christ as the revelation of God's power and love and creativity. Truth is personal. Taking seriously the doctrine of the Word, Protestants are freed to use investigative reason in its proper sphere. (In the example of this book, we make use of the social sciences which look at man in relation to man in the structures of his own corporate experience in family and society.)[5] Such "reason" cannot help us find truly human fulfillment or "salvation." When it sets itself up as an ultimate, it becomes, in Luther's earthy term, "the devil's whore." When a person comes to know God through an encounter with the Person, Jesus Christ, he has an obligation then to use the gift of the mind in his vocation. The doctrine of the Word, the living Lordship of Christ, reminds us that truth is defined in terms of an event, an act, both historical and contemporary in its effect; it is not basically propositional information. Truth comes in encounter, in communal terms, although it never lacks a cognitive content. This affirmation frees the Christian to examine everything in all creation (Christ is King therein), for he is confident that nothing can finally contradict Truth.

Protestant Christians see *the church* as the "Body of Christ" and also understand it as a community of faith. It is the new structure of communal existence which is called into being to announce God's act in the person of Jesus Christ and to demonstrate the new life, the full human life, which is recovered through him. It is a fellowship which proclaims this good news, serves the neighbor in need, and provides a mutual ministry of believers to one another. The primary human reality in the church is not in its leadership, the ordained ministry, but in the common life of the people of God. All believers belong to this community of God and all have appropriate gifts of service to this community and to the world. Within the fellowship of faith, the clergy are charged with the responsibility of keeping the church focused on its task by serving Christ through Word and Sacrament. By this means they help to equip the laity for their discipleship in the institutions and structures of our world in which they are to be "leaven."

The reformers re-evaluated the common life and *Christian "vocation"* in the light of the New Testament and found no warrant for dividing life and work into the "religious" and the "secular." The Protestant Christian is to "be the church" in the area of his daily work and life and to be the church *in the home*. Any useful, honest work, done under responsibility to God, is quite on a par with the ministry or with so-called "religious" work. There is only one vocation or calling, and that is "discipleship" in the situation where we live; it is, in Luther's words, to be a Christ to one's neighbor.

The Protestant doctrine of *justification by faith* is an assertion that God's love is what redeems man and an indication that this reconciliation is actualized in human life in the response of personal faith and trust. No efforts to earn God's love by "goodness" (even by being a "good parent") or "religiousness" or by scholarship and research will avail. "Perfectionism" (even in family living) is a denial of the prior love of God in Christ who accepts us as we are and so allows us to accept ourselves. Here, briefly, are some of the elements of Protestantism's distinctive themes which permeate the reformers' understanding of family life.

In light of the changes in family living sketched in Chapter 2, we are led to ask some pressing questions and seek for theological light upon them; for Protestantism, as was noted in the last chapter, fosters an obligation to believe what is true in the light of the intention of Scripture; it does not make the suggestion that every man has a right to believe what he likes. We have already explored biblical insights into family life; we now approach the question in the distinctive way in which Protestant Christians generally understand the gospel. A number of resources are available for the scholar who wishes to make a deeper study of the Reformation's understanding of the family;[6] here we content ourselves reviewing Reformation perspectives on four questions which appear again and again through the research findings: What is the place of marriage in the Christian life? How is the family related to the church? What is the church family's place in Christian nurture? Can we discover Protestant insights into proper family government?

The Place of Marriage in the Christian Life

In asking, "What is the place of marriage in the Christian life?" we face an entirely different situation from that of the sixteenth-century reformers. In the U.S.A. today marriage is taken for granted as the *summum bonum* of existence. It is the preferred status for the vast majority of our people. Yet the principles of monogamy, fidelity, and indissolubility have, as we have seen, given way to an outlook which is openly tentative, experimental, and individualistic. The seeds of this conflict are apparent in the sixteenth century and even earlier. The reformers, however, were not wrestling with this kind of issue. The question for them concerned the status of marriage as over against celibacy in the Christian life. Protestantism has now so completely accepted the idea of a married clergy that it is difficult for moderns to sense the radical departure in thinking that the reformers instigated. But it is still instructive for our day and problem to see the issues laid out.

Luther and Calvin rejected the Roman claim that celibacy was a higher order of life than marriage. It was Augustine who set the tone for all later Roman Catholic thinking with regard to celibacy and marriage. Because he saw the sexual act as the vehicle by which the sin of Adam was transmitted to all mankind, procreation was viewed as inferior to the state which refrained from it. Tainted with sin and corruption by concupiscence, sex was to be avoided if possible.[7] If a person marries he is never to assume that he enters an estate which is equal in sanctity to that of the celibate; indeed the sexual act necessary to consummate the union is a sin (but "venial" and therefore pardonable).[8] Augustine found himself in a dilemma, saying on the one hand (in accordance with Scripture) that marriage is "good" but on the other hand that refraining from marrying is much better. This dichotomous attitude toward marriage and family has continued throughout Catholic thinking even though occasional voices within that church were raised against it.[9] Thomas Aquinas, official systematic theologian of the Roman Catholic church, follows Augustine faithfully in this viewpoint. William Cole, judging from the standpoint of the New Testament, comments, "Thomas made no allowance for differences of individual temperament in this judgment (that virginity is superior to marriage), as Paul obviously did in I Corinthians 7. He flatly asserted that it is abstractly true that virginity is superior to marriage."[10]

The Council of Trent, as the culmination of the Counter-Reformation, hardened dogmatically for the Roman Catholic church almost all the issues in the area of faith and life which had been left somewhat flexible up to that time. Catholic dogma was narrowly defined within rigid limits; doctrine concerning marriage and family might develop *from* this point but it could never change. Trent affirmed what had been a predominant attitude—that although devout celibacy and virginity were not a condemnation of marriage, they nevertheless were "better and more blessed than to be united in marriage." As a consequence, Cole points out, "a group of divines, holding themselves free from all 'venereal pleasure,' declared by fiat that theirs is an estate superior to that of the weak ones who must marry and they gave detailed instructions concerning a life of which they had no first-hand experience."[11]

Luther and Calvin rejected this claim decisively. Martin Luther scored point after point against the Catholic view that virginity is spiritually preferable to marriage, and while doing so was not above using his penchant for earthy remarks to make his position heard. For example, he dubbed religious celibacy an excuse for running into the cloister to escape from dirty diapers! But although using sarcasm liberally, his argument did not depend upon it. His prime theological reason for preferring marriage to celibacy was his conviction that God ordained that all men were created to live in the conjugal state. In his famous *Table Talk* he asks, "On what pretense can man have interdicted marriage, which is a law of nature? 'Tis though we were forbidden to eat, to drink, to sleep. That which God has ordained and regulated, is no longer a matter of the human will, which we may adopt or reject with impunity."[12] His second reason was that the power of sexual drives was such that marriage provided a remedy for concupiscence. In this he follows St. Paul's thinking. Luther was assured that a life of genuine celibacy was virtually impossible; and he had ample evidence at hand that priests, forbidden to marry, had nonetheless violated their vows of celibacy repeatedly. Both Luther and Calvin regarded marriage as theologically equal to celibacy in status, and a preferable state except to a gifted few. It is sheer presumption, maintained Calvin, to undertake the celibate life unless one has been given this very rare gift to do so by God. To take a vow of virginity and reject the remedy offered for natural sexual drives in marriage is to rebel against God. Singleness, then, is a live option for any person blessed with the special gift of God which allows him to live in a virginal state; but to make celibacy a binding rule on those in church vocations seemed to both Luther and Calvin to be contrary to the divine will.

The need of Protestants to think further today on this matter of "marriage for the many and celibacy for the gifted few" is occasioned by new social conditions which prohibit the marriage of countless contemporary women. The male-female ratio disadvantages them seriously, and no ready solution is at hand.[13]

Like St. Paul and with somewhat the same eschatological motivation, Luther and Calvin knew that the single person unfettered by married cares theoretically might be better able to pursue the study and preaching of the Word of God. But realist that he was, Calvin knew also that marriage eliminated preoccupation with sexual thoughts which so often plague the unmarried and might, by that token, set men freer yet for that service. The chief thing, the reformers maintained, was to serve God with one's whole being. To this end it would be *expedient* for the few to be unmarried and for the many to be married.

For both reformers, marriage served a larger purpose than the satisfaction of irresistible (largely male) sexual urges (and Luther was not without a feeling of ambivalence about the goodness of sex even within marriage). Procreation was considered to be a major purpose of marriage although not so much a primary end as the *fruit* of the conjugal state. The reformers' admonition to propagate was at once the result of the injunction to "increase and multiply" and the practical situation of underpopulation in northwestern Europe.[14] Calvin's caustic words to the Roman priesthood indicted them for evading this social responsibility since most of them were not "gifted" to be celibates anyway. From the theological standpoint, God chose procreation as a proximate means by which his church was to be perpetuated. With a typical sixteenth-century slant on life expectancy, Luther muses in his *Table Talk:* "Twenty years is but a short time, yet in this short time the world were empty, if there was no marrying and production of children. God assembles unto himself a Christian church out of little children."[15] There is little doubt that the reformers were as pro-fertility as were their Roman Catholic opposition.

But marriage as a vehicle for procreation and as a remedy for sexual passion is certainly not the whole story for them. The reformers see in marriage and family social purposes which were equally compelling. Luther described the home as a "school for character," emphasizing the unique value of the tensions and frustrations of family life in teaching patience and humility, squelching human pride, and above all, revealing the urgency of forgiveness.[16] Modern-day Protestantism could learn much from the reformers who were not given to wild-eyed idealism about the Christian home. Our literature, which abounds in references to "married perfection," could take a note from Luther when he astutely observes: " 'Tis a grand thing for a married pair to live in perfect union, but the devil rarely permits this. When they are apart, they cannot endure the separation, and when they are together, they cannot endure the always seeing one another."[17]

Calvin's conception of marriage was generally more affirmative than that of Luther probably because of his greater appreciation of women. He taught that the *primary* purpose of marriage is social; *companionship* is its fundamental aim. In his view of marriage as a high calling, woman is only secondarily an agent of generation because she is primarily a helpmeet. Cole represents his thought pungently when he claims that "Calvin obviously displayed a greater appreciation of woman than any previous theologian, emancipating her from her enforced role as a mere baby factory, or safety valve for the male libido."[18] A wife was not merely a companion of the bedroom but of one's whole life. The decisive biblical words regarding marriage are from Genesis 2:18: "It is not good that the man should be alone." It is a sharing of mind and spirit and not merely sex which spells out for Calvin the deepest values of married life. Yet we must be aware of the sharp differences in his ideas of companionship and the prevailing modern notion of mutual happiness being an end in itself. Sacrifice was embraced in Calvin's idea of comradeship and the union was always subordinate to the service of God. When his beloved wife Idelette died, he testified: "I have been bereaved of the best companion of my life who, if our lot had been harsher, would have been not only the willing sharer of exile and poverty, but even of death. While she lived, she was the faithful helper of my ministry."[19] For Calvin the sexual aspects of this companionship remained in the background perhaps, as Fagley remarks, "because it was regarded as having shameful connotations or because it was thought of so largely in terms of the duty of procreation. The idea of 'one flesh' was preserved but not given the fullness of its Biblical meaning. It would appear in more significant form in the 20th century."[20]

Modern Protestantism has explored the important biblical idea of "one flesh" (Genesis 2:24; Matthew 19:3–11; Mark 10:2–12; I Corinthians 6:16; Ephesians 5:22 ff.) of which even the reformers took little account. It is a concept which informs, more than any other, the contemporary Christian view of marriage. Though the one-flesh relationship is ultimately not definable (but can be apprehended in the experience of Christian mates), the most complete attempt to do so to date has been made by Derrick Sherwin Bailey, an Anglican, in *The Mystery of Love and Marriage:*

> The emphasis in "one flesh" is primarily upon *henosis* which results from the sexual union of man and woman. In Scripture "one" is a rich and suggestive word. In the Genesis passage it may at first have meant simply that husband and wife become "one" in relation to the community—that through marriage a new social unit emerges—but when taken into the context of the New Testament it gains greatly in significance. It implies the resolution of discord, the transcending of superficial difference and antagonisms at a new and deeper level of existence or experience; not an amalgamation in which the identity of the constituents is swallowed up and lost in an undifferentiated unity, nor mere conjunction in which no real union is involved. The singleness for which "one" stands, in its most pregnant use, is organic, not arithmetical, and has a suggestion of uniqueness; it is exemplified at its highest in the mysterious triunity of God, of which the biunity of husband and wife is an analogue.
>
> In marriage man and woman become "one *flesh*." This means that through sexual intercourse in which they consummate their love they restore the original pattern of human unity. . . . Male and female . . . are not independent but complementary, and individuality incomplete until they have achieved the union in which each integrates and is integrated by the other. Although the union in "one flesh" is a physical union established by sexual intercourse . . . it involves at the same time the whole being, and affects the personality at the deepest level. It is a union of the entire man and the entire woman. In it they become a new and distinct unity, wholly different from other relational unities . . .[21]

It is from this understanding of the "one-flesh" relationship (predominant in the New Testament over any reference to propagation), that modern Protestants derive their meaning for marriage. The major Protestant groups have gone on record as viewing the unitive, one-flesh relationship of man and wife as more important—or at least of equal importance—than the procreative aspects of marriage. It is this biblical insight (as well as the need to produce only those children for whom they can properly care and the practical considerations of dangerous overpopulation) which informs Protestants in their almost unanimous approval of scientifically valid methods of conception control. United Presbyterians have put the issue unequivocally in their 171st General Assembly pronouncement:

> Recognizing that in the wisdom of God Christian marriage is a relationship of love and fidelity which involves both companionship and parenthood, and believing that the sexual life within this relationship is given by God for the benefit of his children, and is neither an ethically neutral aspect of human existence, nor an evil which needs to be justified by something else, as for example, by the procreation of children, the 171st General Assembly approves the principle of voluntary family planning and responsible parenthood, affirms that the proper use of medically approved contraceptives may contribute to the spiritual, emotional, and economic welfare of the family.[22]

The Episcopal Lambeth Conference of 1958 contended that three functions of marriage are interwoven: procreative, unitive, and responsible care of children. The first two are not to be subordinated one to the other, nor are they directly related to each other. The report goes on to say:

> . . . No marriage would be according to God's will which (where procreation is possible) did not bear fruit in children. But it is clearly not true that all other duties and relationships in marriage must be subordinate to the procreative one. Neither the Bible nor human experience supports such a view. Where it has been held, the reason generally lay in a fear of the misuse of the sexual relationship or in a false sense that there is, in any sexual relationship, an intrinsic evil.[23]

Protestantism generally would reject the Roman Catholic conjecture that marriage has one primary purpose, procreation, to which all other purposes are to be subordinated. Not only is this argument biblically unsound but is forced artificially by the principles of Thomistic philosophy which is the Roman Catholic's prior commitment.[24] One wonders with Cole whether the elevation of virginity and celibacy above marriage, the subordination of women to men, and the control of the moral theology by the unmarried priesthood of the Roman Catholic church will not always prevent that church's wholeheartedly giving its "full benediction to human sexuality."[25]

Divorce and Remarriage

Any statement about marriage in the Christian life would be incomplete without a word about its possible dissolution. It is clear from their writings that Luther and Calvin both hated divorce; lifelong monogamous marriage is the intention of God, they maintained. Realists they were, however. Taking seriously the fall of man which affected the conjugal state as well as every other area of life, they reluctantly regarded divorce as permissible under certain well-defined circumstances. Both set themselves firmly against the proposal to let the marriage relationship be terminated at will. This was one of the dangers, they held, in clandestine marriage as over against marriage solemnized in a public act.[26] But we cannot turn to the detail of that controversy here. Luther does concede divorce for adultery or desertion and is willing to abide by the laws of secular government in the matter (since marriage is not a sacrament and hence not under the control of the church).

Calvin, in contrast to Luther, allowed several grounds for divorce which are, even in our day, quite liberal. He allowed divorce not only on the grounds of adultery (as did Luther) but for the wife as well as the husband. Adultery was a most serious cause of family dissolution.[27] Calvin also admits three other grounds for divorce or separation: desertion, extreme incompatibility in religion, incapacity for sexual intercourse (as a basis for annulment and remarriage). Both Luther and Calvin regarded the Roman practice, permitting separation while not allowing remarriage, as indefensible and cruel. For Calvin especially, remarriage was not only allowed but encouraged since separated men and women were exposed to temptations which marriage was designed to overcome. Many Protestant denominations have not yet caught up with his position but, at the present time, the whole question of remarriage is being rethought from both a theological and a therapeutic perspective.[28]

Sacrament or Holy Estate?

Calvin and Luther were of one mind in rejecting the sacramental character of marriage. To Luther there is "no higher office, estate, condition and work (next to the Gospel which concerns God himself) than the estate of marriage,"[29] and Calvin speaks of marriage as a "holy ordinance of God." But they were adamant in their contention that marriage is not a sacrament; marriage did not have the status in the realm of redemption claimed for Baptism and the Lord's Supper. Each scoffed at the mistranslation of the Greek "mysterion" to the Latin "sacramentum" in the analogy of marriage with Christ and the church in Ephesians 5:31–32. Marriage preceded the church; it is rooted in God's creation, not uniquely in his plan of redemption. The marriages of the ancients were no less sacred than Christian marriage, they held. Cole reminds of Calvin's sharpness in saying:

> Calvin turned a biting satire on Rome for her inconsistency in declaring with one voice that marriage is a sacrament while with another she denies that same sacrament to those who serve her best, the priests, monks, and nuns. He laid his finger on a further absurdity in the fact that Rome claims that the grace of the Holy Spirit is conferred in every sacrament, while denying that the Holy Spirit is ever present in the marriage act.[30]

Both Luther and Calvin agreed that marriage regulation was an affair of the state, but the latter was more insistent that the state which regulated be guided by church counsel.

The Anglican branch of the Reformation came to adopt a middle ground between Luther and Calvin and the Roman Catholic position. It maintained the sacramental nature of "holy wedlock," meaning by this (with Augustine) that the union of husband and wife is one in which God participates, is effected through their consent alone, and is subsequently sealed by coitus. But that church rejected the medieval conception (reinforced at Trent) that marriage is a rite instituted by Christ, an external sign in a word spoken which effectually *causes* grace to come into the lives of bride and groom.

In Roman Catholic thought, since the sacraments are interrelated (Baptism and the Mass being necessary for marriage to be a sacrament and for it to be effectual), everything pertaining to marriage is put squarely under the regulation and control of the Roman Catholic church. It was this total jurisdiction of the church over the marriage and family question, and the theological errors upon which it was based, which the reformers challenged vigorously. To them, marriage was still under God's ultimate authority (as was the state which regulated it), but this was a vastly different thing than being under the rule of the hierarchy in the Roman Catholic church. And this conclusion of the reformers brings us to our next major question.

The Relationship of the Family to the Church

To introduce this question is to invoke the broader problem of the relation of culture to the church. Should the church be opposed to culture? Or above culture? Or should it attempt to transform it?[31] It is probable that the answer to home-church relationships will be similar to a particular church's way of seeing its relationship to culture. The Christ-above-culture position is that officially held by the Roman Catholic church in the philosophy of Thomas Aquinas. The church home, as we have seen, is under the church's jurisdiction. Luther sensed a polarity between Christ and culture and, consequently, man is in constant tension between the two loyalties and areas of responsibility which always are with him. For John Calvin, finite structures, such as the home, are seen to be "instruments" and not obstacles to God's grace. The problem of church and home for Calvinists is one of re-creating the family so that it might serve God's purposes. If marriage (and family) is not automatically an order of redemption (by being a sacrament) but only potentially related to God through its individual members and their ministry to one another, it follows that the gospel must be communicated *to* the home as to any other order of creation. There is no "Christian family" *per se;* members of the church who live in families must be led to see the way in which the distorted family order must die and be raised to new life under the power of the spirit of Christ.

When the whole family is *in* the church (as described in this chapter), the communication of the gospel enters the family by way of the parents who teach their children. This chain of teaching is the prime illustration of the covenant relationship. The inclusion of children in the Covenant (see Chapter 3) in Calvin's thought is ordinarily by way of the family. It is through the parents that the child derives his sanctification; they represent the church to him and through them the child receives his "ingrafting into the body of the church." When parents are Christian, the church lives in the home and is related to it. This relationship, then, is not the relationship of two things (institutions) which exist side by side so that a detached definition or scientific account can be given of the relation between them. The church is always in dispersion as its members are in the world; the very definition of the church advanced earlier holds it always to be in relation. For this reason it would be better for Protestants to cease using the ambiguous phrase, "the Christian home," and speak rather of the church-in-the-home where Christian nurture occurs.

The reformers rejected the medieval innovation of matrimony as a sacramental rite, denying that God had appointed an external ceremony that transmits grace and confirms his promise to his people. According to the Bible, people receive the grace of God not by exchanging nuptial vows but by responding to God's love in Jesus Christ by personal faith and trust. Experience shows that the family can be a battleground as well as "the gathered of God"; no marriage vows *per se* assure that the home is a means of grace. As in any other institution of society, the forces of alienation as well as reconciliation are present (and perhaps the demonic attitudes are more destructive of persons here than in any other context). The intimate face-to-face relationships of the family can be a hazard as well as a help to the spiritual growth of its members. It is not easier to fulfill the kingdom of God at home. Unless family members are *educated* in Christian faith—and that may be on quite a different level from "instruction"—the family fails to become (as Calvin felt it ought to become) a part of the covenanted people who share in the purposes which that people have in the world. Unless parents are nurtured in the faith, and in turn exercise their vocation in the communication and demonstration of the gospel to their children, the home cannot fulfill its purpose in the sight of God.

For Protestants who eschew the domination of the institutions of the world by the church (since both are under the judgment of God and both are subject to sin and error), the church cannot relate itself to the family through coercion, overt or subtle. It must always fight the temptation to define its life by a redeemed order of law, says Gibson Winter,[32] and to maintain this order as a "new law" within its life as community. In the Roman Catholic concept of sacramental marriage, law is imposed upon the family; and this is just one example of the "sacralizing" of institutional relationships of the community. The attempt to incorporate familial, political, and economic relationships under ecclesiastical control was broken by the reformers. Only in the family and in education was this control ever achieved by the church of Rome. Protestantism, though not free of the attempt to do the same thing (witness Calvin's theocracy in Geneva) has, in the modern day, rejected both jurisdictional and legislative power over the institutions of God's created order. The church's task is basically educational and pastoral. When the church supports fidelity in the marital covenant as essential to the health of the society and of marriage, it does so through pastoral concern and through the witness of the laity as it lives in the world. If we reject the Roman attempt to control the functioning of societal groups through political power, we are left with the question of how we do in fact shape the life of the effective corporate elements of society. If we reject direct intervention, how does the community of faith provide an atmosphere in which all families might grow in health and maturity? According to the reformers, church families have a definite share in the process of education of their own members; this is where we start.

The Church Family's Place in Christian Nurture

One place where the family and church join in Calvin's thought is in his awareness that the home is of basic importance in the nurture of children. In his sermons he frequently reminded his congregation of the teaching responsibility of Christian parents. Indeed, parenthood is a calling which may be quite at variance with the parent's concern about personal, individual success. We are to be "gospel bearers" to each other in the family. It is in the family, Luther contends, that the gifts of love, patience, forgiveness, and obedience are best to be learned. He described parents as "apostle, bishop, and priest" to their children; no more honorable and valuable work could be done than teaching them. In this, the reformers were reiterating a viewpoint which existed throughout the previous history of the church, at least in its early phases. William Barclay describes how the early church, planted in a secular world, relied upon the home for its religious education and sent its children to pagan schools for general education. "The Church saw that in the last analysis the only true teachers of any child are the parents of that child. . . . As the Church saw it, the school is at best only an adjunct to the home. It is the parent who is responsible for bringing the child into the world; . . . The child is the gift of God to the parent, and the child must be the gift of the parent to God."[33]

At the present time this approach seems utopian. Church parents, as we shall see, do not regard themselves as direct teachers of their children in matters of Christian faith; they scarcely know what it is all about themselves. Without the church educating intensively at the adult level, as it did in the preparation of the catechumens in the first centuries of its existence, there is little hope of home religious education being reinstated. Even with that kind of education, one wonders what can be accomplished in an urbanized culture in a family wherein the roles of mother and father have changed drastically.

Protestant Insights into Family Government

The relationship of husband and wife in the reformers' thinking is monotonously like the Old Testament patriarchal view which was reviewed in the last chapter. Calvin's lunges in the direction of women's rights and sexual equality notwithstanding, there is not the slightest doubt in his mind which sex is superior. Because of his endowments and his prior creation, man is to be the master of the house (but not a tyrant to his wife). Luther saw this relationship stemming from the physical structure of the sexes: "Men have broad and large chests, and small hips, and more understanding than the women, who have but small and narrow breasts, and broad hips, to the end they should remain at home, sit still, keep house, and bear and bring up children."[34] Luther granted his wife sovereignty in household matters but nevertheless asserted unequivocally that "God created Adam master of living creatures, but Eve spoilt all, when she persuaded him to set himself above God's will. 'Tis you women, with your tricks and artifices, that lead men into error."[35] If anything, we can see a retrogressive tendency in Luther and Calvin regarding family government. Certainly they were not alert to the modification of the patriarchal pattern seen in the fifth chapter of Ephesians and the seventh chapter of I Corinthians, for example. Women were clearly subordinate, and children to be subjected to their parents. The Anglican stream of the Reformation was not one whit behind in upholding this androcentricity. Hooker, for example, alleges women to be "intrinsically inferior in excellence, imbecile by sex and nature, weak in body, inconstant in mind, and imperfect and infirm in character."[36] Throughout Reformation thinking, as in the Roman Catholic view, this presumed ontological superiority of male over female determines the roles which each is expected to play in the home.

Social science findings have seriously challenged the proposition that the social roles and psychological characteristics of men and women are *directly* related to their physical structure; cultural anthropology has uncovered too many variations to be confident of this assumption. Given equality of educational opportunity, the female of the species has demonstrated beyond any doubt that the opinions of most post-New Testament theologians were based more on arrogance and ignorance than on fact. In the previous chapter we have seen how the New Testament treats the subject of subordination and superordination. How then, does contemporary Protestantism interpret the classical Christian teachings on the father's headship of the family?

Liberal Protestantism in the 1930's and 1940's simply erased the patriarchal tradition by accusing St. Paul and all classical theologians of ignorance of cultural relativities in their own thinking and their own irrational need for superiority. "Democracy" in the family was seen—under the influence of John Dewey—as God's will for family government. But, in the light of "Momism" and other related phenomena in American life, a second look has been taken at the traditional position.

Some contemporary theologians would continue to speak of an ordained position of father and mother in the family structure; ontological superiority of male over female is held to be scripturally defensible. But, as we noted in Chapter 3, husbands and wives are seen as related to each other in *mutual* subjection; "headship" of the male means taking the initiative in service as Christ did. This is a reversal of the usual meaning extracted from the fifth chapter of Ephesians. The concept of lordship, or headship, say these biblical scholars, is thereby transformed into acceptance of service. (Perhaps it is the new societal situation, in which the demonstrated equality of women in many fields is a blatant fact, that allows modern theologians to see in the biblical Word something which is genuinely there but which could not be perceived before. Exegesis tends to grow out of the interpreter's existential situation as well as the "given" text before him.)

A number of contemporary theologians see husband and wife equal as persons and in spiritual status but different in function. To modern Roman Catholic scholars, "the differences are oriented in terms of reproduction. . . . The husband's headship . . . must be defined in terms of the exigencies of the family unity (and) flows from and is limited by his role as protector and provider of the family unit."[37] But, as we have seen in Chapter 2, being an economic provider may actually remove the father from headship of the family in almost every other aspect. Clearly, the traditional concept has been diluted by his vocational preoccupation.

Gibson Winter, a Protestant theologian trained thoroughly in the social sciences, sees the "headship" of the father as a necessary role in the dynamics of a small group—in this case the family. Every group, he holds, needs two complementary roles for successful functioning—that of leader and that of supporter. The leader as "idea man" and initiator of action would be helpless without a person in the group who gives emotional support to him and to other members and reconciles differences between them. When these two persons work together, group cohesion is possible and tasks get accomplished. He suggests that the father is the leader in this sense and the mother the emotional supporter (except in the case of very young children where she is both).[38] Both these interpretations seek to preserve the traditional structural relationships of husband and wife in the family while shedding the false assumptions of the "classical" Christian view. They are indications of a trend in theological thinking.

One of the most creative attempts to date to state the relationships of husband and wife in a biblical yet anthropologically defensible way has come from the pen of Derrick Sherwin Bailey. In his book *Sexual Relation in Christian Thought* he claims that most previous theological attempts to elaborate true conceptions of manhood and womanhood have been trapped in cultural stereotypes. The defense of man's superordination has often been based upon arguments that were essentially empirical: for example, woman is weaker, less intelligent, and so on. But the findings of social sciences have robbed this argument of much of its plausibility since they show that many of the characteristics thought to be intrinsic to the female are the products of cultural conditioning, inadequate education, and so on. The empirical argument for woman's inferiority has been exploded as has the "hollow pretense to superordinate status" claimed for the male. Furthermore, says Bailey,

> St. Paul's idea of a divine law behind the principle of male headship is no more than a literalistic reference from the account of man's creation given in the second chapter of Genesis. In the final analysis, therefore, his conception of the general status of each sex relative to the other stands or falls on a plain question of fact. Is it true, we have to ask, that God derived woman from man—that he made her subordinate, and destined her to remain so for ever? To this, only one reply is possible: no positive evidence of any kind can be adduced in favour of such an idea, while on the other hand there are compelling reasons (both theological and scientific) for rejecting it as untenable.[39]

He goes on to assert that such an idea of male headship has no place in the teaching of Jesus. Nor can the subordination of woman to man have its corresponding counterpart in the relations of the persons of the Godhead. The Fourth Gospel especially, it will be recalled, points to a full mutuality in the relationship of Father to Son, each witnessing to and glorifying the other. Where does this leave us, then, in using the Godhead as an analogy to determine the biblical meaning of the relation of man and wife to each other? Bailey maintains that there is no objective definition of sexual order and of masculinity and femininity available; this is a mystery known only to God. We can have no abstract comprehension of it; nor can it be deduced from biological and psychosocial data about the sexes. This rejection of a hierarchical notion does not mean that the sexual realm is without any order, however. What it is, is revealed in an actual "I-Thou" relation of man and woman in which they see each other as persons.

> True sexual knowledge . . . is always existential and dependent upon a capacity for sincere and responsible relational ventures; it can never be derived . . . from social stereotypes. It is in Christ that sex assumes its real significance, for in him alone can man and woman find the disciplined freedom which enables them to learn

> through their relational experiences something of the deeper meaning of masculinity or femininity. . . . All that can be said is that despite infinite possibilities of variety due to personal factors, it (the sexual order) always remains intrinsically an order of mutual complementation wherein neither sex is subordinate or superordinate to the other.[40]

The question of the parents' relationship to the child has been the subject of less controversy in Protestant thinking than the relation of husband to wife. The differential of age, size, and ability between parent and child undoubtedly has suggested the roles to be taken in family government. In Jesus' acceptance of the child as prototypical of those who were to enter the kingdom, we seem to have a much higher view of childhood than we find in the reformers. Paul, too, in his warning to fathers not to provoke their children to anger revealed his understanding of the child as a significant being in his own right. Children were to obey their parents in the Lord, following the fifth commandment.[41] The reformers' intensification of the father-centered household, together with a conviction of the sinfulness of infants, served to promote the subjugation of children to the wills of their parents (reminiscent of that Old Testament period when father was the "ba'al" of the family). Yet within this stern framework, children were cherished.[42]

Not until the 1800's did Protestant theologians generally re-evaluate the child's nature and his place in the government of the family.[43] Against a background of thought that affirmed that the child is "prone to evil as the sparks fly upward," Horace Bushnell made his major contributions; he wedded the orthodox notion of childhood depravity with the doctrine of growth. Seeing the child as influenced both by internal growth and by Christian family atmosphere, he condemned alike the "no government" or "ostrich government," advocated by the liberals and the harsh methods of the orthodox group which promoted "hopeless despair" in the tender souls of the young.

Modern Protestants, informed by the new insights of psychiatry, have not gone much beyond the enlightened Bushnell in their views of child rearing and family government. Of one thing they are certain: the child is not property, but a person whose welfare we hold as a trust from God. Parents know that in relation to their children, they are both givers and receivers in their family. Full mutuality in family government, being "subject to one another out of reverence for Christ," is the uncharted way of Protestants in the modern day. How they fare in their quest for Christian living in the family will be revealed in Part Two.

NOTES

1. Though Protestantism is "split" into about 250 separate denominations in the U.S.A., approximately 85 per cent of the individuals who make up these groups are members of 12 major denominations.
2. John Dillenberger and Claude Welch, *Protestant Christianity: Interpreted Through Its Development,* p. 3. New York: Charles Scribner's Sons, 1958.
3. A few of the most lucid expositions of Protestant doctrine are *Protestant Christianity* by John Dillenberger and Claude Welch; *Primer for Protestants* by James Hastings Nichols; William Hordern's *A Layman's Guide to Protestant Theology; Christian Doctrine* by John S. Whale; *The Heritage of the Reformation* by Wilhelm Pauck; and Daniel Jenkin's *Tradition, Freedom, and the Spirit.* Historical origins are unraveled in Roland H. Bainton's *The Reformation of the Sixteenth Century.* Definitions of concepts and movements of thought in contemporary Protestantism are available in *A Handbook of Christian Theology* edited by Marvin Halverson. On the knotty question of where the Protestant finds his norm, see *Authority in Protestant Theology* by Robert Clyde Johnson.
4. John L. Thomas, S.J., *The American Catholic Family,* p. 44.
5. Says Claude Welch: "That the church is subject to sociological analysis is not a fact to be deplored as representing an accidental and rather unfortunate aspect of the church's being. It is of positive import for theology, for this is but a reflection of the nature of the church as a humanly concrete body of responding people." *The Reality of the Church,* p. 61.
6. See the following books for different phases of a Protestant understanding of marriage and family:

Derrick Sherwin Bailey, *Sexual Relation in Christian Thought* and *The Mystery of Love and Marriage.*
Roland H. Bainton, *What Christianity Says About Sex, Love, and Marriage.*
Henry A. Bowman, *A Christian Interpretation of Marriage.*
Emil Brunner, *Man in Revolt* and *The Divine Imperative.*
Horace Bushnell, *Christian Nurture.*
William G. Cole, *Sex and Love in the Bible* and *Sex in Christianity and Psychoanalysis.*
Richard M. Fagley, *The Population Explosion and Christian Responsibility.*
Oscar E. Feucht, ed., *Helping Families Through the Church.*
Seward Hiltner, *Sex and the Christian Life.*
David Mace, *Whom God Hath Joined.*
Otto A. Piper, *The Christian Interpretation of Sex.*
Lewis J. Sherrill, *Family and Church.*
Leslie Weatherhead, *The Mastery of Sex Through Psychology and Religion.*
Gibson Winter, *Love and Conflict.*
William P. Wylie, *Human Nature and Christian Marriage.*

Wynn, J. C., *Pastoral Ministry to Families* and *How Christian Parents Face Family Problems.*

7. It is not unlikely that his earlier involvement in illicit sexual relationships conditioned his theologizing at this point.
8. William Cole suggests that whereas Thomas Aquinas, following Augustine, held that Christ had been born of a virgin in order to escape the infection of original sin, neither the Gospels nor the Epistles of the New Testament even suggest that he was born of a virgin to exempt him from the taint of sexual intercourse. This dualistic thought finds its origin in Oriental and Hellenistic cultures rather than in Judaism.
9. Jovinian, a fourth century "protestant" in the sphere of marriage and family, found fault with the excessive praise accorded by the church to unmarried life. It was his contention that God had given his creatures organs of regeneration just as he had given them organs for the intake of food. Why should churchmen make such strictures concerning a physical relation created in us to be used in marriage? Did not all good things come from God? Celibacy was against the nature that God gave us.
10. William G. Cole, *Sex in Christianity and Psychoanalysis,* p. 78.
11. William G. Cole, *Sex in Christianity and Psychoanalysis,* p. 98.
12. *The Table Talk of Martin Luther,* DCCXXVIII, William Hazlitt, ed. and trans., p. 300.
13. Carl Jung says forthrightly: "It is no longer the question of a dozen or so of voluntary or involuntary old maids here and there; it is a matter of millions. Our legal code and our social morality offer no answer to this question. Or can the (Catholic) Church give a satisfactory answer? Should we build gigantic nunneries in order to provide suitable accommodations for these women? Or should police-controlled prostitution be increased? Obviously this is impossible since we are dealing neither with saints nor with prostitutes, but with normal women who cannot register their spiritual claims with the police. They are decent women who want to marry, and if this is not possible, well—the next best thing." Quoted in *Psychological Reflections—An Anthology of the Writings of C. G. Jung,* Jolande Jacobi, ed., p. 107.
14. See Richard M. Fagley, *The Population Explosion and Christian Responsibility,* for an elaboration of this theme.
15. *The Table Talk of Martin Luther,* CXXIX, p. 57.
16. Martin Luther, *Works,* III, ed. Holman, p. 423.
17. *The Table Talk of Martin Luther,* DCCXXXII, p. 301.
18. William G. Cole, *Sex in Christianity and Psychoanalysis,* p. 120.
19. *Sex and Religion Today,* Simon Doniger, ed., pp. 77–78.
20. Richard M. Fagley, *The Population Explosion and Christian Responsibility,* p. 191.
21. Derrick Sherwin Bailey, *The Mystery of Love and Marriage,* pp. 43, 44. New York: Harper & Brothers, 1952.
22. See July 1959 issue of *Social Progress* published by the United Presbyterian Board of Christian Education.
23. *The Family Today,* The Report of Committee Five of the Lambeth Conference 1958, The National Council, Episcopal Church.
24. In discussing the contradictions in Roman Catholic writing on the sub-

ject, Fagley asks why the Roman churchmen cling to one primary cause. He queries: "Why not a frank admission that there are two primary ends? The explanation, I think, is that the philosophical approach of Thomism requires a single primary end or formal cause." *The Population Explosion and Christian Responsibility,* p. 176.

25. *Sex in Christianity and Psychoanalysis,* p. 154.
26. Gibson Winter says, "Luther's attack on Clandestine Marriage was a body blow to the whole Roman system, since Luther contradicted the sacramental notion of marriage by declaring a clandestine marriage null. Luther could not agree that consent or consent with copulation made a marriage. Marriage is a public matter for the community, and is not valid in secret. Gibson Winter, "Marriage and Family in Christian Thought," unpublished paper delivered at the Consultative Conference on Theology. See Appendix VI.
27. It was more than a legalistic act of adultery, however, which Calvin castigated. It was the basic violation of fidelity which wives and husbands owe one another in action, word or thought. The act of adultery was but a physical expression of a spiritual affair, an affair which may indicate the "death" of a marriage.
28. See the insightful study of James G. Emerson, *Divorce, The Church, and Remarriage.*
29. Martin Luther, *Works,* III, 423, 424.
30. William Graham Cole, *Sex in Christianity and Psychoanalysis,* p. 129. New York: Oxford University Press, Inc., 1955.
31. In his now celebrated essay on the problem *Christ and Culture,* H. Richard Niebuhr sets up five kinds of relationships which have existed in Christian thought and practice throughout Christian history: opposition between Christ and culture; fundamental agreement between Christ and culture; Christ above culture; Christ and culture in paradox and polarity; and Christ converting and transforming culture.
32. From Gibson Winter, "Marriage and Family in Christian Thought," p. 11.
33. William Barclay, *Train Up a Child,* pp. 261–262.
34. *The Table Talk of Martin Luther,* DCCXXV, p. 299.
35. *The Table Talk of Martin Luther,* DCCXXVII, p. 300.
36. Derrick Sherwin Bailey, *Sexual Relation in Christian Thought,* p. 201.
37. John L. Thomas, S.J., *The American Catholic Family,* p. 304.
38. Gibson Winter, *Love and Conflict.*
39. Derrick Sherwin Bailey, *Sexual Relation in Christian Thought,* pp. 296–297. New York: Harper & Brothers, 1959.
40. Derrick Sherwin Bailey, *Sexual Relation in Christian Thought,* pp. 281, 289, 301. New York: Harper & Brothers, 1959.
41. Karl Barth suggests that the commandment to honor father and mother was not a tribute to their perfection or absolute right over the child but was given because they had to do with bringing up children as the people of God. We honor them, he maintains, because they bring to children the life-giving story of Israel.
42. Luther, in a kind of detached manner, speaks of children as "far more excelling creatures of God than all the fruits of the trees. In them we see God's power, wisdom and art. . . ." Concerning their health he

says, "When young children cry lustily, they grow well and rapidly, for through crying, the members and veins are stretched out, which have no other exercise." *Luther's Table Talk*, DCCLXXVIII, p. 315.

43. In his *Social History of the American Family*, Vol. II, Arthur W. Calhoun suggests that the public recognition of the child as a socially significant human being in this period antedated a similar recognition afforded the woman and mother.

PART TWO

FAMILY AND CHURCH:
THE CONTEMPORARY PICTURE

- **Parents Speak Through Church Research**
- **Personal Characteristics of Interviewed Parents**
- **Socio-Economic Characteristics of the Sample**
- **Protestantism and Small-Town Values**
- **Problems and Satisfactions of Protestant Parents**

5

Protestant Parents Speak to the Church

WHEN THE CHURCH TURNS TO RESEARCH, it is forced by its nature to face in two directions: toward the picture of the modern home provided by empirical findings; and toward the "normative" statements regarding the family derived from the heritage. In describing the actual situation confronting the church in today's changing family, the church learns to listen to the world. From this information it grasps many clues for the next educational steps to be taken. For its normative insights, it looks to its past as well as to the present. In Chapters 3 and 4, a general Protestant slant on the family was suggested. The nature of Protestantism, we were reminded, will not allow any of the positions described to be taken as once-and-for-all statements of theological understanding of the family.[1] Convinced with John Robinson of Puritan times that "God has more truth and light to break forth from his holy Word," the Reformation stream of Christianity continues to look at the intention of Scripture regarding our current situation, knowing that biblical interpretation is enriched with each new chapter of history, and also that the word of God comes to us not so much in "principles" of religion and ethics but rather addressed to particular situations in dramatic action. The basic dependence of Protestantism is on an *event,* a decisive act of God in Christ that breaks open personal and social life in such a way that new dimensions of depth are recovered within it. So conceived, the normative position of Protestantism is "dynamic" and is expressed in an interaction between a concrete present and a particular past. It is no accident that Protestantism, with this stance, provides both incentive and support for the empirical methodology of the social sciences.

This chapter will include views given by Protestant parents to two of the questions raised in the last chapter: "What is the place of marriage in the Christian life?" and "Can we discover Protestant insights into proper family government?" These questions had not been put to our respondents in just these words but from their interviews and questionnaires, we can derive a comprehensive picture of the answer. And Chapter 6 will describe the religious perspectives of this sample of Protestant parents reflecting upon the two remaining questions raised in Chapter 4: "How is the family related to the church?" and "What is the church family's place in Christian nurture?"

Parents Speak Through Church Research

Beginning in late 1958 more than one thousand parents began to receive standardized letters from their respective churches. Each letter had referred to a curious survey being conducted among churchmen to discover what problems parents face today, the kinds of things families enjoy doing together, and how they feel about their church life. Then it put the question: *"Will you represent the parents of our church at this discussion?"*

It was such an approach, briefly noted in Chapter 1 and to be described more fully below, that brought together the nation-wide sampling of 63 groups of parents from which many of the research data came. For each group a skilled interviewer had been retained to lead the discussions; he was usually a stranger to the group. As might be expected, reactions to this kind of invitation cover an entire spectrum of attitudes, most of them reflecting positive anticipation of the experience (even after it was learned that the conversations were to be electronically recorded). One interviewer later reported of his group:

> *The spirit was excellent and interest ran high from the beginning of the interview. One mother sat near the door because she said (upon arrival) that she would have to leave before the meeting was over to attend another meeting at school. But she became so interested that she never left. One young father had not even time to eat his dinner, but he came. One mother drove eleven miles alone, to and from the meeting.*

So new was this approach in their church experience, that some parents entered the discussion with mental question marks about it. They were accustomed to being given answers through inspiring speeches, but the church seldom before had sought actively to gather their honest opinions about an area of life that concerned them deeply—their families. Curiosity mingled with reticence describes the attitude of many who responded to the invitation. More than one of the interviewers picked up an initial hesitancy in his group:

> *There was a bit of concern at first to know what this was all about. Were they to be lectured? This puzzlement quickly disappeared when they were informed about the general plans of the project and the procedures for the evening. Then they all participated freely and seemed to enjoy it.*

A small minority of the "group interviews" did not develop this open, honest atmosphere for which we had wished. The initial expectations of the experience, external conditions, relationships existing within the group and community, and the attitude toward the pastor (who was never present in the group), and rarely toward the interviewer, all contributed to the inhibited response when it appeared. One interviewer who encountered a tense group atmosphere summarizes its genesis thus:

> *It was a rainy night, and the rural roads were difficult for traveling. The people came with the expectation they were going to be "examined" and hence had built up considerable anxiety. The atmosphere seemed to be tense throughout. Hostile feelings were expressed toward the pastor and the church. In this,* he dryly adds, *there was good involvement.*

A Philosophy of Research

We had learned from a review of hundreds of family research studies, accomplished since the Second World War, that there was more than a little truth in the healthily cynical statement that much research seemed to be a series of scientifically rigorous circumlocutions to prove the obvious. (The principles derived from the research efforts were often a product of a method rather than the data themselves.) Common sense was not often given its due. Yet for the church a problem remains when all this is said: How best do we listen to our families; how do we discover where they are in their thinking, their believing, their doing? A description of many parents' attitudes and practices is far preferable to the intuitive elaboration of a few cases, so often the homiletically conditioned approach of the clergyman. Yet mere description (even of a large number of cases) by itself does not suffice; all generalizing is to some end. One has to know what is wanted from such research.

The purposes of the research emerged after a long process of clarification of what was needed by the several audiences to which we wished to address ourselves: the board of education sponsoring the study, hopefully seeking information which would make more effective an already massive effort at educating the homes of the constituency; the pastors and directors of religious education who are the strategic "movers" in most local church ministry; the parents who (with their children) were to be the participants in any family education efforts which would finally materialize; and finally, our fellow researchers in the family field (many of whom had expressed amazement that the church was interested in objective research). Out of intensive conversations with these groups, three objectives were advanced: *First,* to ascertain what a representative group of church parents under good discussion leadership will talk about regarding the tensions, goals, and resources of family living. The group interviews were to be "reality tests" depicting the readiness of parents to deal with crucial questions under skilled leadership in a church setting. *Second,* we wanted to gather valid information about this sample of Protestant families and their life. The combination of verbal interview and written questionnaire was to be used, each supplementing the other in procuring the information needed. We were concerned to use these in such a way that the parents involved in the research effort were not made "guinea pigs" or "objects of research" but would be led to consider those questions whose answers mean as much to them as to the investigators. As one of our consultants, Nelson Foote, said, "One of the first criteria that would seem to derive from taking any group of subjects as the audience for a piece of research is the degree to which these subjects can recognize it as truly applying to themselves." Whether we have succeeded in satisfying this criterion can be finally tested only by this book's readership. That many of the group sessions from which data were gathered did prove at once a source of information for us and also "functional research," facilitating the increased understanding of the parents, was attested to in a number of evaluations. One of our trained interviewers said of his group:

> *At the close of the meeting the larger percentage of the group seemed loath to leave and remained to discuss things further. Several made a point of expressing appreciation at being invited to participate. One man went so far as to express the hope that the tape recorder had*

failed entirely so that the group could be called together again for another discussion.

To some groups, such as the following, the procedure was of limited direct usefulness, unless the subjects learned something from their own defensive behavior.

This was a suburban well-to-do church. They were unwilling to "let down their hair" because of the competitive situation in which they lived. The respondents were somewhat afraid of saying too much about their own problems. But the questionnaire and personal discussion after the meeting revealed many tensions and anxieties in basic human relationships.

In contrast to this assessment, the majority of the group sessions were considered by interviewers and parents to be of live interest, active participation, and of considerable help in clarifying conflicts, goals, and available sources of help for family living. This plan, then, was our attempt to give these subjects help through the very process by which information was gathered. To use the now well-known phrase by Martin Buber, it would be our hope that research could become an "I-Thou" as well as an "I-It" relationship.

A *third* objective of the parents' study was to give the group of parents the kind of exploratory experience with a wide variety of family concerns that would motivate the members to think further about these matters through the church program. Though no systematic follow-up has been made of churches that participated in this research effort, the last report received indicated the intention of a few groups constituted as they were for the interview to continue meeting together. A number of sponsoring pastors spoke appreciatively of the impetus this group experience had given their general adult education program.

Particular care was taken to insure that the relationship between the researchers and the subjects (in this case the parents) were mutually helpful. Foote again reminds us that even the validity of a study is affected by the quality of these relationships.

Any study intended for its subjects as an audience can be appraised in terms of the kind of relation established between the subjects and the investigator. Not only is their degree of participation likely to affect the outcome of the research in terms of obtaining data, but it also affects the quality of the data in ways that are blithely overlooked when researchers fail to report how they obtained the co-operation of their subjects. In a society where everyone is becoming familiar with social science techniques and findings, and expect sooner or later to obtain some benefit from family research, the relationship of investigator and investigated is bound to receive more attention from the latter if not the former.[2]

To the report of "how co-operation was obtained," we now proceed.

The Research Procedure

The basic sources of information from parents in this study were the recordings of two-hour group interviews held in 63 Presbyterian churches throughout the U.S.A., supplemented by a 25-item, anonymous, pretested questionnaire[3] administered after the group discussion to each parent present. Eight hundred forty-five (845) parents (representing as many families since no two parents from the same families were invited) participated in these interviews. Questionnaires from seven hundred nineteen (719) of these interviewed parents were usable for analysis.[4] To these were added 291 questionnaires completed in miscellaneous parents' groups in the church, bringing the total to one thousand available to us for some aspects of the investigation. It has been established in research methodology that a questionnaire administered *following* a candid discussion on the same general subject has more validity than one completed by an individual when he is "cold." The combination of group interview and the parents' questionnaire did prove fruitful for checking similarities, inconsistencies, and gaps in the data received by the two methods.

What is a "group interview?" It is a guided discussion that focuses upon standard questions interjected by the interviewer into the group for their free discussion. An interview schedule and prescribed procedure, used by each interviewer, provided a common frame of reference for all the groups involved in the study.[5]

The interviewer, a person skilled in group discussion, ideally moves from one question to another without the group members being much aware of the order of the questions. He tries to preserve the impression of a good, spontaneous conversation with the group. However, he tries not to interject his own attitude or experience into the conversation or express value judgments. The interviewer's job, he was told, is to free the group for self-exploratory purposes and to assure group members that so far as his behavior is concerned, they will be protected from denial, contradiction, competition, or other harassment. The group-interviewing job required considerable skill and discipline.

To find people possessed of these abilities, active in Protestant churches, and willing to participate in this project, was no little task. To complicate matters further, well-qualified personnel were likely to be concentrated in the large urban centers, thus compounding the problem of getting a wide representation of church groups in different locales. But finally, fifty-four men and women, representing a variety of disciplines—the ministry (with special graduate training), psychology, psychiatry, social work, and sociology were invited because of their demonstrated skill in releasing groups for depth conversations. The majority of the interviewers possess rich experience in group dynamics, counseling, clinical, or interview survey work related to their particular discipline. About one-third carry some formal teaching responsibility, usually in institutions of higher learning. Writers and researchers in marriage and family living are found among their number.[6] It was a well-trained group.

These men and women not only conducted the two-hour interview and administered the questionnaires but, in addition, outlined from the tape or disc recording the topics discussed, indicating the points of group consensus, involvement, confusion, and avoidance appearing in the interview. A copy of this outline report was sent to the pastor and to the research office by these leaders. This proved to be an invaluable aid in analyzing the transcribed recordings later.

Once the group interviewers had been selected, and their willingness to serve had been assured, the problem remained to win the co-operation of local churches located near the interviewers yet representing a variety of sizes and community types. These were to host the group interviews. The response was heartening; sixty-six churches participated in the program initially. Sixty-three (63) of the recordings received from these groups were found usable in the research program. The final roster of congregations hosting group interviews reveals the variety among them.

TABLE 1 SIZE OF GROUP INTERVIEW CHURCHES

Size of Congregation	*Number of Host Churches*
0–99 members	1
100–299 members	15
300–599 members	18
600–1199 members	17
1200 and up members	12
Total	63

The sample was weighted toward the larger churches; the median average congregation had 460 members (as compared with a United

Presbyterian average of about 350 members). The congregations involved were further differentiated by the kind of community in which they are located according to a fourfold breakdown.

TABLE 2 DISTRIBUTION OF GROUP INTERVIEW CHURCHES BY TYPE OF COMMUNITY

Type of Community	*Number of Host Churches*
Rural	9
Town and small city (under 50,000)	6
City (over 50,000)	28
Suburbs of a metropolitan city	20
Total	63

The sample is underrepresented by the rural and small town churches.[7] In one sense, the research findings can be conceived as in line with the future direction of Protestantism now centering in the heavily populated suburban areas. Currently one out of four Presbyterian churches is located in suburbs of metropolitan cities, but the sense of direction is suggested by a fourteen-denomination study of church development made by the National Council of Churches; over the last ten-year period 19 per cent of new churches organized were urban, 17.5 per cent rural, and *63.5* per cent suburban! Church building clearly follows the population bulge reported in Chapter 2.[8]

Each host pastor (or one designated by him) was given instructions on the physical setup of the group interview, the contact with the assigned interviewer, and instructions for inviting the group of parents. He was, insofar as possible, to select a random sample of up to twenty members from his congregation, and only one parent from each home.[9] In general, the instructions were diligently adhered to, but this was no easy task for the pastor or his delegate. On the whole, a minority of churches were able to get a response from a genuine cross section of the membership, active and inactive; but the largest group of parents were above average in their church participation. (In the sociologist's terms, more "nuclear" and "modal" than "marginal" members responded to the invitation; this result was not unexpected.) The extent of their church participation will be detailed in Chapter 6.

The average interview was attended by 13 parents, six fathers and seven mothers. The groups ranged in size from 6 to 22 participants, only four per cent of whom did not express themselves in the interviews; nearly all completed questionnaires for us. It should be noted that in no case was the pastor of the church present at the interview; his absence seemed in many cases to increase the candor of the respondents. *"I hope what I say will not be taken as criticism of our pastor but . . ."* preceded a number of revealing statements about the ordained leadership of the church. When interviews were completed, the questionnaires and interviews were analyzed. Tabulation on Keysort cards served to classify the questionnaire responses. (All answers given by the parents were cross-tabulated with their sex, age, education, stage in the family life cycle, to their place of residence and degree of church activity.)[10]

One hundred twenty-six hours of group interview recordings were transcribed; this was the verbal product of the 63 groups of church parents. Few silences are to be noted in these two-hour recordings. Some interviews ran even longer than the suggested time and a few ran into minor recording problems. Said one interviewer concerning his inner-city group:

> *The participants were not prepared for a three-hour evening starting at 8* P.M. *with some recording trouble; this made several people anxious by the time of 10:15 (because of the necessity of going home alone in a hazardous neighborhood) but the interest was well sustained until after we adjourned at 11* P.M.

As might be imagined, the analysis of group recordings, even from the transcripts, is no simple task; but from this process a veritable gold mine of information was obtained.[11] The description of problems, goals, and resources of this group of Protestant parents will combine the information of the interviews with that revealed by the questionnaire.

Personal Characteristics of Interviewed Parents

We had anticipated, on the basis of what we knew about church attendance, that more mothers than fathers would attend the group interviews in spite of an effort to attract an equal number of each; we were not surprised to find this to be the case. What did surprise us, however, was the percentage of men among the 845 parents who did attend the interviews (382 or 45.2 per cent) and the relatively greater expression of appreciation for the experience by males. Mothers in the interviews, numbering 463 (or 54.8 per cent of the sample) were not so verbally active in the group; evidently for many of the women the experience had the familiar flavor of an afternoon in PTA or in church circle discussions. To the men it was a more unusual opportunity.

By design, the project called for the participation of parents who were living together with their mates with at least one child under eighteen at home. The figures cited for this sample, therefore, do not represent the picture of marital status in the church at large. It was apparent that some compromises had been made with the sampling procedure at the local level since we found that nine parents (about one per cent) who were widowed or divorced and not now married attended the group interviews. Ninety-nine per cent of the participating parents did meet the requirement laid down. Yet some interesting differences appeared among them. The great majority (93 per cent) of parents were living with their original spouse; five per cent were remarried after being divorced; and one per cent were remarried after the death of the spouse.[12] A survey of magazine readership in this denomination has indicated that about 91 per cent of the church's membership over 18 years of age is married at any one time. It was a highly stable marital group that we drew into the interviews.

The average respondent was in his late thirties[13] and had at least one teen-ager in the family. Parents knew what they were talking about when they discussed family problems in the interviews; for among each 100 families represented, there was a minimum of two hundred and forty children.[14] Forty-six per cent of these families had three children or more; and proportionately more professional workers were found among the ranks of these prolific parents. Though thirty-seven per cent of this sample are thus far "old-fashioned" two-child families, the two-and-a-fraction offspring per family may indicate that Protestants are swinging back to a quiverful.[15]

It seems important for the church to understand that there are many phases in family life which call for adjustments on the part of parents; that new relationships emerge with each state as do the needs of family members. Drawing upon Evelyn Duvall's formulation of the "family life cycle," we sought to get information from our parents about the stages through which they were living. (Duvall's theory holds that whole families change as the children grow; that a family grows through a given stage with its *oldest* child, pushing into new unknowns. As younger children come along, they "arrive in a family somewhat familiar with these normal events and stages of children's growth through the induction given by the eldest.")[16] It was apparent in the interviews that parents whose children were older often served as advisers to parents of younger children in the discussion. (This might well constitute a new expression of the "priesthood of believers" to each other in the life of the church.) The table on page 127 indicates the number of families in various stages of the family life cycle.

TABLE 3 DISTRIBUTION OF PARENTS ACCORDING TO AGE OF OLDEST CHILD

Age of Child	*Percentage of Parents*
Under 2½ years	4.1%
2 through 5 years	14.5%
6 through 12 years	37.0%
13 through 19 years	35.0%
20 years and older	9.4%

Socio-Economic Characteristics of the Sample

In common with a large proportion of American Protestantism, our study describes parents with higher-than-average status in income, occupation, and education. A number of studies now indicate that Episcopalians and Congregationalists share this same profile with the United Presbyterians from whose membership we had drawn our sample; and the same characteristics will be found among some Methodists, Baptists, and Lutherans although these latter three denominations represent a wider cross section of all socio-economic classes. Protestantism as a whole draws its adherents from all class groups in roughly the same proportion as the total population; and our interviews had persons from all socio-economic strata. It was, however, weighted toward the dominant middle-class pattern of the "old line" Protestant denominations. Of the parents surveyed, 93 per cent were high school graduates, and 65 per cent had attended college (compared with 16.4 per cent of the population nationally). A cross section of the denomination's readership of its official magazine made earlier had shown a slightly lower educational attainment,[17] but it must be noted that this reading sample is underrepresented in rural and inner-city areas and by Negro families; the educational achievement figure would be lower if these groups had full-strength representation.

It was assumed in the urban and suburban interviews that children of the respondents would go to college. When a question was raised about the children's educational future one suburban mother said with surprise: *"Why, of course they're going to college. How else can they get ahead?"* These same people tended to be avid readers.[18] The high educational attainment of the respondents did not always guarantee articulateness in the interview; other factors operated to inhibit status-conscious people from going beyond publicly sanctioned topics in their discussion.

Fifteen years ago, only about two-thirds of this group of Protestants would have been found to have made it all the way through high school whereas in this study almost two-thirds were found to have attended college. An adequate picture of the denomination lies somewhere between these two figures.[19]

Occupationally, too, the parents interviewed were a cut above the higher-than-average rank of the denomination as a whole. The biggest single classification of the chief wage earner is "professional and technical"—sometimes called the "egghead" jobs (representing between a quarter and a third of the total membership). In the nation as a whole this classification ranks only fifth in an order of nine listed kinds of work (only one out of ten workers being so classified). Managers and owners of businesses are more numerous among our sample (and among Episcopalians, Congregationalists, and those of Reformed bodies) than in the population at large. But these Protestant groups have fewer farmers proportionately than the 8.7 per cent of Americans who live by agriculture. In contrast, Lutherans, Methodists, and Baptists possess a great many farmers in their memberships; these three denominations, largely, swing the rural balance for Protestantism in the nation as a whole. Will Herberg points out that in the labor movement there can be little doubt that Roman Catholics make up and have long made up (because of the occupations heavily represented among their membership) a considerably greater proportion than they do in the population as a whole. The small number of "operatives," production-line workers, and the like on our rolls (well under one-half of the proportion of the national figure) would tend to support this observation.

It is apparent that we are dealing chiefly with a middle- and upper-middle-class section of Protestantism in this report, classes in which the major, "old line" Protestant denominations are amply represented.[20] Yet even within this sample it is possible to note differences in attitude toward the economic realities of life. For example, financial problems were freely discussed in city and rural interviews. In one out of four urban groups (chiefly inner-city parishes), and in two out of three rural groups in the sample, parents openly aspired to "attain financial security," "pay off debts," or "increase income." Only in mill towns and industrial suburbs did insecurity about a job future and the fear of a depression come to the fore. A number of men in these latter churches, it was reported, worked at two jobs to make ends meet. Financial problems were rarely introduced into the residential-suburb discussions; financial adequacy was more obvious here (as was the fear of losing status with revelations of financial embarrassment).[21] The problem of inadequate income was placed number eight among twenty-five concerns bothering our parents. For residents of the suburbs it was placed further down the scale.

Protestantism and Small-Town Values

Of the present sample of parents, the majority (54 per cent) reported they live in cities of over 100,000 population and their suburbs. Only one-third of them grew up in such locales, however. What happens to Protestant "small town" values in such a migration? There seems to be, says one Protestant social analyst, a nostalgia for the values of rural life which permeates Protestantism (especially its leadership) wherever the church manifests itself in America.

> Although there are large and ecclesiastically influential congregations of almost all the major denominations in all our principal cities, Protestantism's viewpoint remains stubbornly that of the village. As such it has often become entangled in the suburbs' and exurbs' desperate attempts to reclaim synthetically the virtues of village and small-town life. The effort to modernize a pastoral religion by providing it with a split-level, ranch-house façade is one of the more depressing Protestant ventures of our time.[22]

Yet the physical move to suburbia is but a geographical symptom of a shift to a suburban mentality on the part of people in all locales.

Protestant critics decry the "Babylonian Captivity" of the suburban church, claiming that the prophetic voice of the church is being muted by a conformist, comfort-seeking temper. They see danger in the family-orientation of the parish and the insulation of middle-class people from a multiracial, multicultural community with all its intergroup problems. Lashing out with journalistic invective at the suburbanites' tendency to oversimplify ethical situations in an exceedingly complex world, critics of suburban life see it chiefly as escape from reality. Is this blast at suburban life a journalistic shock treatment, or is it cool assessment of the actual situation?

Exponents of a new Protestant suburbia (a temporary situation now with the rapid influx of other faiths) point to the recovery of face-to-face relationships in the midst of a depersonalized world. They speak of the legitimacy of "belonging" in a world characterized by schizoid detachment. They deny that the "mission to the suburbs" must always fail to be mission; signs of a rebirth of an articulate Christian faith are emerging here, they claim. Adult Christian education, now recognized as one of the greatest needs in Protestantism, finds its major impetus and most of its students in suburbia, they remind us. Both detractors and champions of suburbia recall for us this problem: in the midst of an exceedingly complex sociological transition, the relation of church and culture must be rethought.

Because of mass media—television, radio, movies, magazines, newspapers, paperbacks—the same cultural fare is available to all. We can no longer assume that rural and urban people are sharply contrasting types; some differences remain, but the suburban mentality is exercising a leveling influence on both groups. The suburb, offering a recovery of personal relationships (however stereotypified by the novels) without the inconvenience of the farm and isolated small town; emphasis on "neighboring" with ready access to the supermarkets, good schools, and churches, has a wide appeal through all strata of American society. Protestants feel insecure that their psychological abandonment of the central cities has left them in a "minority" status; they are equally distressed when the "amiable syncretism" of suburbia tends to vitiate a prophetic witness. It is a troubled Protestantism which lives in the new suburbia.

Problems and Satisfactions of Protestant Parents

The pastor and his colleagues, often confronted with people in counseling who come with severe family distress—conflict, failure, delinquency, and the like—may tend to overlook the more pervasive tensions which plague most Protestant families. These are not generally the explosive discords that lead to divorce, to emotional breakdown, and to runaway and delinquent children. They are problems, however, which rob them of serenity and effective relations, not to mention effective Christian witness. We approach the typical problems of typical Protestants not from a case study approach. Nor shall we discuss and classify the different kinds of emotional interaction of parish families.[23] It is the general rather than the idiosyncratic struggles that we seek to describe; problems discussed on this level may suggest educational approaches which can be embodied in the local parish.

The Pressure of Time

No problem was as frequently and insistently voiced as the pressure of time and schedule upon our families. "Competition from too many activities, that tend to separate the family" was a constant complaint of these parents, and (we were to learn) of their pastors also (noted in Chapter 7). Interestingly, this problem was not confined to any one type of community; rural, urban, and suburban parents all feelingly report this kind of tension.

Especially in the residential suburbs do our parents report fantastic busyness and the necessity of an overscheduled life. Says one parent:

> *I faced an outburst with my twelve-year-old a couple of Saturdays ago, one that made me stop and think. She said, "I'm so tired of going to a cello lesson at 2 o'clock and a dancing lesson at 4 o'clock. When will I have time to play and ride my bike . . . ?" We have our life all scheduled out and we need it that way. My husband is in school and I work, and everyone must work out their life hour by hour. There's always concern with time—rush, rush, rush! And it takes a terrible toll on me.*

Many of our people, wanting to be "good parents," find themselves ensnared in a dozen community activities, all deemed good in themselves. One spells out what it means to be a "good mother" of school-age children in the modern day:

> *As children get older, parents operate as chauffeurs. I think mothers are particularly called upon to participate in so many activities—civic, school, and church—but they feel as if they are very worthwhile things. On the other hand, once you get caught in those activities, you're stuck. Then I find myself getting quite tense with my children.*

The modern suburban mother is expected to have an unlimited store of energy, and to follow the child into his complicated organization life. What a contrast to the ailing mother of yesteryear when it was fashionable to be delicate! An 1841 *Parents Magazine* reveals the sharp contrast in expectations of the "good mother":

> I must not tease my mother;
> And when she likes to read
> Or has a headache, I will step
> Quite silently indeed.
> I will not choose a noisy play
> Nor trifling troubles tell
> But sit down quiet by her side
> And try to make her well.[24]

The time pressure we find so well illustrated in our reports is not a new thing. In the mid-1800's, perceptive Horace Bushnell indicated both its presence in the homes of his day and a clue to its dynamics:

> The weary comes home to the weary—the careworn meets the careworn. The pressure upon a multitude of professional and business men is really frightful; combined with the necessity of going

> long distances to their places of duty, it produces little short of an absolute separation from their families. There are fathers in the community who are almost strangers to their own children—who do not know one-half as much about them as their teachers. The appropriate work and play and worship of the home cannot be so much as begun in many dwellings, and anything is caught at which promises to relieve parents from work which they can find no time to do.[25]

Here the busyness is centered chiefly in the demands of the father's job; and these demands have increased today. Add to them the tyrannical schedule of a working mother and the problem is compounded. But what *is* new in the picture of the hectic round presented by our parents is *the lure of community activities* upon each member of the family. Especially in the gregarious suburb (but increasingly in rural and city areas as well) do these demands become imperative. Beginning at age three, children's groups are organized so that leisure time is supervised; little activity for middle-class children is allowed to develop outside the orbit of adult control. Such free recreational pursuit is often regarded with suspicion and fear. During a recent outbreak of misdemeanors in a community hosting a group interview, a letter issued by a group of mothers said in part:

> *The great antidote to the sort of purposeless use of leisure which leads to mischief and worse, is the substitution of creative interests and activities. The schools, both day and Sabbath, can do much in this respect—but the vital stimulus must come from parents. This means provision not only of tools for worthwhile activity; but also, much more costing, an ungrudging offer of time and interest in the children's activities by the parents themselves.*

The authors of *Crestwood Heights* found that parents regard the Scouts, Little Leagues, children's clubs, the Sunday school, 4-H and other *adult-controlled, child-centered* organizations as a means of socializing their children. It is here in these associations, they believe, that children learn the extroverted, competitive skills for life. Parents of this social class, therefore, are as liberal in providing their children with this "associational activity" as they are in giving toys, spending-money, or clothing. This is not mere generosity on the parent's part, the authors hold; it is a way of ensuring his child's social status and of forcing the child to organize his leisure rigidly (thus grooming him for later adult status in this kind of community).[26]

But our parents are ambivalent about these organized pursuits. They are convinced that their children need these activities and they want their children to be "a part of everything." On the other hand, they observe that tension mounts, communication in the family deteriorates, and family freedom is crowded out in a seemingly relentless schedule.

> *Many of our misunderstandings are just quick little passes that are made about problems when the children or parents are on their way out,* says one father. *It's a geared society—the children have plans—a very social society. My wife and I are getting worn out just trying to regulate our schedule. The whole thing to me is just a rat race, and it is hard to keep it on the level of a smooth-running family unit. Yet, you wouldn't want your children to operate any other way.*

In one candid group, a parent quoted a magazine article in the interview with which many others agreed: *"The overriding fear of parents in the twentieth century is that their children will not be popular, will not be liked, will be unhappy little odd balls playing by themselves."*[27]

Yet in the midst of this desire for social acceptance, a few parents, especially fathers, are aware of dangers too. They raise a question about dances and nylons in the fifth grade. They feel "growing up too early" is associated with the increased number of adolescent sex problems, teen-age marriages, and premarital pregnancies. (Central city parents are likewise concerned about sexual dangers and cite many examples of harm to their children, but the problem to them is one of conflicting cultural standards not fabricated sociability.)

Parents are frank to say that it is the children's organizations which contribute most to family disorganization and busyness. Interestingly, the adult-centered social groups to which so many belong[28] are rarely mentioned as culprits. (Several parents interviewed in a study of summertime activities in Michigan reported that the country club made the greatest contribution to their families because there "the whole family finds something interesting to do.") A strange reluctance to talk about their *nonparental* roles permeated many of the parent sessions. One interviewer analyzes this interesting fact:

> *Little is said about their own needs that would find resources outside their children. Rather than its being unselfishness, I felt it was a lack of the ability to fulfill self-needs without feeling guilty.*

This reaction is not unexpected in a church group. It was common to hear "irresponsible parents" (those not taking part in these many child-centered organizations) roundly castigated by the participants. One of our psychologist consultants suggests that these parents seem to be motivated chiefly by a sense of duty toward their children and a sense of social insecurity. This, he is frank to say, may reflect not love so much as rejection of both their children and the parental role. *"It's just expected of you; you have to belong to these things,"* says one of the busy parents interviewed. When one seeks to discover the satisfactions these parents find in the associations designed to help them in child rearing, he seldom finds statements more specific than *"they help build character,"* or *"they help children get acquainted."* A few parents, but the number is insignificant, report personal help in taking a leadership position or in *"getting to know the people in the community,"* the latter especially if the parents are recent arrivals in town. Some find they do come to know their children better as a result of their endless chauffeuring and participation in youth activities; for this they are somewhat grateful. But we get the impression upon hearing the tape recordings that the desire to be a "good parent," community member, or typical Protestant—a person active in civic affairs—is the most readily admitted motivation for the rigorous organizational life they lead.

The interviews and questionnaires reveal, with rare exceptions, the confusion of our parents in sorting out the values which guide their choices in this busy world. Few would admit openly (as does one father) of an indecisiveness that complicates the problem:

> *I think it is our indecisiveness which is contributing to the unsettledness of our children. We parents don't know what we want or what we want for them. Society is handing them a whole group of attractive opportunities, and they're grabbing on to what they can.*

Some parents claim that advertising pressures, chiefly on television, make the task of evaluating and selecting even more difficult. Howard Whitman, in a syndicated column, speaking to the woman who rides off in six different directions, counsels:

> The smart wife is like a good field general; she takes an advance look at the terrain before striking out, she sizes up the situation, calmly cogitates, then makes her battle plan. And like a good general, she knows that she can't do everything at once. She must take one objective at a time. And she can't take them all. She must decide which objectives are of prime importance. In a woman's day, this means learning to say no.[29]

A few of our parents would, no doubt, be helped by such advice; they need but a nudge to bring order out of chaos in family living.

But these data convince us that a deeper root for the lack of discrimination in daily activities must also be sought. Psychological analysts note that when the parents' chief conflict is the problem of time, we must look beyond that symptom to a confusion in their sense of identity and individuality. With few exceptions these parents tend to say that everything in community life is equally meaningful for them; hence they cannot choose. Individuality and a sense of solid identity is based upon commitment to some value hierarchy; if these values were clear, the conflict of *time* would not be a major consideration, for one would have the basis of choosing and renouncing.[30] It is this note that theologian D. T. Niles has caught in his assertion that "it is irresponsible . . . to think that Christians can find time and money and strength for everything that everybody else does, and that with spare money in spare time and with spare strength they can serve the ends of God's Kingdom. The great pearl is bought only by selling small pearls (Matthew 13:45–46). Where no pearl has been sold, there obedience to the demand of the Kingdom has not begun."[31]

For some parents the inability to choose may reflect a general problem in human relationships. Much yearning for togetherness is in evidence in the group discussions. Yet one senses side by side with this hunger a fear of close relationships in the group and in the family. A desire for closeness and yet a fear of it—this is frequently the conflict of modern parents. Psychiatrist Paul Tournier reports that "by what amounts to a secret understanding many (families) constantly avoid being alone together. . . . They rush from one activity to another, with magnificent devotion and tremendous zeal."[32] Wanting togetherness, they cannot stand it.

Even as the relationship of families to their community is deeply influenced by broad social trends, so the internal relationships of the family are not immune to the cultural transition of our time. It was sociologist David Riesman in *The Lonely Crowd* who coined the useful concept of the "other-directed," meaning those who habitually accept the standards and influence of others in their living. Other-direction is based on the assumption that individuals in a consumption-oriented society will not be able to know who they are or what they want without first testing the social climate. Such persons, he says, have developed a kind of personal radar system to catch signals of approval before they act. Fewer there are (and we found them chiefly in our rural interviews and among the salesmen of our urban groups) who possess their own inner gyroscope that helps them to keep balance in the midst of clamorous demands. Riesman feels that the modern child is trained in such a way that he often lacks any strong desires of his own, desires which he will try to realize in the face of opposition (especially by the peer group).[33] It would, of course, be a mistake to say that all parents in the study suffering from this sense of time pressure reveal the particular motivations just discussed here. For some, the peculiarities of the situation are paramount; for others, anxiety and confusion as to who they are and what they really want in life add to the problem. Whatever the basic motivations of these parents, a contributing factor seems to be a community pattern that compulsively proliferates groups (ostensibly devoted to the welfare of offspring of these same harried fathers and mothers).

Interpersonal Relationships of the Family

John Sirjamaki observes that our continuing emphasis upon individualism as a basic American value as well as our disapproval of a fixed status among the people, whether of family or social class, tend to contribute to a lack of clan feeling. As a consequence, marriage now tends to be regarded very much the private affair of the spouses and all members of the family are likely to view the family as existing for them —not they for it. Under these circumstances marriage and home life have inevitably become largely concerned with the interpersonal relations of family members.[34] The fact that the family now needs to adapt to highly individual schedules of its members is evidence of the "atomism" which we see in the modern family group. Bringing together these individualized fragments into some kind of working team is then a key problem of its more mature members.

The peculiar frustrations in interpersonal relationships, as reported by these parents, might best be understood if we first note their *ideals for family living.* Answers to the questionnaire item "What kinds of things do you want your children to remember about your family life when they grow up?" sheds light upon the goals against which parents are measuring their present family life. The great majority of these fathers and mothers (almost four of every five) wanted their children to remember loving, happy relationships among them; they craved an atmosphere of helpfulness, sympathy, and mutual respect. The "good family" is the happy family; doing things together is deemed indispensable to this happiness. (This is one reason why the "time conflict" is felt so poignantly.) A father's statement reflects a widespread assumption in the parents' interviews:

> *To me, good family life is a family which does things together, and is happy while doing it. Those things may be outdoor activities*

or church activities or whatever the people themselves get pleasure and satisfaction out of doing.

With this image prevailing, it is not difficult to see why "inadequate recreation and leisure time" should be checked as a problem by almost half of the sample; for it is in the nonwork, recreational context that this kind of "togetherness" finds its consummation; vacations, week-end trips, and play are its typical expressions. Oriented as it is to the week ends and evenings, this Protestant middle-class family wants to invest long hours together to explore hitherto untapped potential for comradeship; it is then they get to know each other and to build patterns of mutually satisfying ways of getting along.

The congenial family meal, so often crowded out by the rush, also symbolizes the ideal family. Here the family may catch up on the goings and comings of their highly individual lives. Few parents are fully aware of the educational gains wrought by the institution of the family meal. Though families (and their schedules) make meals what they are, it is equally true that dining experiences can rebuild the emotional relationships of the group. In an instructive study, James Bossard and Eleanor Boll have demonstrated that various patterns of mealtime conversation are characteristic of particular families. It is a highly educational opportunity for families to become aware of what their family conversations reveal about the dynamics of relationship. For example, there is a kind of conversation that is almost habitually passing judgment by analyzing, interpreting, and describing persons, objects, and events. The chief tone of the conversation may be humor, drama, or matter-of-fact reporting. Comments may be chiefly critical, depreciatory, belittling.[35]

Parents who place the family meal among the most important opportunities for developing congenial relationships have, in their own often secular way, caught the close association of vital Christian faith and its communal "family meal," the Lord's Supper. Luther, in his imaginative and instructive *Table Talk* sensed this important connection. Perhaps there is rare opportunity here for educational opportunities of Christian parents to be developed.

Regrettably often, private concerns and pleasures are found in this group sample to be the chief ingredients of "good family life." With rare exceptions, the church seems to be confronted with the family "curved in upon itself," to repeat an indictment first uttered by Luther. One senses in a majority the unspoken presupposition that in the family one should be able to find complete fulfillment. In this kind of assumption there is denial of the Protestant position that only in God known in Jesus Christ can there be ultimate fulfillment of our humanity as we have seen in Chapters 3 and 4.

It was a small minority of parents (scarcely one in six) who wanted their children to remember most of all the Christian faith and the living of that faith; they desired most of all an awareness of God's guidance and love, service to persons outside the family, and participation in the community of faith. It is true, as will be pointed out in the next chapter, that many parents assume that happy relationships and Christian faith are identical; but theirs is a nontheological perspective. That so many identify Christianity with congenial personal relationships, faith with self-sufficient confidence, and service with occasional spurts of generosity, is a finding which should give the church pause. One hundred suburban parents of our sample told us that growth in Christian faith (as they conceived of it) was best stimulated within their family by recreation together, vacations, grace at mealtime, discussion of behavior problems in the family. Placed far down the list and preceded by eleven other activities were Bible reading and worship which could lead them to grasp the specific and historic events of Christian faith for themselves.

One in ten parents want their youngsters to remember most of all the way in which the family worked out its problems together; the memory that love and forgiveness brought them through rough and smooth times, rewarded by reconciliation and confidence borne of victorious struggle. With these (rather rare) parents there seemed to be a greater recognition of the inevitability of both hurt and healing in family living. They, more than others, uttered expressions of self-reproach concerning their own methods, qualities, and policies as parents, but the reaction was not confined to them. In thirty of the 63 groups, self-reproach emerged as a major or minor theme.

Relatively few parents (one in twenty) wanted their offspring primarily to remember the moral training of the family. These (chiefly rural and small town) folks also stressed obedience and respect of parents as related values. For them, "right" and "wrong" tended to be fixed absolutes and the Christian religion was essentially the doing of the "right." They generally held more traditional conceptions of child rearing than did most suburban and urban parents whose views were more flexible and developmentally oriented. In this, rural parents reflected conceptions of parenthood and childhood which are found more frequently among the lower socio-economic levels.[36] One study of the role of the "good mother" contrasted the answers of working-class and middle-class mothers to the question: "What do you think is the most important thing parents can do for their children in bringing them up?" The choices of the working-class women were three to one for a "moral, upright approach" and teaching the child a trade, if he were a boy, and to be a good housewife, if a girl. The middle-class mothers were about evenly split between that view and "giving a wide range of experiences and helping them to grow up to be well-rounded adults."[37] The tension between the "traditional" and "developmental" conceptions of parenthood is especially noticeable in the city parents; rural and small-town parents are more clearly "traditional"; and suburban parents tend to be "developmental" in their approach.[38]

Relatively few fathers and mothers (one in twenty-five) singled out special events and family activities for a preferred place in the memory of their children. Of course, these had often been included in the ideal of the "loving, happy home" first cited. Often family occasions are "ritualized" and represent what the family sees about itself that it wants to continue. Week-end celebrations, summer vacations, and anniversaries are but a few of these possibilities. Says one mother,

> *What do you want your children to remember? I think tradition is a great thing. Doing the same things year after year, I mean at Christmastime. Even as old as my children are, on Christmas Eve they hang up their stockings by the fireplace. It's the little things you do at Thanksgiving and the Fourth of July. To do those little things over and over are very important.*

James Bossard and Eleanor Boll in their book *Ritual in Family Living*[39] reported the three most common rituals of American middle-class families to be related to family recreation, Sunday plans, and reading. It is apparent from their study that rituals can grow up around religious practices, mealtime, work activities, and even the bathroom. With the advent of TV, new ritualized family patterns have emerged and these we shall explore below. In suburban homes particularly (to cite a sharp change in Protestant social habits) one sees another kind of ritual developing whose principal *dramatis personae* are husband and wife: the cocktail hour. A number of parents report this period of husband-wife companionship just before the evening meal. The children's presence is often regarded as intrusion. One father says,

> *"When I was commuting, I had the kids swarming all over me from the minute I walked in the door. We met that problem by having them settled down and watching TV half an hour before I returned*

home. There were many nights they never knew when I came in. Then we were able to postpone dinner for a half hour so that we could settle down with a good cocktail and review the day."

Whatever the value of rituals, it is apparent that to these parents, passing on a family tradition is far less important than freeing the children to create their own pattern of life both now and when they are married. It is against this background of general ideals for family living that the problems confronted in intrafamily relationships should be seen.

High involvement and interest was apparent whenever *difficulties in parent-child relationships* were discussed in the research groups. Parents reported not only that this subject was of deep concern to them, but that they *expected* the help of the church at this point in their lives.[40] "Parent-child relations" heads the list of suggestions given by parents and pastors regarding pertinent topics for family life education; parents with young children would place high priority on such programs. As one researcher has concluded, "Parenthood is a crisis"; it, and not marriage, is the real "romantic complex" of our culture. The intrusion of a third party on a satisfactory relationship of a couple, even though wanted and planned for, brings new and painful reorganization to most families; and parents are disenchanted with the problems occasioned by a first child.[41] Fathers and mothers in the interviews would agree. It is parenthood, not marriage, that requires the greater step into maturity, it seemed to them.

It is at the point of *discipline in the home* that confusion and dissatisfaction among these Protestant parents is most apparent. Shall we "control" or shall we "guide" the child; should we be rigid or flexible in our training? We have seen that there are differences in these conceptions according to social class; now the evidence is accumulating that there are some religious differences too. Miller and Swanson, dividing their groups of mothers into those whose husbands work in an "entrepreneurial" (most often small business or sales) setting and those working in a "welfare bureaucratic" operation (largely within the corporation), found that in entrepreneurial groups Protestants are more likely than Roman Catholics to emphasize the teaching of self-control and personal accountability in the training of their children. In a bureaucratic setting (most often represented in the residential suburb), the differences between the religious faiths are not so clear and consistent. Perhaps, the authors contend, "bureaucratic experiences are such that they tend to make certain Protestant views more like those of Roman Catholics, supplanting stress on self-control with reliance on external controls to guide the child."[42] The following interview dialogue will illustrate the dilemma between rigid control and permissive guidance in which many Protestant parents feel caught:

> *"Is it better to impose your will and insist that your way be done than to let the child make a decision for himself with the pros and cons given him?"*
>
> *"We keep forcing them all the time; it's the same proposition."*
>
> *"If you want your child to attend Sunday school should you insist he go?"*
>
> *"Occasionally."*
>
> *"Should I insist that my child practice her music lesson?"*
>
> *"I think we tend to insist but not necessarily force, but we do insist. I am most certainly against this situation of letting children do as they please either at home, at school, at church, or wherever. I think it's up to the adults to sort of guide the child, lead them perhaps gently, but lead them."*

Parents are wary of the too-heavy hand; several decades of mental health principles, plus an increase in personality understanding, have helped them to see the child as a person in his own right, not as passive clay to be molded. But now, worry about the child's fears, guilt, and hostility is obvious, whereas up until this century these knotty emotions were overlooked. Susannah Wesley, writing at the request of her son John, founder of Methodism, about her methods of child training set forth her sure philosophy:

> In order to form the minds of children, the first thing to be done is to conquer their will, and bring them to an obedient temper. To inform the understanding is a work of time, and must with children proceed by slow degrees as they are able to bear it; but the subjecting of the will is a thing which must be done at once; and the sooner the better.[43]

Now, as then, the battle of wills is no stranger to our homes; but parents are anything but confident about their own behavior when struggle arises. They report they are often torn between "giving in" and dominating the child. Their uncertainty is nicely illustrated in the group's reaction to one mother who made her daughter "hew the line":

> *"I think some of us let them wiggle us around their fingers. I don't think we lay down the law. Isn't it possible to say, 'You cannot do that unless you do your homework first?' I do it all the time. I made her drop out of choir and a number of things."*
>
> *"Gee, you are really a meanie, aren't you?"* (supporting murmurs for this statement from the group).
>
> *"I'm horrible. She can't stand me."*

Parents avidly explore the source of their own difficulty with discipline (which ranked as the number four problem on the questionnaire). One facet of parental motivation appeared with surprising regularity: the fear of alienating their children. This has profound effects on "family government," a question far more troublesome to modern families than to those of Reformation times (as we noted in the previous chapter). In the suburban interviews especially, one gets the impression that parents are often "cowed" by their offspring and earnestly seek their good will and approval.

> *I think I'm as much at fault about this as anyone else, but we are all too easily intimidated by our children. If a small thing comes up at home you know in your heart that a child should be punished, and still you give in—to keep peace and quiet.*

These parents want to be liked by their children; cringing obedience is no adequate substitute for warm companionship, they aver.

> *My parents would just have to speak softly with a stern look (and the ever-present threat of the switch) and we obeyed. We were very frightened and disciplined. With the children now, we yell and they don't listen to us, and our voices get louder, and* still *they like us. There is really a genuine affection and they talk to me about things I wouldn't have discussed with my parents.*

Once again David Riesman's perceptive analysis in *The Lonely Crowd* comes to mind:

> The inner-directed parent is not particularly worried by his child's resentment or hostility. Nor is he as apt to be aware of it. He and the child are both protected by the gap that separates them. The other-directed parent, however, has to win not only his child's good behavior but also his child's good will. Therefore, he is tempted to use his superior didactic skill to "reason" with the child. And when the child learns—this is a part of his sensitive radar equipment—how to argue too, the parent is torn between giving in and falling uneasily back on the sterner methods of his inner-directed parents.[44]

Protestants may well wonder whether these are the only alternatives open to them.[45] Without being aware of Riesman's analysis, parents demonstrate it repeatedly:

> *We don't set down certain rules and stick to them because they're pretty smart. They wouldn't be normal if they weren't. They can work themselves around you and break you down to a certain extent where they'll say, well, you're a square if you don't do this and this.*

Dale B. Harris, one of our consultants and until recently Director of the Institute of Child Welfare of the University of Minnesota, is convinced on the basis of empirical study made there that parents are hurting their children if they are not definite about their own standards and ideals. Following up on the adult lives of nursery school children of the late 1920's, he finds evidence of effective parental standards. The report is so crucial to the parents' dilemma here described that we quote at length:

> Using several criteria, we have selected a sample of children who came from homes where parents were in general clear about their standards, established limits, made some demands, and otherwise demonstrated how children "ought to be," while at the same time extending approval and love. Another sample was identified, matched in sex and socio-economic status, whose families were notably casual with respect to the routine of child-training, sometimes quite indulgent, not too concerned with guiding the child's experience or education, and casual about the child's interactions with his peers. These families likewise extended affection and warmth. . . .
>
> Children from the more structured family experience, contrasted with those from less structured families, as young adults look back more favorably on their education, and much more favorably on their childhood relations with their parents. They are now more satisfied with their jobs and with their family life. They are, however, less satisfied with themselves as persons; they feel they don't measure up. . . .
>
> Young adults from the more structured backgrounds much more often express attitudes of confidence in the future, belief in work as the way to success, confidence in the good will and essential fairness of others. Young adults from the less structured family experience are much more likely to interpret success in terms of luck or special influence, and to express pessimism about the future, both personally and in national affairs, and distrust of other persons. On the California Psychological Inventory the young people from structured families tend to make scores showing more intellectual efficiency and orientation toward achievement, more interest in and responsiveness to the needs, motives, feelings, and experiences of others, and more concern with how others react to them. . . .

As a behavioral scientist and as a parent, Dr. Harris goes on to give his recommendations:

> . . . I would plead for parents more frequently to demonstrate their own values, the way they feel about personal and social issues. I would urge parents loving their children and attempting to under-

> stand their point of view, to lay ground rules for their youngsters which will preserve the forms of behavior and ideals of conduct that parents believe important. I would urge that parents do this even though holding to standards is difficult and at times quite unpopular with their children. If a parent occasionally re-examines and modifies decisions where later experience suggests that the position was ill-advised, I doubt that serious harm is done to a child by parental firmness. . . .
>
> Let me be perfectly clear on this. I am not rejecting the principle that children learn decision-making by making their own decisions. . . . I am saying that *these parents must explore their own beliefs and make their own commitments clear* instead of hiding behind the argument that on such matters it is better to let the youngster make up his own mind "when he is old enough." Such a parent has already set a model of decision-making by default.[46]

It is precisely at the point of "exploring their own beliefs and making their own commitments clear" that our Protestant parents are having difficulty, we discovered. Consequently, our parents are anxious about their own role as guides. The mother "knows" she must be neither over-permissive nor dominant and "bossy." Fathers report too they find it very difficult to walk the tightrope between "authoritarianism" and "indulgence." When they do have clear beliefs, parents often express contradictory goals for their children: they want high achievement and yet freedom from anxiety; individuality but also acceptance by everyone. Emerging in the interviews, however, are indications that in spite of their confusion about their proper role, parents realize that they cannot be simply a "pal" or "buddy" or "big brother" to their children without defaulting the responsibility of a Christian parent and a Christian view of family government. Although their behavior belies this at many points (even in their own report), the majority maintain that a distinction between parent and child is necessary; but wise love, they are quick to add, can still prevail in such a distinction.

Many things seem to undermine parental judgment these days; and parents in the research groups are able to inventory these: there are no clear-cut rules for all situations in a fluid world and a mobile population. Parents are convinced the child's mental health is important and must be safeguarded but they aren't sure how. The influence of the child's peer group, it is recognized, does modify their own decision making and discipline. The very groups in school, community, and church which parents see important for the training of their children in social living are at the same time a source of trouble. The peer group or "youth culture" becomes the measure of all things, especially at adolescence, and the parents and children have few defenses which the group cannot batter down. Says one distraught mother:

> *That's one of these problems you face not only with cars but with clothing, spending money, with going here and there—even in grade school. Our youngest daughter will come home and say that she just can't wear certain shoes because they're not wearing those shoes today. There are certain days my daughters can't wear green or yellow to school.*

Bewildered as parents are, it is little wonder that the church is looked to by a clear majority for help through its youth program. Indeed, the church youth group and Sunday church school is seen often as a means of indirect parental control and an enforcer of the family's standards. Says one parent with a view of the church as a vehicle for conveying the middle-class conception of the moral life: *"I think the church is just a board to keep them on a certain path that all of us want our children to follow."*

Yet, as it has been pointed out, we train our children to be other-directed, consumption-oriented and to be responsive to group direction; they are taught to compete through their personalities rather than through their skills. Responsible lay and ordained leaders aware of this trend are discovering that proclaiming the gospel to an other-directed generation is a difficult business. Paul's words in Romans 12:2, "Do not be conformed to this world but be transformed by the renewal of your mind, that you may prove what is the will of God . . ." seem to fall on deaf ears.

In addition to the discipline and guidance of children, parents in large numbers reported *dissatisfaction with the children's reaction to household routines*. The use of the television (about which most parents complain),[47] eating and sleeping habits, care of property, execution of chores were among the topics discussed heatedly in the groups.

Television has, without doubt, radically changed the household routines of modern Protestant homes. For one thing, it is viewed by the youngsters for an average of 24 hours per week in the families of our sample, 93 per cent of whom own one or more sets. Social analysts and educators in a plethora of articles have claimed both constructive and destructive effects for the "magic box." It has been said that television encourages withdrawal from community groups, intensifies family contact, expands one's intellectual world, and provides new conversation patterns. It is credited with promoting vicarious living through artificially induced emotion, sloganized thinking and conformity, reduction of participant activities, and a shortened time sense! Our depth-discussions brought forth these opinions and more. In general, rural parents are most favorably disposed to television; suburbanites claim to like it least for what it does to complicate home life. Only a seven per cent minority had no truck with this new mechanism—and they had a fight on their hands:

> *We are peculiar people because we will not have a television set and feel we can live and manage without it. Our son thinks we are odd and he lectured me for fifteen minutes: "You and daddy just like to be uncommon." But you have to stick by your own guns.*

In the modern day, surely, this is the epitome of inner-directedness! Most parents put up with television but are ambivalent about it. It is not an unmixed blessing, say these Protestant fathers and mothers. They credit television with being an excellent "mechanical sitter" for children, a relaxer for parents, and, occasionally, a first-rate educator. But they also decry the quarrels caused by program conflicts, undesirable programing (majoring in themes of violence), and interference with family meals. Inroads are made upon family traditions and upon previously prized creative activities, as the following excerpt illustrates:

> *With this business of television, instead of saying they're glad we're going to have a story tonight (we used to read out of the church's Bible storybook and have fun talking about it and maybe making pictures and doing things like that), now John wants to watch Zorro; he seems more important than Jesus! We used to play games too until we got that horrible TV.*

Some strong-minded parents claim they still control the use of the set in their homes; what programs may be seen, and when, is clearly understood by their bairns.

The widely advertised claim of television in its early days that it kept the family at home, is not considered an asset by most parents; *what* family members do and *how* they relate to each other is more important than just being at the hearth, they say. In rare families, television is a prescription for interpersonal tension, as this discussion shows:

> *"Do you find that TV helps the family?"*
> *"We watch it every night. Rather than sit around the table, we watch TV."*
> *"We would never do that!"*
> *"Does it help?"*
> *"Well—it keeps us from arguing."*

The last generation could not have predicted the impact that television would make upon the family.

Parents are disturbed, too, about *tension between brothers and sisters* in the small family group (this was ranked seventh among twenty-five problems bothering parents during the year of the study). Discussion of sibling rivalry appeared often in city and rural interviews; suburban parents were strangely silent on the subject. The highly organized life outside the home may reduce the friction within the home, as may more spacious living quarters. In any event, crowded housing conditions in the city were seen to contribute to dissension among offspring. One city father sizes up his own family situation by saying:

> *When the children were sharing one bedroom the tensions were tremendous. They were fighting with each other constantly. Now we are in five rooms and they have some privacy. It sure has helped tensions in the house.*

Obviously there are many levels of rivalry, some with deep psychological roots and others which are encouraged by the situation itself.

The interviews gave evidence of some *inadequate understanding of child development* which often served to complicate the relationship of parent and (usually) the young child. Other fathers and mothers, further along in the family life cycle, were often quick to give advice and correct false notions as they saw them. Confessed one mother:

> *"Our little girl is the sort who wants to talk and tell you everything that happened and wants you to understand her or not criticize her too severely. Well, she came home from school one day and said a little boy kissed her in nursery school and that the teacher saw it and didn't mind. I said it was terrible. She said it really wasn't so bad and if I was going to act that way she wouldn't tell me any more."*
>
> *"And she's right,"* replied another mother. *"This is a stage they all go through. But for heaven's sake encourage her openness as long as you can; they clam up soon enough."*

In this way parents corrected and educated one another. One parent said she thought the most comforting thought in the Bible for parents of teen-agers was from Ecclesiastes: "This too shall pass away."

These active church folk focused their discussion upon the parental role and there was a reluctance to move away from this orientation into the *relationship of husband and wife* in the family. Only as our interviewers probed this area were responses forthcoming; even then, they were generally guarded (in spite of the fact that the participant's spouse was not present). In many groups a discussion of mate relations held too much threat for the group to discuss openly. On the one hand, parents denied problems in this area. (Though "husband-wife relations" were placed sixth among eight topics they wanted to see developed in church family life education, pastors gave this higher priority, lifting it to the number three position. Suburban pastors, who carry a heavier than average load of marriage counseling, call for this to be emphasized even more.) On the other hand, there was ample indirect evidence that the relationship between husband and wife was a source of considerable concern for these parents. When it was approached in the groups, the discussion frequently was couched in humor and tension-reducing laughter. An interviewer asks:

> *"Are there problems in family life in the area of husband-and-wife relationships which interfere with happiness?"*
>
> *"How many hours do we have?"* (laughter)
>
> *"Just as long as you like."*
>
> *"It's going to be a long night then! My husband doesn't realize that—well, he joined the church once and thought that was it. He didn't see the need to rejoin when we changed denominations. This has been a real sore spot that he hasn't come along with me."*

In our highly mobile society and with the general absence of kinfolk, the tie between husband and wife becomes pre-eminently important, providing as it does the one enduring relationship in the culture. It is very much on the minds of these people; they want to keep it strong. They tend to value Christian marriage as the relationship between friends; it is often held in greater esteem than Christian parenthood. One of the three most poignant dilemmas of suburban family life voiced by our parents can be phrased in the following words:

> *After all, parents are people too. We should have a life of our own as well as being fathers and mothers. But how can we without neglecting the children?*

A statistical "factor analysis" of selected portions of our data from the parents' questionnaires completed by the Russell Sage Foundation turned up a surprising finding. Much psychoanalytically oriented theory often argues that child-rearing problems and husband-and-wife relationships are inseparable in the family, one affecting the other. This evidence seems to indicate that problems related to the parent-child relation are *not necessarily* related to the interpersonal relations between the spouses.[48] This finding would be in line with what we contended before

—that parenthood itself is a crisis. We cannot assume that a parent's trouble in discipline is a result of tension between the distraught mother and her equally distraught husband.

Since the husband-wife relationship in the modern day tends to be marked by an acute segregation of interests—the man preoccupied with the economic sphere and the wife with parental and community affairs—one is not surprised to find that "lack of time with spouse" was one of the chief complaints aired in interviews. Younger couples are aware of the dangers of living in separate worlds, especially if the husband is in highly technical work. They also reveal, in their remarks, that they are cognizant of the future "empty nest" period of their life when they will be alone with their husbands in the home.[49] Projecting themselves into that future, many of these couples in their early thirties sense that it takes deliberate planning to be together at all. One wife complains:

> *My husband goes to work before we get up and we don't have breakfast together. Very often he is not home for dinner, so maybe only once or twice we eat together. It's not enough. To me, eating together and talking things over is a big thing. If we can't do it now, what about later?*

As would be expected in a research project sponsored by the church, *religious problems* affecting the husband-wife relationship are introduced readily. Many wives complained of the religious lukewarmness of their husbands; it was seldom the other way around. It was frequently adjustment by resignation which we observed, illustrated by such remarks as the following:

> *I suppose there are always differences of opinion and attitudes about religion between husband and wife. But we solved it by not stressing it too much. After you have children there are other problems to replace that, and it's good, I guess.*

An interesting and unexpected finding of the special study of our data (see Note 48) was that the college-educated woman in our sample senses *more* rather than less religious dissension in her family as she grows older. As children begin to leave the home, husband and wife re-examine their own beliefs and church relationship. No longer are these parents involved in the church *through* their children. With this motivation for going to church reduced, their real ideological differences often come to the fore for the first time.

Putting the emphasis they do on child rearing, these parents are distressed by any husband-wife relationships which serve to complicate this arduous chore. There appeared to be general agreement in all groups where the topic was introduced, that parents should not quarrel in front of their children; this teaching of family experts at least has found solid reception. But when the differences between spouses involve child-rearing practices, tension can hardly be avoided, they admit:

> *Well, I think half of the arguments between my husband and me come to whether we are raising our children right. We certainly don't agree on methods too often. For example, my husband said he didn't have to eat anything he didn't like in his family and the kids aren't going to have to. So there's no co-operation. You just can't buck it. You just wear out.*

It is no surprise, then, that the problem checked as the fourth most frequently confronted related to "how children are disciplined."

We have spoken many times of the shifting roles of family members. *Disagreement in their role expectations* of each other bothered many parents in the research study. The problem takes a number of forms; a feeling that one is failing the expectations of the spouse is but one.

> *When I let my house and yard go, I get more and more nervous and upset. Then my husband comes home, and the house is a mess, and he might bring someone with him. He doesn't ever say anything, but I know what he must be thinking. If you don't do things that the neighborhood expects of you, that makes you tense. It's kind of a two-way thing. You have to have a clean house and a happy child, too.*

Feelings of uncertainty about one's role and dissatisfactions with the way one's mate is fulfilling his or her function in the family are not uncommon, especially in the early years of marriage and parenthood.

That the sexual relationship in marriage came up at all in a mixed-gender church group, meeting together for the first time, was remarkable. And, to be sure, the references to it were more in the form of abrupt excursions into dangerous territory than they were sustained exploration of a loaded subject. In the parents' questionnaire one of every twelve parents (mostly men) indicated they felt that sex relationships with the spouse needed improvement. When the subject was introduced into the group interview, parents did not present sexual problems *per se* but cited some frustrating circumstances (for example, the necessity of children's sleeping in the parents' bedroom temporarily because of in-law residents) which cause tensions to mount in both husband and wife with the deprivation of normal conjugal life.

Their concern about the sexual area of life was expressed openly, however, when the subject veered to the activities of their teen-age children. Over one-half of these parents (53 per cent) want the church to interpret sex to their children in a Christian context. This majority demonstrated in the interviews their awareness of the widespread ethical confusion abroad today. But moralistic condemnation, too long the church's stock-in-trade, is not sufficient, they warn. Nor is it adequate, they remind us, to utter vague references to "purity," "sin," and the like. They want their children to have facts from the standpoint of faith; they want to work with the church on this task. Church membership is not insulated from the tendency toward premarital sex relations and they know it. Writes one pastor of an upper middle-class Protestant church in suburbia:

> *The past eighteen months have brought the problem of teen-age shotgun marriages and illegitimacies home to me. During this time, at least five of our high-school young people have been caught in this trap. The other minister in town says the situation is the same in his church. Some of these young people are our leaders.*

Parents are not unaware of these sex problems. A large minority of parents, however, were not so sure the church should step *directly* into the responsibility of sex and marriage education. For some, this was still a tabu subject; one does not talk about it anywhere, even at home. Some think the parents ought to do the whole job, but admitted their inadequacy for it. Others wondered if the clergy (with their allegedly moralistic attitudes) could really help at all. Said one disillusioned man in an interview: *"You know what the pastor is going to say before you go to him—so why go?"* Fortunately, many happily married pastors have been made sensitive through counseling training to the human struggles and emotions which saturate sexual conflicts; we can expect them to be of increasingly effective help, if only in referral.

In the problems confronting husband and wife in their relationship, parents agreed that improving their communication with one another was one way to solution. A father remarks to the group:

> *I think that if a husband and wife can sit down and talk out their problems it is very good. Our talks haven't been too successful along some lines, but in some lines very good results have come. Communication is number one.*

And a mother replies:

> *I think too that there are different ways of communication and it isn't always verbal. My husband has a hard time expressing himself in words. Yet our basic communication is very good—I do it all!*

Laughter, we might add, followed. We observed some interesting differences in the problems selected by husbands and wives as most important. Whether one has attended college or not also seems to make a difference whether particular areas of family life are seen as troublesome. College-educated men differed significantly[50] from college-educated women on three items. Men were much more likely to cite "too little time spent together as a family" as a major problem than were the wives. Women were considerably more concerned than men about "who does what among family responsibilities"; and more women, again, saw a problem in the present "religious life and participation of the family."

In comparing noncollege husbands and wives, only with reference to one problem was there a difference between them. Far more men than women were concerned about the level of their "children's achievement." Many of these fathers wanted their children to go beyond what they were able to accomplish in their lives.

When we look at the husbands alone and compare those with college education to those without, we find no significant difference in what they see constituting a problem in their homes. But among the college and noncollege educated wives, we find some striking contrasts. College-trained wives were much more concerned about the level of the children's achievement, how various members of the family carried responsibilities around the house, and the friendships of the family; considerable discontent was shown with these phases of family life by these women. Noncollege wives, though relatively satisfied in the aforementioned areas of family living, did sense more often (in contrast to their highly educated counterparts) the problem of a lack of closeness existing between husband and wife. The college-educated woman, according to our evidence, does not feel quite so isolated from her husband's life, and she tends to reflect greater confidence about her place in his affections.

We discovered that the participants in the study could be classified as "high" or "low" problem families, depending upon the number of problems applying to themselves which they checked on the questionnaire. "High problem families" are characterized by more than one of the following tensions, in addition to the more usual concerns of parents previously discussed: (1) problems involving the family's present housing and furniture; (2) drinking by family members; (3) general tenseness and low morale in the family; (4) dissatisfaction with the amount of the family's income; (5) the wife's working outside the home; and (6) inadequate sexual relations. Interestingly, wives were more likely than husbands to check (1) and (2); men of the high-problem families tended to mention (5) and (6). On items three and four, no discernible differences appeared between the men and the women; they were checked by both equally. These are the families, pastors should note, who will likely seek their help in family problems at one time or another.

Problems Involving Relatives and the Extended Family

Problems concerning relatives were also discussed freely in the parents' groups even though a minority (13 per cent) of the sample had relatives living with them currently. The great majority of relatives in residence were mothers. Many problems related to close contact with relatives were mentioned. They included conflict in child-rearing philosophies, crowded housing, a conflict of roles when the relative lives within the home, and the dominance and dependency relationships of these relatives with their grown children. Says one wife of her husband's mother:

> *It would make me sort of mad when she corrected the children. We disagreed on that a lot, but she claimed she knew more than me about child raising. But she would get mad when I'd ask her to do any little thing around the house. She was the queen who just gave the orders.*

Even when relatives do not live in the family home, tensions can be generated, our parents reported. A comparison of the children's achievement, for example, can bring hard feelings quickly to the surface.

The over-all impression given by these parents is that life with the "extended family" produces more problems than satisfactions. But there *are* satisfactions as well as complaints. Distance from relatives creates a problem for some because they feel lonely or feel their children are being cheated by not knowing their grandparents and other relatives. Advice and practical help in times of crises, baby sitting, supplemental household help, occasional visits which keep family memories alive for all concerned—all these relationships are cherished.

The Relationship of the Family to the Community

In discussing "the pressure of time," we noted that the family's outreach to the community is a source of considerable tension among our active Protestant parents. But there are other complicating factors too. For one thing, parents are frequently disturbed by the standards and values of the neighborhood and community which clash with their own.

Occasionally the children's friends are wealthier than the family concerned and the children make life miserable for their parents by demanding things which they cannot afford. Differing policies of discipline and responsibility among neighbors can also complicate a parent's life.

> *Our children feel they have more responsibilities than the neighbors' children—they feel put upon. I told them to expect me to be the meanest father in the neighborhood; but they were going to have to do certain things whether or not any other child had to do them.*

In our inner-city, low-income Protestant families, the contrast in standards takes more striking form. Fears of children being hurt, molested, or exploited by neighborhood associates are commonly expressed. It is not community pressure for social precociousness we see in suburbia but the dread of physical harm, addiction, and rape which haunts these parents. *"Is there anything so safe about your child,"* asks one mother, *"that he can't be given a 'reefer'?"* Another confesses:

> *When my son is not within range after dark I go through torture. I was at a meeting where they showed the bodies of the Peterson and the Schuster boys and the contaminated clues. We live in a city where all these crimes go unsolved. So we're always careful with guests, picking them up and hovering over them like a protecting mother hen. But when these real people—people you know by name—are raped and murdered, it becomes part of your individual life.*

Rural people see another kind of problem: they complain about the lack of intellectual challenge in their communities for youth. How can they hope to hold them, they wonder. Often, in farming community interviews, the schools and churches were made to bear the blame for this condition. The claim that officials sent them the "left-overs" in intellectual leadership was voiced by discontented fathers and mothers.

But neighborhood and community are not merely the source of problems; they are a help in time of trouble too—at least for some groups. Only in residential suburbs did we sense any widespread acceptance of neighbors as confidants. Mutual service in the form of baby sitting, household projects, visiting, and special affairs seem to thrive there. More than one social scientist studying the suburb has raised an eyebrow about this intensive "neighboring." As a psychotherapist, Erich Fromm looks askance at married life in Park Forest, the suburb described in Whyte's *The Organization Man:*

> Another aspect of social "adjustment" is the complete lack of privacy, and the indiscriminate talking about one's "problems." . . . "It's wonderful," says one young wife. "You find your-

self discussing all your problems with your neighbors—things that back in South Dakota we would have kept to ourselves." As time goes on this capacity for self-revelation grows; and on the most intimate details of family life, court people become amazingly frank with each other. "No one," they point out, "ever need face a problem alone." We may add that it would be more correct to say that never *do* they face a problem.[51]

In contrast to this "open" pattern, in which children have the complete run of all the houses (much to the disgust of some suburban parents), rural parents were as critical as they were complimentary about neighbors. Reticence to share one's life with them was pronounced among our farm and small-town folk. Nor were neighbors seen as a source of much help to city dwellers either. For them, however, friendships in the church made up for this lack.

Dr. Reuben Hill, of the University of Minnesota, suggests an intriguing explanation for this striking contrast of suburban with rural and urban neighboring practices. In an "open community" (one in which all comers are welcome), "closed families" prevail, with fences, emotional distance, and the need for formal introductions making people relatively inaccessible to one another. In this way the possibility of excluding people one doesn't like is preserved. However, in a "closed community" (where some membership standards tend to exclude all but a certain class of people), an "open family" arrangement is the order of the day. Easy access to each other's homes, peer group activity of a casual and informal nature, and even the disciplining of each other's children is encouraged in the residential suburb. Personal intimacy is purchased at a cost of community exclusiveness.

Problems Relating to the Economic Life of the Family

As might be expected, family problems also center around the economic and occupational life which is invested with massive amounts of family energy. Financial problems, reported chiefly by city and farm groups, claimed our attention earlier. More readily discussable in our groups was the "husband's job and its demands," listed by our 1000 parents as the sixth most pressing problem in the average home. This phrase came to mean many things in the interview discussions, but it most often points up the effect of the father's absence upon the family. Sometimes the absence is created by travel; more often it is reported to be a matter of working at nights, or with irregular hours, or at two jobs. One parent complains:

> *Sometimes for three or four days the children don't see their father. It's impossible to set up any regular time together because some days he works sixteen hours; we can't do anything by habit. He can't possibly get home before a quarter to seven, which is too late for three- and four-year-old children to wait for dinner.*

The limits of this study did not permit us to obtain directly the children's interpretations of the problems the parents report. Some of the reactions to father's being away from home so much of the time can be seen, however, in the parents' remarks:

> *"My husband works at night, and my daughter is thirteen; and she said the other day that she hadn't seen her daddy since Monday. She misses the companionship of her father."*
>
> *"My son came home from college this summer, and it was a shock to hear him say that he really didn't know me and that I always seemed so wrapped up in my work that I didn't know he was around. This shook me and I began to wonder if a man should ever allow his job to take him away from getting to know his family."*

We learned that children were affected by the breadwinner's work and we observed, too, the increased burdens on many mothers due to the father's heavy work schedule. Uncertainty and perplexity is often the reaction of the mothers with whom the whole child-rearing process is left. One wife of a traveling man says,

> *You've got to learn to live on your own quite a bit, with your husband's job taking him away. But you still wonder if you have done the right thing with the children. That's a big problem.*

When the focus of the interview was spotlighted on the wife who works for wages, a lively interest was always apparent—especially in the city groups. (The problem seldom came to the fore in rural and suburban environs where there seemed to be less opportunity or need for the outside employment of wives.)[52] The reasons why most of these women go out to work have been discussed earlier; and the wives from our sample share those motivations. A double standard was raised for men and for women in a number of interviews. The husband could be forgiven for being an inadequate husband or father because of the pressure of his work. "There is not much he can do about it," was often the reaction to such a situation. But the woman is to be *both* an effective wife and mother and a person who can contribute through her skills to society. And many two-job mothers say, in the face of this pull, that they always live with a sense of compromise.

In religiously conservative churches, mothers participating in the interview were frequently forced to defend their "right to work" against the male participants. In spite of the fact that research in child growth and development has failed to lend support to the belief that mothers must constantly be available to their children twenty-four hours a day, some alarmed men predicted dire effects on the children of the mothers who work even part time. On the other hand, suburban husbands (often married to college-educated women) seem more alert to the variety of needs in their wives:

> *I'm speaking for the men now. I come home from work and my wife is ready to go; she is tired from being with the kids and she wants to get out of the home and do something. I think I found one outlet—it's not a solution by any means, but it is an alleviation of the problem. My wife works two or three evenings a week. It's an income-producing occupation (it pays for our vacations) and yet it is relaxing for her, gives her a needed change.*

No mother who works outside the home minimized in the group the struggle of caring for the home and family after a long day's work. Exhaustion was no stranger to these women. But the heaviest burden was carried by the wife whose labors outside the home did not receive the wholehearted support of her husband. When wife and husband did not share the same attitude toward her work, troubles of a more serious kind were almost always in evidence.[53]

One other job-related concern appeared frequently in the discussion of parents; the necessity of *moving* because of job transfer; or job opportunity. Surprisingly few of our interviewed parents reported any major problems connected with mobility. This is due, in part, to the fact that a lower over-all proportion of the people of this sample moved during the year, compared with the general population.[54] Mobility, especially among the young executives, seems to be taken as a matter of course. Some recent arrivals to the community expressed loneliness for familiar friends and relatives and for regional folkways, but most respondents took these things in their stride. Evidence from other studies points up the fact that the effects of mobility upon the home depend upon a number of factors.

For one thing, it is important to note who makes the move necessary. The psychological effect will differ for the coerced service man and for the self-motivated professional man to whom a move means advancement. The degree of change is also important; moves within short distances and to relatively familiar territory may leave only slight dislocation. The presence of friends and relatives in a new area often cushions the shocks involved, say our parents. How often one moves is important to the family's balance too, we discovered. Only a few of the parents in this study revealed a transiency pattern which seriously disturbed family equilibrium. And, fortunately for them, most of their communities seemed fairly cordial to the newcomers. It was rarely that an interviewed parent felt strong barriers to the presence of his family in the community. For these the church (sponsoring the interview) often proved to be a community of acceptance, they reported. Moving one's residence, then, by itself, is not generally disruptive to the family's health; in fact, our parents note, it can be the occasion of a greater teamwork than ever experienced before. Of the church's place in welcoming new families, more will be said in Chapter 6.

Parents View the Wider Social Scene

Countless hours of analysis, dissection of interview protocols, and subsequent reflection upon the many revelations of these middle-class Protestant parents left us with an impression that is sobering for the church: family life is discussed as if it were isolated from the broad currents of society and world events. It is disconcerting for official Protestantism with its world-wide mission and awareness of the complexity of our social life to notice that the typical parent insulates his private family life from the political and economic trends which affect his life so deeply. To be sure, some issues intrude so persistently that they cannot be ignored. One cannot close his eyes to the movement of a minority group into a previously all-white suburb. In a few interviews this was *the* searing problem besetting the parents. Interracial churches, set in the heart of a convulsing city, usually dealt with pressing social issues and the church's mission to them quite directly; but these were a small minority. Few of the church groups were without their socially alert parents, anxious about the nuclear age and atomic radiation, concerned over international tensions and war. One tells of his aspirations for a better world for his children:

> *I really think this better world (not just a happier one necessarily) can't be built simply through our leisure activities or pleasures. It takes a stronger kind of growth, a movement beyond our own community into international concern and world missions. But it seems so awfully complicated that I can't resolve in my mind in a few words. I don't know where to start, I guess.*

Hand in hand with this kind of concern there appears to be a sense of resignation and helplessness about anything which they might do. Theodore Gill caught the mood of these parents in observing:

> It is not just the fact that home-made holocausts could now arrest history that frightens us. Far more bemusing is the impression that sweeping, world-sized political, economic, sociological, and psychological trends and currents have more to do with keeping catastrophe on leash than do all our private intentions. The real terror today for sensitive people ought not to be the bomb or the missile but the terrible attendant debilitation of life and spirit in a generation which not only doesn't know what to do but doesn't really think you *can* know what to do any more.[55]

The retreat to private concerns, so obvious in our fathers and mothers, may be born, then, not merely of childish egocentricity but also of a terror in whose presence they feel lost and helpless. If faith rather than despair is an answer, as they often aver, we must inquire now into the nature of the faith they hold.

NOTES

1. Indeed, we have seen that dogmas change in every tradition, *e.g.*, consider the meaning of sacrament as applied to marriage in Roman Catholic circles.
2. Nelson N. Foote, "The Appraisal of Family Research," *Marriage and Family Living,* Feb., 1957, p. 10.
3. See Appendix VIII for sample questionnaire. This particular form had been reduced from a lengthy, open-ended essay type, pretested on 100 parents in the Philadelphia area. As a result of this process, it was possible to simplify the form to a check-list type of operation, retaining but four of the original open-ended "postcoded" questions.
4. This constitutes 85 per cent of those questionnaires submitted. Most of those disqualified for analysis were filled out by parents attending churches not using the "Christian Faith and Life Curriculum," official course of study for the United Presbyterian Church in the U.S.A. Since part of the research mandate called for information from the parents on their use of these materials, those questionnaires not furnishing this crucial information were set aside. A few of the questionnaires (two per cent) lacked personal or socio-economic information necessary to cross-tabulate many of the findings; these also were omitted from analysis.
5. This detailed interview guide was prepared for each interviewer by the Office of Family Education Research of the United Presbyterian Board of Christian Education. Three general questions, spaced about forty minutes apart in the two-hour period, provided the skeleton of the guide:

1. What sorts of problems are parents concerned about these days? What kinds of tensions do you observe in family living in this community?
2. What do you think of when you think of "good family life?" What satisfactions are you working for and finding in your family?
3. What types of solutions help families to overcome their difficulties? Where do families find help achieving what they want? If discussion faltered, a number of probes were used by the interviewer, for example: "Is there anything else you'd like to say about this . . . How do others of you see this . . . Could you give us an example of that . . . Is this what you are saying: (reflecting the interviewer's understanding of a confused statement) . . . What are the effects of this upon the family . . . or, How does this come about?" If the discussion did not touch upon certain key areas related to the subject under consideration, the interviewer introduced them for the reaction of the group. For example, under question number one, any of the following areas might have been probed: What about problems related to how parents get along with children . . . how children in the family get along with one another . . . the religious life of the family . . . how husbands and wives get along . . . relatives . . . community and neighborhood influences? This kind of "pinpointing" pattern was repeated with each question if parents did not volunteer information regarding key subjects. Occasionally, a projective question was introduced and found to be productive, *e.g.*, "What memories do you want your children to have about your family life when they grow up?"

6. See Appendix III for the list of interviewers. Twenty-five possessed earned doctors' degrees (Ph.D., M.D., Th.D., or Ed.D.); and ten were candidates for the doctorate. Twenty-three of the interviewers held Master's degrees, and thirty-nine of them were ordained and claimed the B.D. degree (often in addition to other degrees). About one-third of this group were personally coached in the procedure outlined by the authors; the others took their directions from the interview guide.
7. This bias was occasioned chiefly by the place of residence of the interviewers upon whom we had to depend. Furthermore, and sad to relate, it was found to be much easier to gain the co-operation of pastors in suburban and urban churches than in rural charges.
8. This sampling is in line with the distribution of the United Presbyterian Church *population* which finds about 62 per cent of the membership located in metropolitan areas, and 77 per cent of the readers of *Presbyterian Life* (the official denominational magazine) so located. In contrast, less than one-half of the membership of Methodist churches lives in metropolitan areas. Episcopalians are chiefly metropolites, with almost three out of four adherents residing in the cities and environs.

   Regionally, the group of churches as finally selected is heavily Western and somewhat slights the South. These proportions reflect accurately the trend in the growth of the denomination making the study (and is in line with the direction of the national migration). However, the sample belies the actual current situation in that the far Western states do actually fall below the national average in church membership in all denominations. The actual distribution of host churches is as follows: Northeast region, 17 churches; Midwest, 17 churches; South, 6 churches; and West, 23 churches.

9. A standard procedure was devised by which pastors were instructed to invite a parent whose name fell at a certain interval on a numbered, alphabetized church membership list made up of families who had at least one child under eighteen living at home. (Forty-seven per cent of the church membership generally would so qualify.) Fathers and mothers were to be selected alternately and only one adult respondent was to have been invited (by standard invitation) from any given family. The size of the interval was determined by the membership of the church.

10. No relationship is reported among these various factors unless the percentage of difference between groups is statistically established at the "5 per cent level of confidence," at least. This means that when group differences are cited, it is only when they are of a magnitude that will occur less than 5 per cent of the time (and often less than 2 or 3 per cent of the time) by chance.

    In a special study, Dr. Orville Brim, Jr., of the Russell Sage Foundation, and Dr. Edgar F. Borgatta, of Cornell University, in co-operation with the authors, analyzed 500 questionnaires chosen at random from our 1000 with reference to the number and type of problems that are related to the socio-economic characteristics of the family. Characteristics of "high" or "low" problem families are also depicted in this study. Some of the data are used in the analysis to follow, and the complete co-operative study is now in press.

11. The categories for analysis were "empirically" derived, *i.e.*, constructed after actual inspection of thirty transcriptions of the interviews. Seven main categories for the content of the interviews were devised: (1) relationships within the family; (2) relationships of family or family members to church and/or Christian faith; (3) relationship of the family to the community; (4) relationship of the family to neighbors or neighborhood; (5) relation of family to the occupational world and to the economic structure; (6) relationships of the nuclear family to the extended family; (7) the relationships of the family to mass media, nation and world. One hundred forty-one subcategories were arranged under the major heads to classify the great variety of responses recorded. A transcription protocol frequently fell into one or more content categories; they were not all mutually exclusive. The degree of consensus, involvement, confusion, and avoidance at various points of the discussion, noted for us by the interviewers, added a deeper thrust to the analysis. Differentiations in the content among rural, urban, and city groups were not extensive, but what differences were revealed will be reported. Thirty-five interviews, drawn from the sample of 63, were analyzed in closer detail. Because one person alone might tend to classify the responses differently from another, a check was made by the authors with two other judges of a sample of the material; it was noted that the "interjudge reliability" approximated 85 per cent agree-

ment when the transcription material was classified according to the seven major category heads.

12. By all indications we can expect the remarried group in the church to increase in the years to come; at the present time one of every eight marriages consummated in the U.S.A. is a remarriage following divorce or the death of a spouse.
13. Thirty per cent were under 34 years of age; 45 per cent were between 35 and 44 years of age; and 25 per cent of the parents in the study were over 45 years of age.
14. The approximate figure is given because the questionnaire called for a check in an appropriate box that indicated family size; the last option provided was "*four or more* children" which allows us only a minimum estimate of median family size. A closer investigation of 100 suburban families in our group indicates a total of 290 children among them.
15. The first five months of 1960 showed a drop of almost two per cent in the national birthrate according to the National Office of Vital Statistics. It is neither clear whether this decline will continue nor certain what its causes might be since the marriage rate continues to be high.
16. Evelyn M. Duvall, *Family Development*.
17. This readership survey made in 1952 revealed 83 per cent to be high school graduates, 55 per cent attending college, and 33 per cent graduating from institutions of higher learning.
18. A readership survey of this group of parents, completed in 1952, found 69 per cent of them claiming they read at least one book a month.
19. A survey made in 1945 and 1946 for the Federal Council of Churches by the Office of Public Opinion Research at Princeton (and subsequent studies since) pointed out that educational differences between Protestantism's largest denominations and Catholicism show that the Roman Catholic population tends to have less formal education than do the members of these Protestant bodies. (Other subsequent studies have confirmed this.) It is also clear from present trends that Roman Catholics will be producing a higher proportion of college graduates in the coming years as the immigrant origins of much of that population recedes into the background. It is interesting to note, however, the differences among the Protestant denominations represented in the study. Lutherans, with 56.3 per cent nonhigh school graduates approximated the level of the Roman Catholics with 57 per cent. Two out of every three Baptists (taken as one group) were found to possess less than a high school education. Episcopalians with only 35.3 per cent of nonhigh school graduates, and Presbyterians with 37.1 per cent resembled the Jews' educational level (36.9 per cent) at the upper end of the educational scale.
20. The average income of families engaged in the study and in the denomination has a total cash income of between $1,500 and $2,000 higher annually than the national norm. (Our residential suburban families, taken alone, indicated an average income of almost $9,000 a year with about 12 per cent of the mothers employed outside the home full or part time.) Most of these people own their own homes, and 84 per cent have lawns to mow compared with 64.2 per cent of the general popula-

tion. Over 90 per cent of the denomination's families own a car compared with the U.S. census average American car ownership of 72 per cent, and one out of every four of these constituents have two cars.

21. In a study of 83 young suburban couples, William H. Whyte, Jr., claimed that they were handling their financial affairs "atrociously," owing about $1,000 per family and owning an average equity in savings of only $850. He contends that "they are most pleased, even insistent, that the schools should teach their children . . . thrift. But it is in much the same spirit that many of them send their children to Sunday school, in expiation." "Budgetism: Opiate of the Middle Class," *Fortune,* May, 1956.
22. Truman B. Douglass, "The Job the Protestants Shirk," *Harper's Magazine,* November, 1958, p. 46.
23. A particularly useful book of family case studies to consult for this purpose is *Family Worlds: A Psychosocial Approach to Family Life* by Robert D. Hess and Gerald Handel.
24. "My Mother," *Parent's Magazine,* March, 1841, as quoted in *The Mother's Role in Childhood Education: New England Concepts 1830–1860* by Anne L. Kuhn.
25. See Horace Bushnell, *Christian Nurture.*
26. See John R. Seeley, R. Alexander Sim, and E. W. Loosley, *Crestwood Heights.*
27. The reciprocal needs of young people and their parents must be seen together in viewing these internal pressures. This theme is well developed in *The Creative Years* by Reuel Howe.
28. One study of our constituency indicated eight of every ten adults belonging to clubs not connected with the church. These were chiefly community, fraternal, and professional organizations.
29. Howard Whitman, "Keeping Our Sanity—VII," *The* (Philadelphia) *Evening Bulletin,* April 8, 1957.
30. From a conference with Dr. Paul Pruyser of the Menninger Foundation, one of our research consultants.
31. *The Preacher's Task and the Stone of Stumbling,* p. 114.
32. Paul Tournier, *The Meaning of Persons,* p. 145.
33. David Riesman, Nathan Glazer, and Reuel Denney, *The Lonely Crowd.*
34. John Sirjamaki, *The American Family in the Twentieth Century.*
35. James H. S. Bossard, Eleanor S. Boll, and Winogene E. P. Sanger, "Some Neglected Areas in Family Life Study," *Annals of the American Academy of Political and Social Science,* November, 1950; and James H. S. Bossard, "Family Life: Conversation Is the Key," *Presbyterian Life,* January 25, 1958.
36. Evelyn M. Duvall discovered two types of responses to an open-ended question put to 433 mothers of varying socio-economic strata: "What are five things a good mother does?" The typical "traditional" mother (according to her classification) stated that a good mother keeps house, takes care of her child's physical needs, trains him to regularity, corrects, reprimands, punishes, and scolds him, and "makes him good." To the traditionalist, a good child is one who is neat and clean, obeys and respects adults, respects property, is religious, and works well. The mothers

with a "developmental" point of view, in contrast, see the good mother as one who helps her child to develop socially, provides stimulation to learn, guides with understanding, relates herself lovingly to the child, and who is a happy growing person herself. The "good child" is one who is healthy, happy, loving, eager to learn, and growing as a person. "Implications of Different Conceptions of Motherhood, Fatherhood, and Childhood, Arising Out of Various Studies," *Human Development Bulletin,* January, 1950, pp. 18–20.

37. Lee Rainwater, "The Family Relationships of the Working-Class Housewife," an unpublished paper, July, 1958.
38. It should not be assumed, however, that the ideal conceptions of parents necessarily affect their behavior. A sophisticated college-educated group will almost always describe family ideals in terms of developmental concepts. We do not know either whether the difference in behavior (allegedly stemming from the parents' ideals) makes a difference on the child's behavior. We have some evidence at present that more "acting out" or behavior problems come from traditionalist homes and more neurotic, "inner conflict" problems come from developmental families. It is a fair guess from our data that the great bulk of our homes hover somewhere between these two conceptions of good parenthood.
39. University of Pennsylvania Press, 1950.
40. When we asked parents to list those areas of family life in which the church's help was most appropriate, they listed parent-child relationships, the family's religious development, its participation at church, the way the family makes decisions, and determining the standards of the community.
41. E. E. LeMasters, "Parenthood as Crisis," *Marriage and Family Living,* November, 1957.
42. Daniel R. Miller and Guy E. Swanson, *The Changing American Parent,* pp. 171–172.
43. Quoted in the reference above, p. 11.
44. David Riesman, Nathan Glazer, and Reuel Denney, *The Lonely Crowd,* p. 72. New Haven, Conn.: Yale University Press, 1950.
45. Theologically speaking, Christians cannot be considered either inner-directed or other-directed since the Christian response is the interaction of God's freedom and ours. As Roger Shinn has said, "This image of man differs from David Riesman's image of the autonomous man, who maturely chooses his goals; for though it recognizes choice, it starts from Christ's words: "You did not choose me, but I chose you." (Quoted in *The Christian Century,* September 24, 1958, p. 1073.)
46. Dale B. Harris in a paper presented to the annual conference of the Child Study Association of America, 1958, and subsequently abstracted in the "Bulletin of the Office of Family Education Research" of the United Presbyterian Board of Christian Education, September, 1958. See also *Presbyterian Life,* May 17, 1958.
47. According to the parents' questionnaires, it constituted the most annoying problem, in the eyes of mothers.
48. *Relations Between Family Problems,* Orville G. Brim, Jr., Edgar F. Borgatta, and Roy W. Fairchild (in press).

49. James H. S. Bossard and Eleanor S. Boll, in a study of 440 married persons, unique in that it collected information about them from their brothers and sisters, discovered a critical period of potential unhappiness for married women in the late forties and early fifties. This crisis period seems to be related to the fact that (1) their children no longer retain their earlier dependence upon them; (2) their husbands are inadequate affectionately and sexually; and (3) the menopause may cause emotional and physical complications. For men, there seems to be a similar crisis in the fifties. Here, however, the frustrations and unhappiness tend to center around occupational rather than sexual matters, which often are surmised in novels. The men who have achieved some degree of occupational prominence and success are often ideologically isolated from their wives; and those who have failed frequently use the wife as a scapegoat for their lack of success. "Marital Unhappiness in the Life Cycle," *Marriage and Family Living,* February, 1955, pp. 10–14.
50. To the statistician the "t" scores on these three differences were 2.90, 2.00, and 2.00, respectively. All other differences noted are of about the same magnitude.
51. Erich Fromm, *The Sane Society,* p. 157. New York: Rinehart & Co., Inc., 1955.
52. Whereas in the total U.S. population more than 30 per cent of all married women are in the working force, in this segment of Protestant population, less than 20 per cent are employed full or part time outside the home. In the residential suburbs, we found only 12 per cent of the wives held full or part time jobs.
53. This complaint is included in the "high problem" families of our study.
54. We estimate that 13 per cent of our Presbyterian households move across county lines in any one year as over against about 20 per cent of the total U.S. population. Many inner-city and suburban church households outstrip the national average, however.
55. Seminary Sunday sermon on the CBS "Church of the Air," January 11, 1959.

- Interpretations of Faith
- Some Correlations
- As Parents View the Church
- As Parents View the Clergy
- The Church in Their House
- Religious Problems of Protestant Parents
- Men, Women and the Church
- And Togetherness
- The Yearning for Relationship

6

Protestant Parents and Their Faith

IT HAD BEEN OUR INTENTION to interview parents who represented a broad cross section of the churches' life, the active and the inactive, regular attenders and sporadic, new members and old. Elaborate formulae, described in the previous chapter, had been devised to insure as representative a sampling as possible within the limitations of the research design. In spite of these efforts, the groups in our 63 church interviews ended up with parents who were unusually active in the life of the parish, and who were more loyal to the church than average members. This could be discerned from their attendance record at stated worship services, in their work on behalf of the church, and in their considerable experience many of them had in teaching in church school. In addition, it will be recalled, the interviews tended to draw persons with higher-than-average attainments in education, who held better-status jobs with substantial income. The representation was somewhat askew.

We might therefore have expected an unusually enlightened response to the Christian faith and an articulateness about the Reformed heritage in theology. But this we did not find. They seldom displayed any sure grasp of the distinctive elements inherent in Protestant Christianity. It was not uncommon for them to reveal some embarrassment about any religious tenet or practice that made them seem or feel different from their neighbors. And the fact that many of them were church officers and Sunday church school teachers made but little difference in this general picture. Merton Strommen's Lutheran Youth Research team had uncovered a similar situation among their sample of 1666 young people, from whom the active officers of youth groups showed no less confusion about matters of their faith than the inactive and the chronic absentees.[1] A similar corroboration of the trend was discovered by Robert W. Lynn, in his interviews among fifty church families of Denver,[2] who found that the average mother in those interviewees

> does not understand the uniqueness of the Christian faith or its claim on her life. All too often her understanding of the Christian message, whether she is a nuclear or a marginal parishioner, is that of a denuded gospel, a patchwork of beliefs in the Golden Rule, the Ten Commandments, and "moral and spiritual values." I was often asked, "Aren't the Brownies and the public school in their emphasis upon moral and spiritual values doing the same thing as the church?"

Among our interviewees also, there were many who felt their faith had no unique qualities that could not be duplicated among other worthwhile efforts. One parent voiced it: *"For me, religion isn't going to church. If you're out with your children enjoying the sunshine and fishing, don't you think they're getting enough?"* A general vagueness about unique qualities in Christian faith and practice led many a parent to equate his religious beliefs with moral rules, with "spirituality" or some pleasurable communion with nature. For an age whose theological sophistication had reportedly improved, when laymen were reading books by Tillich, Niebuhr, and Barth, such answers were sobering.

Interpretations of Faith

One way of discovering how parents feel about the faith of the church was to ask them the projective question, "What would you hope for your children in the life of the church?" The query could hardly help bringing out what these adults themselves thought about the community of faith. This question evoked essay answers on the questionnaire; and these were combined with data gathered from the group interviews of parents. It is apparent from all the replies that a great variety of opinion and conviction existed within the sampling of parents. The range of positions stretched all the way from a naïve naturalism on one extreme to perspectives taking their form from the expressions of the recent theological renaissance at the other. But the wide middle ground is characterized (and not particularly caricatured) by Will Herberg who writes:

> This is at least part of the picture presented by religion in contemporary America: Christians flocking to church, yet forgetting all about Christ when it comes to naming the most significant events in history; men and women valuing the Bible as revelation, purchasing and distributing it by the millions, yet apparently seldom reading it themselves. Every aspect of contemporary religious life reflects this paradox—pervasive secularism amid mounting religiosity, "the strengthening of the religious structure in spite of increasing secularization." The influx of members into churches and the increased readiness of Americans to identify themselves in religious terms certainly appear to stand in contrast to the way Americans seem to think and feel about matters central to the faiths they profess.[3]

Insofar as our respondents were reflecting a philosophy of religion consistent with Herberg's criticism, they had strayed far from Protestant theology. And a number of them fill out his criticism. Their vagueness and confusion about the church and its beliefs run through a great many of the recorded comments. What has been dubbed as "objectless faith" came to the fore in a number of interviews. There is even a prevalent faith in faith itself. One parent expressed it well: *"If you can have the faith that things are going to work out all right, I think you can work toward better things."* The tautology in "positive thinking" could hardly be better exposed. The historic Protestant faith, briefly described in Chapter 4 bears little resemblance to this naïveté with its "works righteousness." Other comments had also shown these parents to hold a theory of vocation that was far from the normative Protestant doctrine of the priesthood of all believers. These descendants of the Reformers could hardly be said to be continuing the Reformation.

Nearly half the parents had avoided any theological reference when they spoke about their faith and church life. For them, something designated as "fellowship" was often lifted out as the chief value. Yet this fellowship was nearer to a modern definition of sociability than to the *koinonia* of the New Testament. Their loneliness even within the crowd of fellow members was sometimes poignantly revealed. Some frankly defined their reason for coming into the church as wanting to have "a sense of belonging." Some parents with an anxiety all too common, described how they thrust their children into a conglomerate of activities so that they would feel accepted in *"Scouts, boys' clubs, church school, everything we could find,"* as one of them stated it. The confusion of religious life with group activities could not have been altogether the parents' responsibility. Many a parish church has described its purpose and program in terms of meetings and calendar events. They have what

Robert W. Lynn, in a memorable phrase, has called "a surfeit of groups and a hunger for community."

We confirmed the fact that Will Herberg is unfortunately correct when he charges that the religiousness characteristic of America today is often "a way of sociability or belonging" rather than a way of reorienting life toward God. The religious experience that might have reached "down to the core of existence, shattering and renewing, merely skims the surface of life, and yet succeeds in generating the sincere feeling of being religious. Religion thus becomes a kind of protection the self throws up against the radical demand of faith."[4] When we reflect that superficial religious slogans are displayed for us at PTA, or the American Legion, on posters in buses and on billboards, it is not difficult to see how parents would begin to express themselves in terms of "religiousness without a religion."

Easily this general religiousness blends into a popular current amalgam of Christianity and Americanism. "The American way of life" was frequently mentioned in the interviews as synonymous with their religious faith. One parent phrasing it for many mused: *"It seems to me we should find out what the purpose of our life is and what we're trying to do with our life as Americans, as parents, and as Christians."* Then he asked, *"What's the difference between being a Christian and being an American? Is there any difference?"*

The late Bishop McConnell, colorful leader in American Methodism, could have had an answer for him. One time he observed, "We ought not to send foreign missionaries on the same ships as United States Marines. It just might confuse the natives." But many of the interviewees would not have understood such irony. So long had they listened to sermons about Christianity as a bulwark against communism that many of them could define their faith only in terms of an anti-Communist drive.

We have here documentation for what Eugene Carson Blake has dubbed "America's humanistic nationalism." He describes this phenomenon in acid terms:

> This ideology is what an American is if nobody tampers with his attitudes. His articles of faith are science (in its engineering applications), common sense (his own ideas), the Golden Rule (in its negative form), sportsmanship, and individual independence. . . . I have called this a humanism not because he doesn't believe in God. He does, but his god is not to be confused with a transcendent being to whom he owes duty and life itself, but rather his god is a combination of whipping boy, servant and even a useful ally in dealing with religious people, who otherwise might get in his way.[5]

Paradoxically, religion in terms of patriotism is just the kind of religion against which the Old Testament prophets had inveighed. William Hordern writes:

> We have been developing in America precisely the sort of folk-religion that Amos, Hosea, Isaiah and Jeremiah so bitterly condemned. We speak glibly enough about "this nation under God." But how often do we mean "this nation under God's judgment"? What we imply is that God is always on our side. A recent song hit turned up about "the Bible on the table and the flag upon the wall." This seems to identify religion and patriotism so closely that instead of trying diligently to find God's will for us we blithely assume that what we want for ourselves must be what God also wants us to have. There can be no more sinister heresy than this one.[6]

Misunderstandings about the distinctiveness of Christianity were rife. For many, if not most, the Christian faith was either coincidental with moralism, or with spirituality, or else about the same as communion with nature. For such, Herberg's accusation was just: "Religion can become a very convenient dodge word. It can mean almost anything the user wants it to. It has no cutting edge. It is very pliable."[7]

Yet there were exceptions to this broad, shallow outlook upon Christian commitment. A minority of the laymen did have the capacity and willingness to grapple with personal and social issues in terms of their faith. Their responses were more encouraging. One father, for instance, began to challenge his group as to whether family togetherness was an ultimate value. He insisted that religious faith is meaningless to him apart from his relationships as a parent. Yet even he could not declare his position without an initial apology:

> *I guess I should feel a little bit guilty sometimes for my feelings. It seems like increasingly we have been talking as though a successful or happy family were the ultimate goal in life. And I don't feel this way. I think that probably the raising of my children will be the greatest challenge that I will ever face in life. But my own relationship with other people as well as with my children, and my understanding of Christ and carrying out whatever may be God's will for my life, is also important to me and doesn't necessarily relate to the kids directly at all.*

Interestingly, this type of intimate depth-revelation in the group seemed to call for more personal involvement than many were ready comfortably to accept. Participants frequently resisted such a confession of faith by placing the issues on an easier level: *"I think that you're setting a very fine example in feeling this way, and in putting God in first importance. Your children are going to feel the same way."* Not only this man but others found that when they had dealt frankly or insightfully with a subject of personal commitment, the very next comment might be one of cheerful and mild detraction. Evidently "religiousness without a religion" has so long been a substitute for faith that it is hard even to hear another speak from any other orientation.

"Deeds not creeds" has been a hallmark of American activistic churchmen ever since John D. Rockefeller popularized the motto. Some parents, however are skeptical of this old rhyme, and indicated an appreciation for theology as "the thinking activity of the Christian." One such thinker got a rush of rejoinders when he opined: *"If you have any theology that is sufficiently mature to withstand your own searching, then you can make sense out of it for your children."*

At once, several other parents in the group interview refuted his word with such arguments as:

> *"No, I don't agree. You know as well as I do that the only way you can make sense out of this is in the realm of your human experience, not in any school of thought."* Or,
>
> *"Yes, but you have all the interpretations. And who is to say that I am right, or you are right, or the other one is right? The children are individuals. They have a right to their opinion, which is one reason I have always liked our church because it is flexible to that degree."*

Without pausing to wonder how the last comment would have sounded to a pastor of the church, we can note the peculiar resistance of other parents to the idea that a father might act as "priest of the family" or interpreter of religious values. The insecurity born of uncertainty breaking through these remarks is typical of numberless parents whose grasp on a Protestant understanding of the heritage of faith is unsteady and disconnected.

However, a refreshing few of the parents had been attempting to understand what implications the Christian faith might have for child-rearing practices in their homes. One mother expressed it for others when she asked, *"Isn't it how we interpret our relationship with God, our very own relationship, and how we wish to pass this down to our children? And yet, often it's what we learn or how we react to what is happening in our religious education, knowing that God does not impose his will on us, that makes us realize we cannot impose our selfish demands on our children."* To hear this voice expressing warm acceptance, based upon the fact that God himself accepts us and our willfulness, was to locate one of the scattered few who knows that theological connections lie between what one believes and how one lives in relationship with others. Indeed this could well represent a clue to the church concerning its oft-repeated attempts at parent education: the door to this strategic work may be found not in the courses about child behavior and popular psychology where Christian educators have so long supposed, but in grappling with the issues of our Christian faith. From such experience, with all its overtones of maturation in the faith, many a father and mother might find as an invaluable incidental that they have better understood their task as parents.

Some Correlations

Analysis of the questionnaires filled by these parents showed that it was those who were also teaching in Sunday church school who tended as a group to theological references in their discussion of these questions.

Parents who had no teaching responsibilities in the church school emphasized that they wished their children would gain a knowledge of the Bible from the church. Curiously, this goal is played down by those parents who are regular teachers and substitute teachers. They are more apt to reply that fellowship in the community of faith and discipleship are the goals for their children. Mere information about the Bible, and for its own sake, cannot seem as essential to them. Their understanding of Christian education would keep them from seeing it as mere book learning. We hypothesize that what parents want for their children from church life changes with the parents' relation to the ongoing parish program. As their experience and understanding broaden, so does their expectation. It must be obvious that teaching in itself consists of one powerful (and often overlooked) form of parent education. The strong predilection for moralism and unthinking definitions of Christian education—for example, the memorization of little verses—cannot long endure within the rich experience of a teaching job.

In a few instances, our cross tabulations found correlations between what parents valued for their children in the life of the church and the job of the family breadwinner. Salesmen as a group, for instance, have a much stronger than average desire for their children to gain character training. Good habits and sound principles that can guide them in their decisions are especially valued by the sales group. In the terms of Miller and Swanson (see Chapter 2), they would represent the "entrepreneurial" segment of church life. In Riesman's familiar epithet, they are more inner-directed.

Skilled workers, on the other hand, were among those who picked out Bible knowledge as the goal for their children. These who were craftsmen, foremen, and kindred workmen also laid stress on the desirability of institutional activities of the church. Seldom did they put their hopes for their children in terms of discipleship. All in all, though, the parents had expressed a striking variety in their assessment of Christian faith. The dynamic elements of these expressions had come through the interviewing. Only half, or just an edge over half, were able to relate to personal life any understanding of the historic meanings of the Christian faith, its events, and their meaning. The analysis of the questionnaires and interviews for this combination of 1000 parents had been a melancholy experience. It graphically showed how much additional Christian education is needed by even the active adults of our parish churches today.

As Parents View the Church

Our survey of theology, as reported in Chapter 4 had raised the pertinent question of how the family is related to the church. There we reviewed what this relationship should be in terms of Christianity. It turns out, however, that contemporary parents understand their own relationship in very different terms. Theologians who write books about Christian doctrine have one type of definition of the church; but parents, we were to learn, have quite another. Sermons and books, curriculum lessons and study groups, Scripture lections and commentaries have all laid stress upon the church as a redeeming and redemptive community of faith who are called by God in Christ to a priesthood of all believers. For the parents in these group interviews, however, the image of the church is more an institution, an instrument for special ends, or a traditional way of expressing religious preferences.

The Institutional View

It was the institutional view of the church that prevailed. Seen as primarily a building with an employed staff and a scheduled program, this was the "within the four walls" concept previously mentioned. Remarks recorded from the interviews leave us with the strong impression that for these people the church means a bundle of organizations, a mass of activities, and a crew of willing volunteer workers (well, some less willing than others) who are engaged in about the same basic business as "other character-building agencies." Not infrequently then, the church is seen as a corporate (and usually authoritarian) teacher of morality; for character building in this context has come to mean being told about high moral standards and good character. Even with church school curricula broadened beyond the old-fashioned and limited view of Christian education which held it to lessons concerning goodness, many a Sunday school teacher goes right on teaching every lesson moralistically. Justification by faith might be propounded from the pulpit, but righteousness by works continues to be taught in neighboring classrooms.

Thus viewed as a policing organization, the church appears to many as a good thing for a town to have, like substantial banks, swim clubs, or a city dump. In such a view, the final object of the Christian life may well be reduced to going to church and participating in whatever contributions it makes to civic and community life. As one parent expressed it, *"The church can do what it has always done to help us with our problems. It can give us those things to do that bring us together to worship, and then these other matters will be solved by doing worthwhile things in the church."*

When institutional aspects of church life prevail in the thinking of the people, there is bound to be greater concern about keeping the wheels turning. As a result, parents sometimes complain about being loaded with too much responsibility. They speak of being caught in a veritable beehive of activity, all aimed at nurturing the organization rather than ministering to the world. That they are not alone in such a caricature can be seen in the results of the questionnaire returned by pastors, and described in Chapter 7. Over half of the pastors had reflected an opinion that parents in the church owed institutional participation, loyalty, and support above any other expectations. Parents were hardly inaccurate in their supposition that organization efficiency is what most pastors want.

Over and again the parents were to report that their chief complaint about this institutionalized church was that it split up their family instead of unifying them. Awkward scheduling of events, overorganization, overloading of parents with meetings, and far too many church responsibilities were heatedly detailed by the interviewees. They called for more whole-family activities, in family worship services at church, in planned recreation, and for a type of Christian service in which they could participate together.

The overly organized parish church came in for heavy criticism.

To parents it resembles nothing so much as a three-ring circus in which father and mother are separated from each other as well as from their children by the numerous specialized groups in the frenetic activity of something called The Program. Among the unhappy comments about this bouncing institution, we uncovered complaints about ill-conceived family nights that promote more confusion than fellowship, or infant days at church that fulfill a promotional plan to gather babes in arms but end in upsetting both babies and their parents. Other complaints cited poor planning of the many events that make Sunday not only the busiest but also the most tension-fraught day of the week. Time and time again, the parents begged in one way or another to have this hyperactivity reduced.

It may be that many worthy activities, once planned to nurture Christian people, now require people to nourish them. Institutional activities are easier to understand and to promulgate than are the demands of actual Christian discipleship. But unless church leaders come to terms with the real purpose of the church as a redemptive fellowship with a witness and a mission, unless they consider carefully the growing resentment against the circus aspect of some parish life, trouble is in sight. People may continue for a while to support a busy schedule; but their activities will eventually lose meaning and mission.

The Instrumental View

Human nature being what it is, it is not surprising that many parents have a concept of the church that is largely instrumental. For them the church is useful chiefly for other things over and beyond itself. This essentially utilitarian idea of the church was expressed in a variety of ways. Church membership can improve one's mental health. It might open the way to social status in the community, to job advancement or to developing a more desirable neighborhood. The faith that the church holds then is quickly understood to be good because it is useful in promoting other, major values. Church life can play its assigned part in helping family unity or in helping persons to fill out their lives according to this view. As one father said, *"There has to be a balance. You can't be one-sided in anything, especially in modern-day living. You have to have some religion; you have to have some sports; you have to have some activities of all kinds and try to keep the thing balanced. That's our biggest problem, I think."*

One emergent fact that is clearly marked in the data is the parents' expectation that the church will be a help to them in their family living.

Whether it is expressed as pious hope (*"I think religion itself can be the greatest unifying force as far as the family is concerned"*), or as the confidence born of experience (*"When our family had its trouble we went straight to the church to see the pastor"*), it emphasizes the degree with which many parents depend upon their church community.

Not surprisingly, some of these same parents are rather firm about sending their children to a church whose door they themselves seldom darken. As one mother confessed, *"My husband is very, very strict about the children always going, and I am, too. But he'd just as soon stay home and do other things. And when the children get to the age of about fifteen, they'll be saying, 'Why do I have to go every Sunday when Dad doesn't go?'"* Most experienced churchmen could tell her that it won't take that long!

SYNCRETISM

Another view of the church held by many of the interviewed parents could be stated: The church is an expression of religion, not especially sharp or distinctive. For many, a kind of denominational syncretism prevails in which church origin or background is of little importance. Occasionally it was not even Protestant. A seeming tolerance tends to minimize the basic differences between faiths. Denominational distinctions mean very little to these parents who are seeking a congenial fellowship. Some of them could have even stepped out of the pages of William Whyte's *The Organization Man;* for it was in that book that church members were found to unite with the congregation that happened to have its building located along their traffic pattern as they drove out of their residential suburb. This way they were able most easily to join friendly neighbors who had gravitated to the same church for the same reason.

We could not escape the impression that "a little child shall lead them" into the life of the church. Parents seemed most willing to unite with a church fellowship where their children felt at home. One of them put it this way: *"When we move, our children usually determine where we go to church. Wherever they get acquainted and like the kids, we go there. We visited another church and found that they objected to dancing, so we joined here."*

Another parent, who must have been spokesman for a host of church samplers, explained it this way: *"We just started out to visit all the churches. Being non-Catholic, you can do that. You can go where you please and choose a church, which I think is wonderful."*

Some added light could be thrown on this interdenominational mixture by a pretest we had run in three Philadelphia suburbs prior to these interviews. Sampling just 100 suburban parents on that occasion, we found that over half of them had previously been members of some other denomination than that to which they presently belonged. Some of them had been members of two or three denominations in their moves. The past affiliations of the respondents ran nearly the whole gamut of Christianity: Methodist, Episcopalian, Baptist, Congregationalist, Lutheran, Reformed, United Brethren, Christian Science, Disciples, Unitarian, Roman Catholic, and community churches. The ease with which families can move from one church to another was noticeable. One cannot escape the persistent reports that suburban syncretism has so muted church preference that Jewish and Roman Catholic parents are also found sometimes sending their children to the nearest Sunday church school, regardless of its creed, because it is convenient.

Yet there were some parents within the interview groups who took their Protestant stand with deadly seriousness. They had no easygoing tolerance if they lived as minority groups in areas that were overwhelmingly Roman Catholic, Mormon, or Jewish.[8] Their day-to-day struggle to keep their distinctive form of faith alive precluded any easy syncretism, a term which, it may be remembered, G. K. Chesterton once defined as "religion going to pot."

The Church as Fellowship

These views of the church were not, of course, held exclusively and uniquely by any one parent. Those who had an instrumental view might very well also have a syncretistic view. This observation is certainly true for the next category: the church as a fellowship. Those who stress fellowship as *summum bonum* of church life could defend the institutional view as well. The concept of fellowship might, as we have noted, be confused with sociability; but it was held dear by many. When these parents had been asked to check off a list of church-related experiences in ranking order of their helpfulness, "Personal Friendships Within the Congregation" rose to second place, next to "Sermons and Congregational Worship" itself. Remarks in the interviews had filled out this impression; for they could be quoted in a spate of references to their yearning for a deeper relationship with pastor and people at the church.

An interesting side effect of the interviews was the hope that parents expressed in continuing this very kind of experience. For many, as the previous chapter shows, it was the first time they had ever been invited to come into a church meeting simply to talk about themselves and to share concerns about family life. The great majority of them said they would like more of this kind of opportunity to share and to study together.[9]

The Church as Redemptive Society

Not so many of those who attended the interviews described the church as a redemptive society; but some did, and their understanding of a more normative Christian doctrine stands out because of its very scarcity. Theirs was a distinctly theological view; they understood the fellowship of the church to be the people of God who share a redemptive mission to the world. A man in one session epitomizes this view through his remark:

> *Here's a term that we've used wrongly all the way through. We talk about "the church," but that's us, the Body of Christ. We're "the church"; so maybe it's a matter of our not doing enough for other people in our church and outside. Maybe this is the thing I'm looking for. I criticize the teaching staff; and yet I'm an adequate teacher myself. I could do a good job.*

But parents from inner-city churches, especially if they were in an interracial parish, would reflect a responsible philosophy of church life. Their sense of social ethics was likely to be clear and keen. They were eloquent in taking the church to task for not speaking relevantly to the social conditions that cry out for change. These people are often quite aware of social problems in urban areas and of their Christian obligation. One of them with a rather vehement conviction about the priesthood of all believers turned to another parent in her group and said, *"You have been thinking about an older idea of the ministry. Actually when you join the church you are a minister. We believe that the laymen are the Christians that keep the religion going and we hire our minister in our church only as a sort of co-ordinator."*

Such articulate Protestants were not numerous. But their presence was felt. They brought an enlightened view of the lay ministry (if not always a complete understanding of the ordained pastorate) into these discussions; and in a setting where the interviewer seldom offered an answer, it was they who corrected unbiblical and anti-Protestant heresies. One clear voice comes through a tape recording of an interview that was held in a Western church: *"What do you want—to have Christianity fed to you by the pastor in a spoon, touching you with the holy bread on the lips, instead of reaching out and getting it for yourself?"* The irony is heavy; but the doctrine is sure. Such a parent, exceptional though he or she was among this sampling of 1000, brings a refreshing note to the data. The Protestant doctrine of the church, which insists that the Reformation obliterated not the priesthood but the laity, is still strongly espoused by some.

As Parents View the Clergy

If parents in the research sampling had such diverse notions about the meaning of the priesthood of all believers, it could hardly be expected that they would be unanimous in their estimate of the clergyman. Even those who could verbalize the approved answers about a minister's task fell back into contradictory concepts about him as a person. Unconsciously they would lapse into a curious identification of the man with the church. When the interviewer said "church," many parents were inclined to think "pastor." They cannot help seeing the parish church personified in its clergy; and many tended to speak in this vein. Nevertheless, they did tend to see him in a variety of different guises.

Some would most quickly categorize the pastor among the helping professions. Perhaps because of personal experience or previous knowledge, they know him as a counselor, a pastor, or a resource in time of trouble. One mother, giving no indication of the experience from which she had learned this truth, said: *"Mr. W. is a wonderful minister. In the average church I don't think you could go so freely and expect so much help."* For another parent, the fact that the pastor was available was in itself comfort enough to aid the solution of problems whether he was called in or not: *"I find comfort just in knowing that the pastor is there if I need him. I solve a lot of problems just in knowing he is there, and that if I want to go to him, he will welcome me."*

These parishioners had shown a clear preference for the pastor as a counselor over any other member of the helping professions. Even if a personal or family problem becomes too deep or involved for the pastor to work with, many of these parents would want to take it to a psychiatrist or other counselor only upon his recommendation. The referral role of the clergyman is seen by them not only to be an important resource, but a feature that makes them more confident too.

That such a preference for a clergy-counselor is no isolated impression from this particular sampling of church members is demonstrated in a recent survey conducted under the auspices of the Joint Commission on Mental Illness and Health. Of those interviewed, about one-seventh actually sought help for their emotional problems. Of these who consulted "experts," 42 per cent went to clergymen and 29 per cent to general physicians. Only about one-fourth sought psychiatrists, psychologists, or social agencies for aid. Furthermore, of those who sought help from the clergy, 65 per cent said that they were helped. Less than half of those who consulted psychiatrists felt that their treatment had benefited them.[10] These new statistics lift to prominence a now common conviction that there is no longer any question as to whether the pastor shall act as a counselor; the only question is how well he performs this demanding task.

For all their diffusion of interests, and their reported secular tendencies, these parents found themselves drawn to the church as their peculiar home. They reflected a traditional desire for the pastor to call on them.[11]

It is important here, however, to indicate something of the residential correlations to these answers in our research study. It was suburban parents, for the most part, who advanced a positive view of the clergy as counselors. Rural churchmen had been particularly critical of their pastors, sometimes pointing out that ministers needed more training or that they should get around the parish more frequently. City parents were sometimes inclined to be critical in a less obvious way. They were more likely to say that their pastors were too busy, and that for this reason they would hesitate to call upon them for help. Some were quite explicit: *"I feel that our ministers are called upon for so much community business that the people in our churches feel neglected."*

The Preacher

Through the questionnaire, parents had the opportunity to list what church-related experiences had most helped them to understand themselves in family relationships. It will be remembered that at the top of their list they placed "Sermons and Congregational Worship." Lest this unevaluated item lead us to put too great emphasis on the strength of the pulpit, it is useful to make comparison with the interview sessions. Here the parents did not often refer to their ministers as preachers or make frequent reference to his sermons. When they did, the feeling about preaching was mixed.

Some were enthusiastic over the inspiration they received from the preaching in their church; they could identify sermons by subject and relate them to a better understanding they had gained in family life. Thus from one father:

> *The sermon last week was on marriage and I was very impressed with it. I'm pretty well acquainted with sermons, and I appreciated this one because I went home feeling a great deal better. And I can recall times when I've had rows with my wife over some issue, and a pointed sermon has helped us through.*

Needless to say, many derogatory thoughts would have gone unexpressed in these groups. But there is a minority of voices that speak out candidly in their wish for a more prophetic preaching to be addressed to those conditions in society that affect homes and families. Many of these comments can be traced to urban churches with an interracial membership or those located in interracial neighborhoods.

The pastor himself holds a self-image of the preacher. He had shown this in the questionnaire described in Chapter 7. The time he spends on preparation of sermons, and the high point he considers his preaching to be in "the ministry of the Word" each Sunday morning can but buttress the impression that the clergy take their sermons more seriously than do most pewholders. But the results of years of seminary training, of reading uncounted books and periodicals on the subject of preaching have emphasized in his thinking the central importance of proclaiming the Word in traditional Protestant prophetic preaching. The trouble plainly is that when the parishioners are gathered to talk about the church and its ministry without the presence of the pastor, they reveal that they haven't been hearing much prophetic preaching lately.

The Minister as Administrator

Relatively few parents spoke of the minister as an administrator in the interviews; but this does not mean that they do not consider him to be one. If they conceive the church to be an institution, they are speaking out of an underlying assumption that someone is executive director of that institution; for in our increasingly bureaucratized American culture, institutions and administrative functions are intimately linked. The research consultants who reviewed these data and aided in their interpretation, saw the point. They had found evidence of his hectic administrative life with its hurry from one chore to another, its activism, and its continual promotional work. With Joseph Sittler's description of the maceration of the ministers they would agree:

> The very vocabulary that has been common in the church is eloquent. The parish has a "plant"; its nature or purpose is specified in terms of a "program" for which a "staff" is responsible to a "board." The "program" is evaluated in terms of palpable production

which can be totaled with the same hard-boiled facility as characterizes a merchandising operation—and commonly is. The minister, like it or not, is the executive officer.[12]

The Youth Leader

Parents seem somewhat more aware of their expectation for the minister to be a leader of young people. This assignment of role clearly grew out of a yearning quite as much as from the experience of witnessing the pastor work with the youth. The bruised parents of adolescents expressed hope that the minister would be able to hold the interest of their young people. Feeling their own authority for this age group slipping as the adolescents gain greater emancipation, they welcome additional support from the church. Some parents were frank to say that the last vestige of parental control, indirect though it is, is found in the young people's fellowship at the church. Evidence from the interviews shows that some pastors do considerable counseling in regard to youth problems, both with the young people themselves and with their fathers and mothers. To the extent that he can act as an objective friend in some of the intrafamily tensions that arise where adolescents and parents disagree, the pastor is engaged in a significant ministry.

The Minister and His Critics

Our interviewees ran true to form. Anywhere in American society the inquirer would find the clergyman rated on a wide scale between adoration and contempt. He is seen in one guise as "Elmer Gantry," a rascal; in another, as the fatuous comforter in the play, "J. B."; in still others as the heroic adventurer of the recent TV series, "Crossroads."

Their most devastating criticisms, however, uncovered the problem about which he himself feels most sensitive: his vocation. When some described him as the busy ecclesiastical mechanic, rushing about his chores with a speed that makes it impossible for him to pause long enough to deal with some of life's deepest meanings, they were noting a concern he also deeply feels. If accusations were uttered that he spends too much time trying to keep his own organizational pots boiling, or in ballooning up activities into a parish program, he could second these with vehemence. Today's pastor is painfully aware of the "administrivia" that commandeer his time, of the nagging details that drain off his energy, that force him into pat solutions for weighty problems, and demand that he put more emphasis on doing than on thinking.

As the following chapter shows, he finds his most satisfying work in ministering to his people, in working on an interpersonal level with parishioners, in study and proclamation of the Word of God. That his professional life allows for so little of this deeper kind of ministry is a question that needs to be referred back to the people who attended the group interviews. In sessions of this same genre, with wide freedom to speak out concerning the issues, and share in common concerns, the churches' laymen—who have their own responsibility in ministry—could profitably review what the clergyman's place is in the community of faith. Such a searching inquiry could redound not only to his benefit but to theirs.

The Church in Their House

Inquiries into Protestant theology had pointed up for us a contrast that could hardly be ignored. The theological question that would not be quashed was, What is the church family's place in Christian nurture? We have seen in Chapter 4 something of the normative answer; but it was necessary also to discover the actual situation among the families in our study. Answers, unmitigated by very much contrary data, have made clear that today's Protestant families do only a minimum of worship as family groups, refer all too seldom to their church literature on the Christian family, and tend to a vagueness in theological understanding that pervades their household conversation and common life.

The one family subject that receives more pulpit attention than any other is family worship. This traditional ideal of Protestant families gathered together for Christian worship has been handed down from generation to generation in sermons and church literature. Whether the households actually preserve the tradition from generation to generation is more open to question. Extolled in thousands of magazine articles, sermons, and references every year, regular worship in the home was seldom found among the families we surveyed. They confessed that they just didn't know how to go about it, how to assemble all their busy family in one spot to sit still long enough for the ritual, or where to turn for adequate materials. Families with a spread of ages among their children (a frequent situation) speak of the difficulty of holding the attention of the squirmers and of how the age differences complicate the problem of understanding. A few candid parents say outright what others may feel; that they are not especially interested in the practice nor convinced of its helpfulness.

Yet seven out of ten families represented in the survey regularly have grace at family meals. Some parents obviously mean by this that the children do all the praying for the family, utilizing the graces they have learned at Sunday church school. The natural ease with which a child can handle this little liturgy is apparently a source of discomfort to some fathers and mothers if their children bow heads and offer prayers in a public restaurant. Some told how they stealthily turn to see if anyone sees their offspring in this too-pious act. At any rate this trend means an appreciable increase over the previous generation's practice; for many of these parents explained that they had never known mealtime prayers in their own childhood homes. When we consider the use of Scripture or devotional readings in connection with worship, however, the picture changes sharply. Less than one family in twenty replied that they follow such a liturgy with daily regularity. More than half of these active church families confess that they have such worship at home less than once a year—if at all. Although American Protestants are confronted with an unassailable demand to face up to Christian nurture in home and church, because the schools are not open to them for this purpose, they have yet to devise a consistently effective educational plan that will enlist more than a minority of families even in regular Bible reading.

These discussions had recalled some guilt about the status of worship in the family, and an eagerness on the part of many parents to improve the situation. Especially did those parents who had children under the age of six indicate a readiness to inaugurate such a rubric in their homes. Whenever some parent would testify to satisfaction or to regularity in Bible study and worship at his home, the air was filled with questions as to how it had been accomplished and what advice he might have for the others. One mother, speaking from what proved to be rather a rare experience among these church homes testified:

> *We try to bring God into our family life every day somewhere through our discussion. Whether it's when we're washing the dishes, or making beds, or just talking about what the kids had done, or in saying their prayers. But we make out of it an everyday conversation so that God is not just "The Man Upstairs," but someone who is a part of our life. We don't understand him all the time; and I get mixed up too in my interpretation. But still we talk about him. I want my children to gain a close feeling to God so that when they grow up they will know they have a God to depend on. That's my highest ideal; and I want that for my family, no matter what else we do.*

If they were not worshiping regularly at home, at least they were getting to church. Two-thirds of them are in church at least three Sundays out of every month. Impressively, these parents attend church worship with a faithfulness that reflects their high interest. The high evaluation they placed on congregational worship and friendships within the congregation had surprised us. Plainly the common worship of the church, together with its face-to-face relationships there, count for much in the life of today's families.

The Uses of Literature

An assumption underlying much of Protestant practice is that reading is instrumental to faith. The historical tradition that has put its emphasis in everyone's reading the Bible for himself has necessarily put a premium upon literacy. When missionaries begin their evangelistic work in a new territory, often their first objective is to reduce the language to a phonetic alphabet in writing as a prelude to teaching natives to read. So important is literature to Christian education and the mission of the church that Protestantism's most frequently encountered symbolism is in the printed word.

It is useful, therefore, to ask what weight reading has with churchmen, and how deep an impression this religious literature makes. As reported in Chapter 2, every major American denomination now has made parent education a feature of its curriculum materials. The variety of this literature is impressive, the sheer volume considerable. There are magazines for parents, quarterlies designed to be used co-operatively by teachers and parents both, letters printed to parents of children at various stages and ages, take-home sheets with suggestions for discussions and projects, family periodicals, family reading books, activity kits for parents and children, and new items introduced yearly. In spite of this rich variety, the high quality of much of the writing (though not all, by any means), the ready availability of the literature, and a spirited promotional effort to get parents to read it, the results are not conspicuously encouraging.

Child development literature can hardly be said to accomplish its great purpose if these 845 parents in the group interviews are at all typical. They testify that such writings sometimes increase their anxiety. Many parents are critical, and some are appreciative of the help they receive through magazines, pamphlets, and books. But the rush of critical comments gave a clue as to why so much of the literature had remained unread by these very fathers and mothers. One mother in a Southern town put it this way:

> *I still think that some of the tension between parents and children comes from this reading and magazines that have been coming out, saying "You are doing right by your child" or "You are doing wrong by your child." You begin to wonder why you are such a failure.*

Two other parents joined in. One observed, *"I think magazines are an awful bore."*

Another confessed with a gesture: *"We have a stack that high, and I haven't had a chance to go through it. I'll probably miss an awful lot; but I'd have to read the rest of my life."*

It begins to round out the picture if we review what magazines are to be found on magazine tables in the homes from which the parents come. According to an independent readership survey, the most widely read magazines among the homes from which our sample was selected were denominational magazines, *Reader's Digest, Life, Better Homes and Gardens, McCall's, Saturday Evening Post, Ladies' Home Journal, Time, Good Housekeeping, Look,* and *Coronet.* A cursory glance at the list will show that over half of these periodicals regularly carry family guidance features, and all of them have frequent articles on family life.[13] But these seemingly helpful features meet with mixed reception from parents. Some expressed genuine gratitude for articles that had made a noticeable difference in their attitudes and behavior. Parents volunteered: *"It gave me an entirely different concept,"* or *"After reading this article, things became a bit easier for all our family. It helped us immensely."*

More often, however, doubts were raised and concern was voiced:

> *You just get your house all set nicely so it looks good to you, and then you open a* Better Homes and Gardens, *and you think it looks just terrible. You see these ads with the beautiful woman draped in lovely lingerie, leaning over the cute baby, and you feel kind of . . .*

Here sympathetic laughter drowns out the woman's voice. The interviews turned up the usual proportion of concerned mothers who peruse the books of Dr. Arnold Gesell to learn if their children are conforming, those who feel they must be doing everything wrong after reading any piece on child guidance, and a good many who knew a whole set of books and concepts only by their titles, and yet had no compunction against stating firm opinions about them.

Church Literature for Parents

Spot studies in several national church bodies have forced a rethinking of any plan of parent education that relies chiefly upon the printed word. One such body, after some years of publishing study books for adult classes, now estimates that less than one per cent of those classes have been successful. Another, following considerable experience of publishing family reading books and study units for parents' classes, now questions whether one church in fifteen has been able to use these effectively in parent education.[14] Our own survey had involved parents whose denomination publishes a series of curriculum magazines designed to be used both by parents and by teachers. The magazines are graded according to the stages of the children at about three-year intervals. Thus, there is a parent-teacher magazine for each of five age groups; for four-and-five-year-olds, for six-through-nine, for ten-through-twelve, junior high age, and senior high age. Checking only those questionnaires in which parents said they *receive* such magazines in their homes, and could identify the titles of those they receive, we discovered what appear to be important correlations between the use of parent literature in Christian education and the life of the parish.

Parents who are active church members, but who have no teaching responsibility in the church are unlikely to look at such literature. Six out of ten seldom or never read any part of the parent-teacher magazines that come to their homes. Many men in our sample had simply indicated that they were not well enough acquainted with the parent-teacher magazines to answer any questions about them. If, however, these parents were recruited to teach occasionally in the church school, 70 per cent of this group did read at least one or two articles; and many read most of the magazine's contents. But if they were regular teachers in the church school, the chances are that eight out of ten such parents would make use of the magazines to some extent, over half of them quite carefully reading most or all of the material. We cannot escape the probability that the major reason in their stepped-up use of the materials was that they were to face a church school class Sunday after Sunday. The fact that the same magazine included both teaching plans and parents' articles increases the likelihood that their first interest was lesson preparation.

Nevertheless, as these parents were teaching some time or other in the church school and were forced to the magazines for material, the probability is good that they were also exposed to features designed for parents *per se*. Although it can hardly be seriously suggested that we sign up every last parent in some teaching post of the church school, there is a clue here. Active involvement in the Christian education enterprise of the church is in itself one form of parent education. To be enrolled in it is to be open to contacts that may have effect upon one's parenting.

We found also that the pastor's attitude toward such literature had a noticeable effect upon its use by parents. Where, for instance, he refers to the magazine topics and their purpose in his preaching, parents in that congregation are more likely to read them. If his own family turn to these magazines and make use of them as resources, congregants will also more likely do so. If he leaves such magazines at homes when calling, integrates announcements with magazine themes, or calls attention to them in recommendation, congregational use goes up.

Another correlation, not very hard to fathom, is seen that in those churches where adults have an active, satisfying educational experience, there is also more reading of parent magazines for parents. The stimulation of an adult group is an incentive for many to read, if only to be armed for the next discussion meeting. Some parents speak of "the content becoming alive" when they can compare their own interpretation with that of others. Encouragement to read follows more naturally when there is some possibility of sharing their knowledge with others.

It became clear from analysis of the data that parents do not read parent literature for the sheer joy of reading. They will read it with a function in mind—a problem to solve, a class to prepare for, a discussion in which they expect to share. Combined with these experiences, reading makes more sense to them. Patently, it is inadvisable to rely upon literature alone in family education. No available data or record of experience would encourage that.

Religious Problems of Protestant Parents

Among people who think of the church solely in institutional terms, it is inevitable that some of their grievous problems have to do with showing proper loyalty. Parents in the interviews would allude occasionally to their own attendance record at church services and their participation in the church; but they also projected their guilt feelings into remarks about their children. It is not unusual for Protestant parents to carry about with them the unexamined assumption that adults need the life of the church less than their children. Christian education for years has suffered from the widely accepted notion that its efforts are confined to children, and then in Sunday school for the most part. This "kid stuff" philosophy has its logical result in fathers who devote Sunday to golf and the newspaper, albeit indignantly insisting that the children get into their Sunday best and get over to the church.

It was the youth whose church attendance received attention in interview discussions. No matter what area of the country is considered, and whether the community be urban, suburban, or rural, this nagging question of interest and attendance in the church was brought forth. Parents proved quite ambivalent about "forcing" their young people to go to church. Sometimes they explicitly related the problem to their own flagging zeal; more often, however, they simply left unmentioned that they suffered from a similar quandary in regard to self-discipline. Usually, the issue was left in organizational terms: *"I wonder if it's right to make Sally go to church."* Seldom was the lack of interest expressed as doubt or confusion about the Christian faith.

Something of the parents' same lack of courage already analyzed in regard to discipline of children shows up here. Outer-directed parents, unsure of themselves and their authority, hardly feel competent and firm in matters of religious practice. But another side of the question is found, of course, in the church itself. When the youth does come into the church, what does he find there? By this question we do not mean, what features will he find that attract and hold his interest, but rather what sure foundation will he find for his own developing philosophy of life? A church whose energies are spent largely in keeping an organization in repair and well lubricated will not be the most hopeful place to look for a prophetic ministry. Dietrich Bonhoeffer, noting something like this same situation in the church under Nazi Germany wrote: "The church has not dared to proclaim the divine authority and dignity of parenthood in the face of the revolution of youth."[15] His concern that those parents had not felt much doctrinal support from the church in their task of rearing youth could find echoes in American churches today.

Ignorance of the Faith

Adults might feel content for many years about their knowledge and depth of understanding in a score of subjects, were it not for children. With the coming of their sons and daughters, however, the crisis we know as parenthood begins, and a good part of that crisis is centered in the daily challenge of answering questions. No one doubts that the parent is on the spot. His is the job of interpreting life from day to day. He (more often, she) is obligated to catch up on a body of knowledge in a few minutes' time (a concern which increases the commissions of encyclopedia salesmen). But sometimes more importantly, the parent is forced to think through questions about meaning and standards that might have been deferred much longer. These questions, largely in the realm of values, turn up most consistently along with problems of faith and assent. The directness with which we communicate those things in which we believe makes it inevitable that our children will pick up our attitudes, absorb some of our values, and question us closely about others.

A mother in an Eastern city looked at our interviewer and said plaintively, *"You can't get away with leaving out interpretation now because the kids today ask questions."* Then she added more pensively than accurately, *"They never used to."*

This is the very uncertainty that has sparked some adult education efforts in the churches. Most of our interviewees had admitted to being confused about the meaning of faith and ethics in today's world. The majority claimed, as one persuasive man stated it: *"Parents need as much help as children in understanding Christian faith."* With this an overwhelming majority of the parents agreed, as tallies of the questionnaires show. Though there was argument over what should be the nature of adult education in churches, two preferences achieved some recognizable consensus: (1) Parents were interested in neighborhood groups that could meet in homes; and (2) they feel the need for short-term content courses that would cover such issues as theology, social questions, parent education, Bible study. The very experience of being in a group interview where they could talk over basic matters with an informed resource person (the interviewer in this case) led to the next suggestion. They showed a strong preference to have such groups staffed with adequate leadership who could aid them in making the content relevant to family living.

For this desire, the parents had also the support of our research consultants. They too were aware of the churches' need for adequate leadership in such a venture; for most of them were also churchmen. One of them put the case all too plainly in saying, *"Churches have failed in the crisis of leadership because they have not enlisted their most capable people in their most urgent tasks."* All these consultants had urged that the churches step up their activity in adult education and offer enough variety that adults in different circumstances and abilities may find educational opportunities that speak to their needs.

Protestants in the Minority

A strange, new feeling has been stealing over American Protestant homes in recent decades. It is the eerie impression of being outnumbered at least in the centers of influence—the cities. Protestants of all denominations have a clear plurality over the other faiths combined in the U.S.A., but there are now numerous local areas where they are in a distinct minority. This, as many a Jewish family could have informed them, has its profound effect upon family life.

In those interviews that were held in such areas, we found our Protestant parents to be preoccupied with the concern of their minority status. Those who live in communities that are predominantly Roman Catholic, Jewish, or Mormon (a church usually designated as Protestant, but possessing an aggressive in-group *esprit* that makes it difficult for others in their neighborhoods they dub as "Gentiles"), report that they need more help than they are receiving from their churches. They feel the need for assistance in understanding what to do about associations and friendships, both for themselves and their children who are frequently rejected by the other children or exposed to proselytizing. They were also deeply interested in how to achieve and maintain a distinctly Protestant identity. And they had always with them the severe problem of developing tolerance toward the standards of the majority groups that surrounded them.

"The children across the street were teaching our Susie the catechism; and they told her that unless she blessed herself when she did certain things she would not go to heaven. And she just can't understand it," explained one mother in an East Coast city interview. And a typically boyish aspiration was reported by one father from another neighborhood: *"We had a problem with our boy wishing he was Jewish because the Jews got out of school for their special holidays."* Then he added more seriously:

> *As Protestants we have not been a minority long enough to know what to do about it. We haven't pointed up our heritage; and now we understand that we haven't been preparing him to uphold his position. We want to give him enough fundamentals of our religious background that he can understand what his personal faith can mean to him. We want him to know that there are reasons for our faith, that our reasons are valid and will stand the test of time. We can do this and still have enough tolerance to show that we don't want to take away the other person's right to worship.*

This thoughtful father was not alone in his motivation toward a deeper level of Christian education. The neighborhood religious picture had often given parents an unexpected opportunity for such teaching in the home. The interfaith arguments of their children had brought hard questions back to parents. In their struggle with these, and in consultations with each other, some had begun to hammer out the firm rejoinders that would help because they were based on biblical foundation.

It was for this type of additional assistance they were asking when they turned to the church for informed leadership.

These parents are likewise impressed by another factor in mixed-religious neighborhoods, namely, the intermarriage picture. From contacts comes dating, and from dating many a wedding. That marriages across faith lines have markedly increased since the end of World War II is attested by a number of studies.[16] The tolerance felt by many Americans for such mixed marriages is by no means shared by all; and many of these parents living as a minority group in neighborhoods overwhelmingly populated by adherents of another faith, have become defensive. They did not often articulate their reasons in terms of the risk of marital instability, the problems of child rearing, or the possible awkwardness of in-law relationships. This was a matter that they felt deeply; and their objections were emotionally conditioned. Out of this depth of conviction they had urged that the church's educational program aid young people to understand their heritage of faith, and help them to develop wholesome, promising friendships.

Significant Omissions

What was left out of these interview discussions was occasionally as important as the topics included. Significantly, very little serious consideration was found about ethical dilemmas in the employment of the breadwinner. We know from other discussions about the Christian's vocational life, that this area represents a deep concern for many men. Yet they did not easily connect it with their discussion of family life. Paradoxically, they had shown a real interest instead in vocational guidance for their children. Out of eight different areas of family life education which these parents had ranked in order, "Christian Interpretation of Vocation" rated third for inclusion in the church program. What they may have meant here, however, is a basis for making a choice of vocation. But any amount of testing for aptitudes and inclination will be inadequate if there is no basis in values for understanding one's work life. This is clearly a job for church education.

One man from a Western city was conspicuous for his courage; for not many men touched on the topic he laid open:

> *Are there really two codes of ethics in our world—one for spiritual attainment, and one in your everyday work where the dollar comes in? Here's your religious life on one side, and your business life on the other. Why, we have an altogether different language at*

work from what I would ever use at home in the evenings. In order to get anything accomplished, you have to talk like the other fellows.

But such a man was unique; for the most disconcerting omission in these discussion interviews was the lack of insight into the relationships between occupational values and family living. As we have noted in Chapter 2, the occupation of the husband has become a fundamental basis for the family's status. It often determines where they live, who their friends are, what their recreation will be, and how their children are reared. The imperialism of the job is seldom challenged. Yet the effect of the occupation on family values is hardly recognized, and is considered to be out-of-bounds in these church-sponsored discussions! The church is more often seen to be relevant to the nonwork, leisure time aspects of these parents' lives. Perhaps the church itself has brought this condition upon itself by an insulation from secular life. The church seems hardly aware at times of the technology and commercialism that make up the context of our workaday world. Church life is too much confined to a world of its own. We get caught up in a whirl of religious activities, concerned with programs overlaid with a spiritual vocabulary, and the fellowship of a worshiping clique. This has contributed to what one pastor calls "a file cabinet set of adjustments" that can be pulled out for each role—Sunday, Baptist deacon; Monday night, an Elk; Tuesday, a typical high-pressure salesman; Wednesday, chairman of the PTA . . .

If the church is to do anything with this need for a Christian interpretation of vocation, and get it beneath the level of inconvenience (father's absence on trips makes home life harder, or the working mother finds a new schedule is necessary), we must be ready to expect more rather than less problems from parents. If all of life, including our work life, is brought into the sphere of Christian obedience, parents may be forced to embrace the cultural conflict which they often seek to escape through insulating one role from another—and retreating into the life of the contemporary parish church.

Men, Women and the Church

Seldom mentioned aloud in the interviews was a matter that showed up sharply in the questionnaire response. (More than once was the design vindicated at the point of having both these research techniques checking each other.) The remarkably different outlooks of fathers and mothers in regard to church came through vividly in the anonymous questionnaire. One of the most striking, though it was hardly surprising, was demonstrated in the greater church interest manifested by women in the sample. We found that father is apt to attend church services and meetings less than mother. Among those who attended at church worship only once in every three months or less, men had the larger representation by far. The man reads Christian literature much less than his wife, whether it be denominational magazines or the parents' materials published by church educational boards. Moreover, his wife is more likely to say that she finds such material helpful, even when both of them do read it. It is the woman, also, who plays a more prominent part in the teaching and leadership tasks of the church school. Robert W. Lynn in his parallel study, had noted the same phenomena:

> In the majority of instances, the role of father does not involve either his relation of religious teacher to his children in the home, or in relation of the parent co-operating in the home with the church school. And so it is mainly the mother's "job" to teach in the church school or to co-operate in the home with the church school teacher. Some churchmen have complained of the laziness of the Protestant father concerning his children's Christian education; but, if I may say so, the explanation of laziness is a lazy explanation on our part. The father's phenomenal ignorance about the curriculum of the church school is "selective inattention" due in some measure to his present role definition. In saying this, I come dangerously close to a kind of environmental determinism. I do not mean that society determines his role and that therefore the father is not responsible. Not at all. Rather, the church must seek to understand how the restriction and reduction of the father's traditional prerogative as the priest and teacher of his family is directly related to the increasing centering upon the occupational role of the source of his identity. Our pious chatter about "the Christian family" and about "the responsible parent who co-operates" often serves to intensify his sense of guilt about the conflict between the claims of job and family.[17]

And Togetherness

It had been a frequent charge, often sternly voiced, that churches tear family members asunder by scheduling programs which do not allow them to remain together in their religious life. These essentially competitive features, parents contended, mean that church leaders continue to think of members in individual terms rather than in their family relational context. The errors cited were numerous: church programs so highly departmentalized that it is not unusual for married couples to be separated in religious education, or for parents to be completely omitted from the education plans of the church. Though it is true that there are demonstrable advantages to the graded system of religious education, we in Protestantism may now have overdone it, and to our own hurt. Those few churches that are now experimenting with other plans may be pointing to an entirely new development: having whole families in Bible classes, fathers, mothers, and the children; or recruiting husband-wife combinations to do team teaching in church school; or scheduling night sessions of vacation church school so that the entire family may attend. These more experimental plans have achieved nothing like the acceptance of the long-established graded system; but, in their favor, it can be said they do not vitiate worship by family groups, or eliminate the possibility of a joint educational approach for parents and children as is the case in many church schools.

To the dismay of many parents who were interviewed, the church appeared to be working against its own interests and stated policies. They had pleaded for a conscientious home study of curriculum but then preempted so much time for age group activities that the family was left with little time to fulfill its part. One mother pointed out that her church had suggested Sunday afternoons for family discussion of the church school lessons, and then had soon thereafter announced youth meetings and choir rehearsals for Sunday afternoons. When the church claims so much time, parents feel, not unfairly, that the leadership is promoting war on its own program. *"Maybe,"* as one irate father said, *"they don't know what they're doing."*

A reorientation of church programing would be necessary to reduce the divisiveness now caused by neglect. To think of family units instead of individual contributors might necessitate an entirely new procedure in office administration. A survey within the Indianapolis Family Life Clinic of 1958, sponsored by the National Council of Churches, discovered that few churches even have family records that show the kinship of family members. One father in the interviews noted the intermittent demands from churches for time, energy, and funds to support a variety of organizations and purposes which are justified in themselves; but which, when they are viewed collectively, just happen to disrupt family life. Church activity does tend toward meaninglessness when it fails to take into account the persons in families and their need for supportive structuring and relationships.

Churches, of all things, ought to be involved in building an educational enterprise around family groupings and cease causing divisions within parish homes. One especially critical man spoke out at an interview: *"The church often asks me to do things that have not the remotest connection with my family life, and that could better have been omitted."* Another voiced the need for the support of the church in their family problems of atomization: *"Frankly we need things arranged to bring us together. Most things are now arranged to keep us apart."*

And a weary mother spoke for a legion of "chauffeur Christians" about the ferrying service so many parents run as they drive back and forth between church and home: *"Carol is starting to come down here now, getting into a lot of activities. I have to cart her back on Sunday and come down myself a half-hour later. Then I bring down the boy for another meeting. When we're home, they're down here. When they're home, we're in church. How are we ever going to get together? This church isolates parents from their children!"*

Surely because of the general resentment voiced by parents who feel that their families are split by multiple demands, the churches must re-examine what they expect of families. Parents are in agreement that their religious life should include a program that allows them to remain together in families for a greater portion of time. They have seen too much of overorganization, and the overloading of some few parents with too many responsibilities.

Many of our informants heatedly demanded that the churches take into account the whole family when planning programs. Instead of so many unco-ordinated meetings, they would like to have family worship services, recreation events for families, service opportunities for family groups. There is a warning here in the repeated remarks by parents indicating that they feel "pushed around" or "exploited" by their churches.

All this underscores the point that these parents want what has come to be called "togetherness." But a close reading of the research data could raise the question as to how much they could endure of this highly vaunted togetherness. Many parents (and fathers were quite specific about this) wanted discussion groups on an adult level; nothing was mentioned about admitting their children. We cannot escape the inference that some families appear to have been together too much, and at excessively close quarters. Churches who move to satisfy these requests for family group activities would do well also to calculate to what extent such requests are made because of the current fad for togetherness. They could do well to listen also for indications of other family concerns. The interviews were peppered with mention of problems that must have been complicated by the tensions and difficulties inherent in just being together. Between the extremes of splitting the family at the threshold of the church and forcing them together more than they can stand, there must be a mean. Our clue is that it lies in the area of solving the scheduling conflicts of parish program, providing for more meaningful whole-family events, and in establishing those educational plans that enable persons better to understand themselves and their relationships.

The Yearning for Relationship

It is apparent, then, that church members have quite enough meetings, but their yearning for relationships, their oft-mentioned loneliness, means they would welcome the personal touch. *"What we need,"* one man said quietly, *"is less meetings and more meeting."* One-third of the interviews disclosed that the atmosphere of the church is too unfriendly and formal to be satisfying. These parents want a deeper relatedness to the leadership of the church too. What else is behind their insistent request that the pastor do more visiting in the homes? They want a two-way conversation about the important matters in their lives; and they feel the church allows too little opportunity for this.

"I know it's very difficult in a church of this size for everyone to get to know the minister," one mother averred, *"but in the church where I grew up, the pastor could call all the people by their first name. This is important."* This old-fashioned yearning shows that the traditional expectation for a clergyman to call in the homes of his parish has changed but little in this day of the so-called "pastor-director." To the neglect of home visitation, some of our respondents attribute the inability of pastors to understand their parishioners or to know what the situation is in many parish homes.

The real and poignant loneliness with which some, but certainly not all, of these churchmen are struggling represents a special opportunity for parish churches. Persons who fail to find recognition and acceptance in their apartment dwellings or community life look for a friendly, helping hand to reach out to them. Part of this problem relates to the high rate of mobility and the not unnatural rootlessness that our people must feel at some time or another. Families on the move frequently lose any sense of being wanted as they come out of a known community into an unknown. The church is equipped as no other agency to orient the newcomers and to provide a ready ground for new roots.

Churches, though they may be aware that one person in five moves each year, still operate as if they had a steady, continuing constituency. As Reuben Hill has observed, the newcomer is almost expected to introduce himself and to win his way into the in-group. In effect, he is to say, "I'm not part of this group; may I come in?" He advances hesitantly into his new neighborhood where he finds people have a façade of aloofness, but he need not enter so hesitantly into church life. Here his first impressions are unusually sensitive. He tests first to learn if this new environment is different from his old home. He tends to magnify both warmth and coolness, as many a pastor has learned. The church that is organized to identify new families and is ready to work with them can offer help, and introductions, and a new measure of security.[18]

Often the church constitutes the one familiar spot in an otherwise strange community. If only the parishioners will remember their natural function of welcoming the newcomers, much that is now unstable in family life might be stabilized.

NOTES

1. Merton Strommen, *et al.*, "Lutheran Youth Research." See Note 11, Chapter 1.
2. Robert W. Lynn, "Fifty Church Families and Their Role Expectations." See Note 41, Chapter 2.
3. Will Herberg, *Protestant-Catholic-Jew*, p. 14. New York: Doubleday & Company, Inc., 1956.
4. Will Herberg, *Protestant-Catholic-Jew*, p. 276.
5. *The Christian Century*, Oct. 15, 1958, p. 1178.
6. William Hordern, "America's Religious Revival," *Advance*, June 28, 1957, pp. 4–6.
7. Will Herberg, *Protestant-Catholic-Jew*, p. 290.
8. Roman Catholics outnumber Protestants in 12 states now, according to a study reported by the National Council of Churches' Bureau of Research and Survey. Sociologists are beginning to describe the U.S.A. as a "post-Protestant" culture.
9. It is interesting also to note that where churches already had a pattern of such groups meeting in adult education, they showed a better understanding of historic Christian faith than churches without such adult education.
10. Data from Gerald Gurin, Joseph Veroff, and Sheila Feld, *Americans View Their Mental Health*. New York: Basic Books, 1960.
11. Of interest is the paper delivered by Luke Mader Smith on "Laymen's Images of Parish Clergymen" at The Society for the Scientific Study of Religion, Harvard University, Oct. 31, 1959. He found that laymen of all groups expect pastors to visit them, counsel them, and be a "reference group for the laymen." "In spite of growing individualization in the larger society, religious leaders are still most effective in that area where relationships must be extended but also stabilized by ascription." And there is other evidence that church members prefer to look to their church for guidance, from a series of interviews conducted by research representatives of the National Council of Churches. Parents were asked in that survey (held on a house-to-house basis without any reference to religious affiliation) to indicate which organizations contribute most to their family life. The largest number of parents, 71, indicated the

church, with 38 reporting the PTA, and other organizations receiving scattering mentions. (Lauris B. Whitman, Helen F. Spaulding, and Alice Dimock, *Study of Summertime Activities of Children in Relation to the Summer Program of the Churches, National Council of Churches, 1959.*)

12. Joseph Sittler, "The Maceration of the Minister," *The Christian Century,* June 10, 1959.
13. In one of those slick popular magazines that habitually adorns the coffee tables of countless American homes, there recently appeared a passage of more or less enduring worth. Because of its emphasis on the family, we repeat it here: "What is your family really like? What are its goals? Its needs? Its interests? What do you believe in? If you know—with certainty—you will have a successful living room."
14. Orville G. Brim, Jr., reviewing the effectiveness of literature used by parents, cites four research studies that employed control groups in a complete experimental design in order to test results: "One of these, a comparatively small study concerned with improvement in factual information about children's health, reports a favorable change occurring in the parents involved. The other three major studies have all been concerned with changes in parent attitudes. One of these three reports that no changes occurred; the other two report positive effects upon parent attitudes. However, in these two there are certain deficiencies in the selection of the control groups and, in addition, the positive changes reported differ from one study to the other; thus, the findings of each are open to various interpretations." *Education for Child Rearing,* p. 311.
15. Dietrich Bonhoeffer, *Ethics,* p. 49.
16. See for instance James H. S. Bossard and Harold C. Letts, "Mixed Marriages Involving Lutherans—A Research Report" in *Marriage and Family Living,* Nov., 1956, p. 308; and also John L. Thomas, S.J., *The American Catholic Family,* Chapter 6.
17. From the unpublished paper "Fifty Church Families and Their Role Expectations" (used by permission of the author). Another research study, that should give us pause, found that a father's church affiliation had direct effect upon the family's over-all participation pattern. See Sarah Frances Anders, "Religious Behavior of Church Families," *Marriage and Family Living,* Feb., 1955.
18. Some research would indicate that the welcome extended by church members is more likely to lead to a newcomer's entrance into church participation than is the pastor's rather expected hospitality. (Roy G. Francis, Charles E. Ramsey, and Jacob A. Toews, "The Church in the Rural Fringe," *Minnesota Farm and Home Science,* Feb., 1955.)

- **Pastors and People Share the Ministry**
- **The Pastors Are Polled**
- **The Clergy View of Family and Church**
- **Pastors Evaluate Their Ministry to Families**
- **Counseling and Home Visitation**
- **Preaching and Corporate Worship**
- **The Teaching and Educational Ministry**
- **The Pastor and His Home Life**

7

The Church's Ministry to Families

AS THE LAYMAN LOOKS AT THE CLERGYMAN and reveals what he sees he illustrates, more than he knows, an incipient clericalism. It is true that he often considers that the minister has a different calling from himself. But more tragic for Protestantism is his tendency to denigrate himself as a part of the church. The unordained Protestant usually views himself as a layman, not only in the professional sense of being unqualified to speak in a highly technical field (in this case theology), but regrettably and heretically as a person of lower status than the pastor in the church. Too often the Roman Catholic notion of the "sacred" life being higher than the "secular" life in the world has filtered into Protestant thinking where it has no place. To Protestants there is but one "vocation" and that is discipleship to Jesus Christ wherever one is called to work and live. It is ironic, therefore, that the movement which in its original genius taught the "priesthood of all believers," should slip into an attitude which all too frequently attributes to the ordained pastor both jurisdictional authority and superiority of spiritual power. It is apparently both a misunderstanding of biblical doctrine and an inordinate need for status which leads some pastors to perpetuate this sharp division of clergy and laity. Beyond both this error and sin, however, we can sense in pastors today a genuine confusion concerning who they are and their function in the modern church. Consequently, Protestantism is seeking both the theological and the empirical means to understand the place of the ministry in the church.[1]

Pastors and People Share the Ministry

The layman's tendency to see the minister generally as executive head of a religious organization is understandable. For one thing he has been led to believe by the omnipresent American organizational pattern (and often by the clergy themselves) that institutional expansion is an expression of authentic Christian witness. He notices, too, that whatever the minister prefers to call himself, his actual practice is related largely to organizing, administering, and promoting, even in his preaching and pastoral work. And once a conventional pattern of institutional activity becomes normative, people come to expect it, and to demand professional leadership to guide it. No one can keep up with the complex modern church on a part-time basis. This being the predominant reasoning of the laity, the ministry receives its identity, not so much from a theological understanding of the church and its mission, as from the practical necessities of an ongoing organization, the functions of which are devoted to enhancing the religious life.

Lined up against the tendency to see the church solely in terms of sociological realities, Protestant biblical scholars and theologians have been calling the church back to an understanding of its theological character and the ministry to its primary role. They do not deny that the community of faith will always have an institutional face and that this makes up a part of the theological understanding of the church.[2] They insist, however, that it is far too narrow a conception to see the church in terms of its formal leadership, codes, and cultus without asking whether the biblical view permits such sociological categories to say the last word.

It is the biblical view, they assert,[3] that all believers belong to the *laos,* the people of God in community, and that they all have the requisite gifts appropriate to their calling. "As against most Catholic theory and not a little Protestant practice . . . it needs to be asserted unambiguously that the primary reality in the Church is not the ministry but the congregation (or the common life of the people of God)."[4] This is not to minimize the importance of an *office* of the ministry of Word and Sacraments whose service it is to keep the whole body focused on its gospel, its mission, and its witness. But when the church puts its *primary* emphasis upon the "service of the sanctuary" and upon an institution with creeds, sacraments, and orders, it almost invariably draws attention away from the ministry of the whole membership in the ordinary life of the world. The peculiar position of the laity, we are reminded, is that living and moving in the context of the day-to-day world, they are in continual dialogue with it and are commissioned to witness to the Lord of the church in their service. That they need the nourishment of the church at worship and study to fulfill this mission and to be a Christocentric brotherhood goes without saying. And in this task the pastor is to develop the "equipment of the saints for the work of ministry" (Ephesians 4:12).

It is with this realization that pastor and people serve together that we describe the ministry to families now existing in a large part of Protestantism. We cannot assume that the ordained pastor's ministry is the only service being performed to families in the church. Yet, practically, one must recognize that the pastor's ministry often sets the tone for the people's service to each other and to the world; pastor and people bear a reciprocal relationship to one another in this ministry. For our basic information about the ministry of the church to families, then, it was necessary and desirable to go to pastors themselves. This we did through a lengthy anonymous questionnaire.[5]

The Pastors Are Polled

No questionnaire can be constructed without first determining the goals and purposes which the instrument is to serve. Three purposes informed our study: first, to discover a valid picture of the minister's way of serving families both directly and in collaboration with laymen; second, to discover the readiness of pastor and church to move into certain areas of education for family life;[6] and third, to tap some selected attitudes and opinions which could subsequently be compared with those of laymen on the same subjects.

The content of the questionnaire represents, in large part, the collective curiosity of numerous staff people of the denomination (see Appendix) whose departments were already to some extent involved in Christian education for family life. It was they who were encountering obstacles and they who had most to gain from such a survey. Many more topics were suggested than could be used, as might have been expected.

The process of building the questionnaire itself proceeded through a number of steps after the content priorities were decided. A long, open-ended instrument was devised and pretested with 35 neighborhood pastors whose on-the-spot comments, reactions and questions aided us in simplifying and abbreviating the form. Numerous ambiguities in wording were clarified. All but four open-ended questions were converted to multiple-choice or ranking-type queries which included the most popular answers received during the pretest. Thereafter, a revised version was mailed to 100 pastors all over the nation. Their participation also helped us to eliminate some questions and to rearrange others. After these two searching pretests the final questionnaire[7] was developed and printed and prepared for mailing to 3541 Presbyterian ministers; and from that number a gratifying 74.7 per cent (2645 questionnaires) were returned for tabulation and analysis.[8] In this large return, all regions of the country were adequately represented.

Because of budget limitations a sample of the return was selected for tabulation: one thousand (1000) questionnaires, in all. The following tables reveal some of the characteristics of this group of pastors.

TABLE 1 DISTRIBUTION BY SIZE OF CHURCHES SERVED BY FULL-TIME PASTORS

Size of Church Served	*Percentage of Pastor Respondents*
1 to 99 members	19.8
100 to 299 members	38.1
300 to 599 members	19.7
600 to 1199 members	13.1
1200 members and over	9.2
No answer	.1

Since many of the smallest churches are without full-time pastors it proved harder to get an adequate representation of them for the study; therefore, *every* questionnaire returned by a pastor serving a church of less than 100 members was used in the analysis. If a pastor served a "larger parish," composed of more than one congregation, we asked him to report on the program of that church which possessed the most adequate records and program.

TABLE 2 DISTRIBUTION OF CHURCHES BY TYPE OF COMMUNITY

Type of Community in Which Church Is Located	*Percentage of Pastor Respondents*
Rural	35.3
Urban	37.1
Suburban	25.0
No answer	2.6

Relatively few pastors, it can be seen, were unable to identify the kind of community in which they lived and worked. Quite a number were frankly confused, however, since their community was undergoing great transformation. Many formerly rural environs were taking on the earmarks of a suburb with housing tracts replacing grazing land, for instance. To these transitional areas sociologists have attached the title "rurban."

TABLE 3 POPULATION OF COMMUNITIES IN WHICH CHURCHES ARE LOCATED

Population of Community	*Percentage of Pastor Respondents*
One family to 1,000 persons	20.3
1,000 to 5,000 persons	21.8
5,000 to 10,000 persons	11.9
10,000 to 25,000 persons	11.6
25,000 to 50,000 persons	8.2
50,000 to 100,000 persons	7.1
100,000 to 250,000 persons	7.1
250,000 persons and over	10.3
No answer	1.7

It will be noted that the majority of these churches are found in communities under 10,000 population. Smaller churches predominate in these towns as might be expected. However, in the case of the suburbs we generally find larger-than-average churches.

TABLE 4 AGE OF PASTORS IN THE STUDY

Age of Pastors	*Percentage of Pastor Respondents*
Under 35	30.6
35 to 49	36.0
50 or over	33.3
No answer	.1

The table above shows an approximately equal number of pastors in the three age groupings.[9] Interestingly, the smallest churches have a larger than average number of both younger and older men staffing them. Some interesting differences related to the pastor's age were to be discovered.

About three out of four (72 per cent) of the respondents were the only professional persons on the church's staff. We were not surprised to verify that a larger number of multiple-staff churches were to be found in metropolitan areas of the country.[10]

The marital status of the pastors in the study reveals that 95 per cent of them are married; 4 per cent are single; and 1 per cent are widowed and not remarried. Only one respondent of the 1000 listed his status as "divorced." No attempt was made, however, to determine the number of pastors who might have been widowed or divorced and subsequently remarried. The great majority of the pastors have children, as can be seen from the table below:

TABLE 5 FAMILY LIFE CYCLE STAGES OF PASTORS IN THE STUDY

Age of Oldest Child	*Percentage of Pastor Respondents*
(Unmarried	4.0)
(Married but childless	1.9)
Birth to 2 years	15.0
3 through 5 years	12.7
6 through 12 years	19.0
13 through 19 years	18.4
20 through 24 years	8.7
25 years and older	20.3

In the analysis of the questionnaire[11] the answers to each of the 120 questions were cross-tabulated with a set of "basic variables" (that is, characteristics of the pastor or his church) which would allow us to see the relationships of the findings to each other. The six key items which were correlated with all the answers and with each other were: (1) the region of the U.S.A. in which the church was located; (2) the type of community; (3) the size of the congregation; (4) the age of the pastor; (5) the church's status as single- or multiple-staff; and (6) the degree of use of church curriculum materials by the church and pastor. This breakdown allowed us to note the differences in attitudes and practices among our clergy and relate them to these various characteristics.[12] Some of the differences among pastors will be noticed as we reveal their views of church and family.

The Clergy View of Family and Church

Pastors, it turns out, are somewhat divided in their assessments of the comparative places of church and family in regard to religious nurture. Although the majority indicated that they consider parents to be the chief religious educators of children, a sizable percentage had experienced enough disillusion on this score to register a series of exceptions and protests. One-third of all the pastors, for instance, could assent to this proposition only if the parents thus responsible were also active in the church. To them it was clear that fathers and mothers could hardly pass on to their children a faith they themselves did not possess. Even with this qualification, however, it is possible for most parish ministers to agree that the home is our most powerful influence in Christian nurture; and the church school at best can be only a supplement. With George A. Buttrick they would be inclined to agree that the home is so far ahead of any other educational institution that it has no serious rival.[13]

One out of four pastors had the diametrically opposed view. For them the church school was of paramount influence; and though they could agree in theory to the parents' prior weight in Christian nurture, to them the facts seem to point to the main job's being done by the formal educational arm of the church. A distinguishing correlation arose from the data at this point, showing that clergymen who responded this way were most likely to be either younger clergymen serving as sole pastors in small-to-medium-size churches or else those who were serving at the time in a collegiate ministry in some larger church. In either case, the likelihood is that we are dealing with a fairly recent graduate of a theological school. He has received his specialized training at a time when there has been additional emphasis on Christian education both as a practical theological discipline and as a professional ministry. As a new, more self-conscious professionalism arises among church educators, there is reason to expect that those who have an investment in this work will better understand the power of the church school and more optimistically view its possibilities. Concomitant with these circumstances, these same ministers had been exposed to a curriculum briefing program on behalf of church school materials that began in 1947 and has continued unabated ever since. The sheer impact of this continuous contact, together with a constant improvement in educational materials and leadership training, could but be expected to spark a new group of apologists for the church school. Even the increased attention to the doctrine of the church in seminary courses and current literature would, in spite of itself, have called new attention to the church's institutional and organizational life in which the church school so fully shares.

Interestingly, only a very small number of the clergy, just one in twenty-five, showed any acute awareness of the influence of community standards on the family. They had said that although parents are theoretically the most powerful contacts in children's lives, those parents are strongly swayed by community patterns and opinions. With Reuben Hill and other sociologists, they would consider the family as one institution dependent upon other institutions in society and responsive to the surrounding environment.

Though statistically small, an identifiable minority reflect a somewhat filiarchal view. They took the frank position that parents hold but little authority and that it is *children* who act as the chief religious influence in the home. Experience had led these pastors to credit children with bringing their parents into the church, forcing attention on curriculum materials, or altering family patterns to the extent that prayers would be introduced at mealtime. That fathers and mothers learn from their growing children would have been witnessed by these pastors in their parishes, and perhaps felt within their parsonages also. Nowhere do youngsters wield a greater influence upon the education of their parents than in the realm of faith. Something of the goodness of God, his love, and his creation can be communicated through little children whose honest outlook and unclouded eyes can open new vistas to adults.

Pastoral Expectations from Parents

An open-ended question (that is, one which called for the pastor to fill in the answer with his own words) had asked: What does the church expect of Christian families? Once more the institutional bias shows through plainly. Somewhat more than half of our respondents, 56 per cent, framed answers that stressed family participation in the institutional life of the church. They detailed this as meaning support of the church program, both financially and personally, assisting with the educational features of the church, maintaining enthusiastic backing for the church from the family, and being present at the public meetings and services of the parish. Although this was a cross-section answer that came from all types and ages of pastors, one group is represented here significantly more often than would have been expected from their total portion of the sample. They are the middle-aged clergy who serve alone in their parishes. Their emphasis upon institutional loyalty is marked. This observation might not be so noticeable were it not for the contrast afforded by younger pastors who are serving in multiple-staff churches; for they offer institutional answers less often than could have been predicted, judging upon their representation in the total sample. Only a longitudinal study that permits subsequent surveys with this same sample over the years could confirm an allegation that these men increase an essentially conservative interest in the church-as-institution as the years go by. Certainly this hypothesis alone is incapable of baring the whole reason. We have only to review that recent graduates of theological seminary have had more intensive study in theology with its renewed accent on church as *koinonia,* as well as their entirely new discipline in pastoral psychology (stressing the meaning of persons and their particular needs quite apart from the ability of those persons to play their part in increasing the effectiveness of the church organization) to realize that younger ministers will be motivated differently in their responses.

It would be easy at this point to be misunderstood. Let it be pointed out that we are not holding out the institutional view of the church for ridicule. Except for unusual and isolated instances such as the "No Church" movement in Japan, the Christian church does not exist apart from its life in institution. As John S. Whale has said:

> Empirically considered, the church is necessarily visible and institutional. This wonderful and sacred mystery is mediated to us through the visible and empirical; sacred Scriptures; sacred rites and sacraments, the outward, visible and efficacious signs of inward and spiritual realities; sacred offices of Christian ministry; sacred seasons, buildings, forms. Life in the spirit is never disembodied; it is incarnate in a Body whose organs are Word, Sacraments, and Ministry. Indeed the visible church is the divinely given medium whereby God's sovereign grace is shed abroad. It is the "means of grace" from which all others draw their life. It is the supreme agency of mediation, following upon that of the Incarnate Son of God himself. That is why the visible church is rightly known by all Christians as "an extension of the Incarnation."[14]

In analysis of the questionnaires, our concern is not that pastors understand the church to be an institution. They can hardly do otherwise. The concern, rather, is that when given an opportunity to define in their own words the relationship between families and church, a majority could reflect a view so manifestly out of balance. Unless the church is understood to go forth not only as a visible institution but also as "The Church Triumphant," and as the Body of Christ, a society already conditioned to feeling that much of life is lived in conformity to institutions will all but forget that the genius of the church is its existence in tension between the inspiration of the Holy Spirit and the historical tradition of order and practice, between their own parish and the grandeur of the ecumenical community. Without a constant recognition of this profound tension on the part of the clergy, laymen can hardly be expected to feel that they have much connection with what centuries of Christians have known as The Church Invisible.

Another possible explanation for the predominantly institutional bias of the parish minister is his common belief that loyalty to the institutional church provides a steppingstone in Christian growth. Thus, it is alleged, persons who first become interested in the church as an organization can by this means advance to the worthier end of seeing the church in terms of mission and of evangelism. This idea would carry more weight, were it not for the evidence that too many churchmen get mired into the means and never move on to the next admirable stage.

Now it is important also to show that an impressive number of responses, 31 per cent to be exact, did display a more inclusive view of the church when they answered this question about what the church expects of families. Their category of replies can be classified as faith-centered. They had stressed a loyalty to Christ, a commitment to Christian witness, an understanding of missionary outreach, of prayer life, of growth in the faith, obligations in evangelism, and so on. It is fascinating to trace the cross tabulations of such replies and to learn who answers what. We dare not burden the reader with complete statistical correlations at every point; but it may prove informative to illustrate from occasional examples what trends are noticeable. Here, for instance, occurs a conspicuous gap. One class of clergymen who did *not* reply in terms of faith-centered categories were the administrative pastors in larger-than-average churches. It was such a man, often the senior minister of a staff in a church of 600 to 1199 adult members, who was least likely to couch his answers in faith-centered terminology. This statistical observation permits of no illogical generalization, such as an inference that the senior staff member in a larger church so assigns specific responsibilities that someone else is responsible for the religious side of parish life. It does permit the rather easily documented suggestion that ministers who are charged with the administration of a growing, demanding organization are understandingly tempted to begin to think more in organizational terms than once they had.

The third largest group of answers here occur in the home-centered category. Almost 27 per cent[15] are recorded as understanding their Christian families as those who specialize in religion at home. Their concepts emphasized that Christian parents are expected to fulfill their baptismal vows, to prepare opportunities for Christian nurture in the family, to set a Christian example to their children, and to pray in their family fellowship. Such an opinion helps to fill out the previously reported finding that pastors are convinced that a strong link exists between church and home.

Questionnaires also are capable of picking up some feeling content in answers. A minority of responses, a scant four per cent, picture the church as expecting entirely too little of parishioner families. They would seem to subscribe to a not unfamiliar view that the community of Christian faith does not demand enough today from its members, and that as a result they invest more loyalty and interest in nonchurch activities than they ever think of putting into spiritual life. Without pausing to look down the interesting byway available here, and separating once again the institutional from the noninstitutional aspects, we briefly note that to many church members the Christian yoke has become altogether too easy and their burden all too light because they fail to hear with understanding the gospel's word about the cost of discipleship. It can fairly be concluded from these data that the average pastor tends overmuch to interpret his church life in subjective terms of its organization and only secondarily, and sometimes seldom, as commitment and witness to its Christian faith in home and community. Not unmixed with such a finding is the current building boom in church plants, the growth of church membership, the comparative prosperity of an organization that knows little of sacrifice and is mindful of the needs of others only when prompted by carefully organized campaigns, popularly known as "One Great Hour of Sharing," "The Every Member Canvass" or "Religion in American Life."

Expectations of the Church

The relationships existing between church and home have a converse side, namely, what the parents expect of the church. We had gathered data on this subject from the parents themselves, as reported in Chapter 6. Yet it was useful to ascertain also what pastors themselves believed that parents expected from their church life. This would supply a clue to what they felt their pastoral ministry ought to be. Their image of parental expectations ranged from "everything" to "nothing." That is to say, there were some pastors, one out of every four, who contend that parents expect the church to take over the entire task of teaching their children, relieving them entirely of any responsibility; there were others, about ten per cent, who give a wholly opposite view, namely, that parents really expect nothing at all of the church. A surprising number of these comments were made with strong emotional overtones, some even in bitterness. If parents made excessive demands upon the church, calling for more than the pastor feels they have a right to ask, or if on the other hand they thought so little of this phase of family life that they anticipated nothing at all from the church, their pastors could respond in terms of disillusion.

However, another portion of pastors would respond that parents, as they know them, really expect the church to present Christ and his gospel. They represent about one in five pastors in the sample, and have a higher than anticipated representation of suburban pastors. Another group of about 17 per cent would say that parents assign to the church the task of making their children religiously and morally good; and it was the younger men, recent graduates of seminary courses in which "moralism" is castigated, who responded so. A scattering of other replies emphasize expectations of a religious school program, a spiritual guidance program, a worshiping community, and a counseling service of reassurance and sympathy for their problems in personal and family life.

A sparse three per cent seem to feel that parents would look to the church merely for assistance in the Christian education of their children. Since this is the dominant philosophy of current home and church curriculum programs, the smallness of the group is a blow. Official interpretation of recent Christian curriculum programs has often laid stress on the role of the church to augment and assist the parents who are understood to be the only real communicators of the faith. The minuscule proportion represented in this answer may well be attributed to knowledgeable pastors who by now have enough experience to see through this debatable proposition.

Not only does the ratio between a helping church and an educating parent turn out to be impractical, but it also fails to face up to the fact that few parents (regardless of their pedagogical abilities) are able long to act in the capacity of teachers to their own children. It is enough, some authorities contend, for the parent to be a parent without visiting upon him the compulsion also to be a teacher. The relationship is conspicuously different; and it may as well be candidly admitted that children are able often to learn far more from a teacher outside the family than from mother or father. Moreover, a close reading of curriculum studies from a dozen denominations would show that irrespective of this interpretation of church-assisted parents, the curricula themselves are not edited that way. It could have been sheer realism that led most pastors to see the home-church relationship as something different from the official stand that holds the church has only to act in auxiliary capacity in Christian education.

Difficulties in Christian Family Living

Church families experience severe difficulty in attempting to measure up to standards of Christian living in their homes. They know it only too well, as their interviews disclosed; and pastors proved to be painfully aware of the same situation. When queried about obstacles present in their communities that militate against the building of Christian family life, they listed a number. Some of these are highly specific, others noticeably vague.

Far and away the most frequent obstacle reported by the pastors was this: a plethora of outside-the-home activities compete to separate the family and fan domestic friction. The pastor is well aware of the multiple activities in community life that divide households and dissipate their sense of unity. He has seen the little leagues, drama groups, extracurricular school activities, ski clubs, dances, garden groups, and bowling teams cut into family morale until it is all but impossible for fatigued parents and children even to be civil to each other, let alone live in a spirit of Christian charity. (There is, of course, a subjective aspect to this opinion that the parson holds about his parish homes. We were to learn that he himself feels keenly that manifold pressures upon his own time create conflicts in parsonage life; it was not unnatural that he would carry over something of this feeling into assessment of parish families.) Not unexpectedly, the clergymen in large churches of 1200 members and up cite this as a serious problem. Theirs is a busy and varied program that often feels the competition of community affairs; and they are usually located in booming metropolitan areas whose richness of cultural and recreational offerings could intensify competition for time and energy of families. Frequently their members are also active in numerous other civic and community causes and the numerous obligations they carry outside the home contrive to prevent sufficient attention to the rituals and collective life essential to Christian practices in the family. Those parishes which feature the most intensive educational program on behalf of church and home feel keenly this matter of the competition of time because adequate study of curriculum takes time and is better managed when it is buttressed by family discussion.

As a side issue, it is interesting to note that those pastors who serve parishes of less than 100 members infrequently report this concern. It may be that the rural communities, where so many of them are located, draw upon church members less for leadership and participation outside the church. Yet this would be debated by rural area experience wherein there are often as many and as hectic demands upon persons as in any urban community. The changing face of rural America shows substantially less of the bucolic, leisurely life than once it did. A more convincing guess, and one that is better founded upon handy evidence, is that the smaller rural churches have so modest a program beyond Sunday worship services that they feel the sting of competition less. If, as we surmise, these pastoral responses are heavily weighted by subjective considerations, this would be a potent factor.

A second concern, checked by almost as many pastors, reveals their judgment that sheer ignorance of the meaning of Christian family life and how to practice it, is an outstanding obstacle for these homes. Not a few Protestant clergymen cast admiring eyes on the traditional rituals in the homes of other faiths. To have some integral counterpart to the lighting of the Sabbath candles or the Seder feast in Jewish households, or the symbolism of crucifix and madonna figures on the walls of Roman Catholic households would seem to them to strengthen the reminders of family religion. Moreover, some see in the Cana Conference and the Catholic Family Movement an organized and self-conscious approach to educating families about religious teachings, and cannot help wishing that they had something as tangible.

Failing to establish a firm practice of daily worship within family groups, and concerned that comparatively little of the organized educational program for parents is getting through to family life, it is altogether understandable that Protestant clergymen are eager for the kind of group life and liturgy that will catch the imagination and loyalty of families. They know that in early Reformation homes, the children were instructed at the hearthside, that they learned the meaning of the priesthood of all believers and justification by faith at their mothers' knees. If Protestant homes of today are to live in historic remembrance of their heritage, they will need a more pervasive reminder than little devotional magazines and unread curriculum quarterlies. Pastors are doubtless perceptive in identifying the obstacle to Christian family living as an inside problem, namely ignorance of the meaning and practice of Christian faith.

As was usually the case with questionnaire items, a list of other answers fell into a heap of minority opinions after these top few categories. A number of pastors attributed to indifference and sin the lack of substantial Christian family living in their communities. Some feel that the disappearance of the family altar can be held accountable. Others seriously advance that newer architectural trends have eliminated the dining room from low-cost housing, and this works against the reading of the Bible in family groups because a venerated and habitual locale for this liturgy had been omitted. Blame is also placed on the fact that employed mothers are away from home so much, and the increasing trend for women to enter remunerative employment works against Christian family living.

Divided religious loyalties are credited with being another obstacle to Christian family living by some pastors. Although this proved not to be a widely spread problem in the sampling, where it was prevalent, it was deeply effective. The pastors had been questioned as to what percentage of their families had an interfaith make-up, that is to say, where one or more members of the immediate family is not an adherent of the Protestant faith. The median average turned out to be four per cent; and a full fifteen per cent of the churches reported no interfaith families at all. Paradoxically the smallest churches in the sample, those with less than 100 members, proved to be the most homogeneous and the most heterogeneous in this regard. Small rural churches seldom have interfaith families within their membership; but the small inner-city mission churches quite commonly have religiously split families. An easily understood geographical pattern stands out of this finding. Churches in our survey from the West and churches from the Northeast areas of the nation report the largest number of interfaith families. These regions also have heavy Roman Catholic populations. Proportionately fewer churches of the North Central and Southern sections of the country include many interfaith households.

Statisticians, in analyzing questionnaires, sometimes speak of "wastebasket categories," meaning by this untechnical jargon those items that fall into the remainder list after the significant top items have been tallied. Few conclusions can be derived from these remainders because they are simply left after a respondent has checked off the items most meaningful to him. Here at the wastebasket level of our survey we found categories that in themselves appear to be dynamically important, yet in their rank order here are statistically not significant. Some of them were checked by less than one-half of one per cent of the sample. These included such obstacles as neighborhood problems through the unchristian standards set by surrounding families, difficulties with liquor because alcoholic drinks are too easy to obtain and use, and tensions that are created at work but expressed in the home.

Perhaps this last classification, the very bottom of the list in order of rank, is significant not because of statistical considerations but for a negative reason. The fact that pastors thought this was so unimportant is strange because much of contemporary literature and experience points up the fact that work tensions do ricochet into the home. William Whyte's *Is Anybody Listening?*[16] describes how the business man brings home his office worries with his attaché case and how these pervade the whole atmosphere of the home. The numerous family advice columns syndicated throughout the nation's newspapers repeatedly advise wives how to reduce the tension in a home-coming husband at evening time so that the entire household will not be disturbed. Women's magazines are replete with articles on this topic and make many a suggestion: first feed friend husband a hearty dinner and only then discuss problems with him, or spirit the children out of his sight until he has an opportunity to loosen his tie and read the evening paper, and so on, sometimes *ad absurdum.*

The irony is even more pronounced when we add up two other factors. The parents themselves had been asked just what things disturb them and need improvement in their family living; and they ranked "Husband's Job and Its Demands" among the first six in a list of 25 possible items. But more interesting was the introspective look the pastors cast at their own parsonage families. The pastor had been given the opportunity to rank a series of categories in their order of importance to him when asked what family problems ministers most frequently have. First and top by a clear lead was his opinion that too many demands on the pastor leave him without time for his own family. Just why the clergy would be so painfully aware of the pressure their own professional work brings to bear on family life and so oblivious to the same phenomenon in parishioners' homes is puzzling. It may, however, be related to the sharp and unfortunate distinction made by innumerable clergymen as well as laymen between what is designated as sacred and what is considered to be secular. The pastor so often has a Sunday-oriented view of his parish breadwinners. He knows them best in their dark suits, pursuing what for them is a leisure-time activity, and removed both by days and miles from their life of work. The removal of man's work from home to a plant some distance from home has years ago so separated his life's poles that most of his acquaintances know him only in one or the other of these situations. It is the misfortune of the minister to recognize him chiefly in his nonwork, home, and church aspect of living. He seldom sees his parishioners in their workaday world or understands the burdens they bear there and carry with them as they leave. This partial view of a man calls for correction if the pastor is to deal with the whole person and minister to his complex of needs and circumstances.

There are, of course, notable exceptions to this picture. Some ministers are acutely aware of the professional, business, and laboring hours of their parishioners; they call on them at their place of work; and they comprehend something of the effect such work has upon family relationships. It ought always to be recognized in these statistical interpretations that the broad and general averages are achieved *because* there are extremes which figure into the calculation. Admittedly some Protestant clergymen are alive to the work-connected home problems of their people; that is how it ranked at all in the list. The remarkable thing is that so few ministers could be sensitive to a problem among their parishioners when they themselves found it so vexing.

Pastors Evaluate Their Ministry to Families

Through a semiprojective question, pastors were asked to assess the value of their pastoral services to parish families. To do this, they wrote into the questionnaire blank just those two functions that seemed to them most effective in their contributions to family stability. Replies elicited by this query give us insight not only into which ministerial tasks can be productive, but also into those phases of his work that the clergyman himself feels are important and worthwhile.

In order of rank from those mentioned most often to the least, we find (1) pastoral counseling, (2) visitation in parish homes, (3) preaching on family life subjects, (4) the pastor's personal attitudes and family life example, (5) the general Christian education program and organizational life of the parish, (6) his promotion of families worshiping together in the church, (7) his promotion of families worshiping together at home, (8) special family events planned by the church, (9) married couples' clubs, (10) personal evangelism, (11) use of the curriculum materials designed for church and home.

There is no justification for concluding that the preponderance of individual pastors would rank their ministerial tasks in just this order. We can only observe that the majority of pastors answered in a way that combines to make this average, and that the list represents an analysis of replies from 1000 typical pastors, anyone of whom might differ sharply from the broad and general listing. For a closer examination, we shall group the most significant of these into three categories and scrutinize some of their meanings. These are counseling and home visitation, preaching and corporate worship, the teaching and educational ministry.

Counseling and Home Visitation

Counseling and calling in the homes of the parish go so naturally together that it is difficult to speak of one without consideration of the other. The pastor is a counselor not only when he meets persons in his study upon appointment, but also (and perhaps especially) when his visitation routine takes him into the homes of the congregation. One man attached this note to his returned questionnaire: *"I have learned to be sensitive to the need for counseling, so that there are few of my pastoral calls that do not involve a counseling situation to some degree. Even with new families I frequently, if not almost invariably, find some point of need expressed by the persons I visit."* In fact, some pastors do all their counseling work through informal contacts in visiting, while drinking coffee with a man at a local restaurant, or even, as one respondent says, "while talking with a parishioner at the street corner before the traffic light changes." Overlooking a question about how effective traffic light counseling may be, it is enough to note that pastoral contacts with parishioners take many forms and are given a high priority by pastors in their ministry to families. Counseling and visiting work prove to be a time-consuming factor in the pastor's busy schedule, the questionnaire demonstrates. Together they approximate the total hours each week that he puts into preparation and preaching of sermons.

If counseling is to be defined as the discussion of personal problems presented to pastors either in the office or during their calling, the total time required for most men each week would not be enormous. The range of hours runs from less than one hour to more than forty for the 1,000 pastors whose records we sampled. Rural pastors cluster at the small end of this continuum; as a group they do little "clinical" counseling. One of them ventures why this is so: *"I have found that members in rural churches are more reticent about their personal problems than city people; in fact, those who do talk over their problems with me most readily have come from urban backgrounds."* Younger pastors also have less opportunity for pastoral counseling even though they consider it important and have been trained in this skill relatively recently. The newer understanding of the pastor's role in counseling has come as much from the therapeutic disciplines as from theology; but both these fields have prominent places in seminary curricula today. It may be some years in a young pastor's experience, nonetheless, before parishioners comfortably confide in him. His youth and his lack of experience work against his effectiveness in this field, if only because parishioners incline to trust the middle-age minister more, and more readily seek him out.

It is the middle-age pastors as a group, as a matter of fact, who more often listed counseling as a chief contribution of their family ministry. And if these men are in multiple-staff churches, the odds are increased markedly that they will spend a premium amount of their work week as counselors. Larger churches with a staff of ministers not only have more calls made upon them for counseling, but often provide more opportunity for it through formalized procedures of appointments; they may have rooms that have been set aside for this ministerial function, and particular assignments for one or more staff members to specialize in this work. Yet, taken as a whole, pastors are spending a median average of just about five hours per week in counseling about personal problems. But it was a difficult estimate for ministers to make. As one of them wrote, *"My best counseling may be done on the sidewalk, or in a right word to people coming into or going out of the church service, in my conduct and attitude while visiting, or in administering the sacraments. In terms of this, it is impossible to state a particular number of hours spent in counseling."*

It does seem clear though that if we account for a man's span of ministry, and allow for the first few years when formal counseling is rare, add in the considerable visitation that the clerical caller does week in and week out, this ministry calls for an appreciable portion of his time. Even though the younger parson may counsel seldom (one of them ruefully reviewed the concentrated training he had received in pastoral psychology now followed by so little experience in the field and lamented: *"Here I am, all dressed up with no place to go!"*) and rural parsons may not label much of their visiting as counseling, a close reading of the research data confirms that the clergy are deeply immersed in that which has been known historically as the cure of souls. It may be less in the form of psychological services after the manner of psychiatry and more in the field of pastoral care; but the contemporary cleric is indubitably making a contribution here in his ministry to persons.

Pastors leave no doubt whatever as to the high value they put on this phase of their ministerial experience. When given opportunity to list the work that afforded them the most personal enjoyment and sense of accomplishment, they unhesitatingly delineated counseling, preaching, and visitation. Teaching and study followed close behind with the leadership of worship. But leadership recruitment and training, and administrative detail trailed far behind. Such a list would, of course, reflect to some extent the normative view of the way a man's ministry should be; but even allowing for this relatively subjective note in the line-up, it is an important finding.

The average pastor appears to be testifying that he likes best those phases of his labor that bring him into face-to-face contact with his people. His is a highly personal work, and its satisfactions are chiefly in terms of lives touched, of persons helped, of people who mature in their faith. Not only that, but the average clergyman, for all his extroverted behavior, is at times a lonely man. He carries confidences he dare not share, even with his helpmeet. He values friendship, yet may feel unable to have close intimate friends in his parish lest he be tempted by intimacy to reveal closely guarded secrets of his people—or sometimes because the very selection of an intimate friend raises resentments among parishioners who have not been so favored. Moreover, his very life in prayer with its intercessions on behalf of persons whose needs he knows so well, his inevitable sense of spiritual inadequacy for the high calling he feels, and with his periodic bouts with doubt and "the dark night of the soul" will increase feelings of aloneness. So much the more then will he find satisfaction and reward in those areas of his pastorate where he is in contact with persons.

Types of Family Counseling

Counseling in the Protestant ministry is not an end in itself. It is a portion of the entire pastoral task; and much of its function is educational. The pastor who understands his counseling task apart from the entire ministry of Christian education not only may fail to meet the larger obligations in his calling, but he may also turn out to be a poor counselor. One pastor returns an extra note with his questionnaire to say: *"A hard core of common sense is most needed, plus hard study in his own biblical field. All other learning seems futile if the minister lacks these."* Some of his finest educational opportunities come through face-to-face contacts with persons who bring questions that require counsel. The parent puzzled by a child's behavior, the family experiencing the hurt and guilt that accompany grief, the timidity of a bride before a wedding: these present an educational opportunity as well as the chance to aid persons to work through their feelings.

The pastor's first line of work, of course, is theological. His best counseling techniques, by far, involve connecting the teaching of the gospel with day-to-day contacts with people. His aim is to assist them in gaining spiritual maturity. Even to embark upon this course, he more than most people will have to keep grounded in the great verities of the Christian faith and to wait upon the Lord to renew his strength. Unless he remains unremittingly aware of his peculiar vocation, his counseling could slide into a professionalized attitude of mere helpfulness or a reference service disconnected from the compassion and work of the gospel ministry.

The great majority of problems to which he counsels even in as broad a definition of pastoral care as we have been indicating, will be of family nature. Premarital guidance, counseling with parents or individuals at times of baptism, conferences at occasions of confirmation, comfort in periods of bereavement: all these developmental stages in family life bring the pastor into his counseling ministry. But so do crises that are laid before him; marital strife,[17] parents-children tensions, severe illness, deep disappointment, emotional illnesses. Seldom, if ever, are these critical problems without their family connotations or their educational opportunities in the Christian faith.

In the course of pastoral counseling a minister will come up against problems that he cannot cope with alone. They call for referral or consultation with specialists whose training has better fitted them for such work. Often these are in the area of psychoneuroses; and the pastor is keenly mindful that they require therapy more than they do Christian education or even pastoral care. In the survey, we had asked the pastors about those problems in which they would generally feel the need for referral or collaboration with some counseling specialist. In order of their rank, these were the most frequently mentioned: Sexual inversion, for example, homosexuality was checked by nine out of ten pastors; persons whose personal or family problems are connected with deep neuroses had been checked by four out of every five respondents; half of the men indicated that drinking patterns connected with family strife were out of their line; slightly under half did not feel that family conflicts are in their line of work when they have reached the point of physical violence; one out of four indicate they cannot counsel with a quite close acquaintance they know especially well; a similar proportion feel unqualified to discuss sexual relations with couples planning marriage; another 25 per cent do not feel equipped to counsel in cases of illegitimacy and would refer these; and only 14 per cent (although even this number is puzzling among our married clergy) would not touch problems of parents-children relationships and family discipline.

We had learned through interviews with representatives of the helping professions that they agree there are several counseling areas from which the ordinary parson should steer clear. They had clearly indicated that counseling with deep emotional problems is the province of the psychologically oriented counselor. They see a division of labor in preventive and remedial work, feeling that the church specializes in the former and they regretfully in the latter. Their frequent point that the church fellowship itself serves in an educational way to support persons and strengthen mental health is a reminder to the pastor that in this ministry he seldom works alone.

For diagnosis and treatment, the pastor does well to make referral to a psychiatrist whose province this is, these experts had insisted. Just what the pastor in an isolated rural area could do, however, is quite another question. Men who had returned the questionnaires included those who were 120 miles from the nearest psychiatrist; and he was more often than not on the overloaded staff of a mental hospital. In many counties of modern U.S.A. (the estimates run up to 50 per cent), the pastor may be the only professional person who has had any training in the psychological sciences. Nor is this situation rapidly improving, because the trend is away from the farm and the situation worsens as more resources are lost to rural America annually. The challenge in this migration calls for an even more adequately prepared ministry, alert to the early symptoms of personality troubles. He must be able to mobilize the resources of the total life of the countryside, and must be in close working relationship with the welfare department of the county, the home demonstration service, the 4-H clubs, and all rural institutions. Many a rural pastor does a remarkable job without even knowing how much he accomplishes in pastoral care. By going about their normal work, some of them perform functions in marriage education, and helping personalities to develop and adjust, without ever calling attention to this work.

With the decline of rural church strength in recent years, and the frequent assignment of the youngest and least experienced men to rural pastorates, there is cause for deep concern over what counseling services can be available to farm areas. If the pastor is often to be the only trained counselor within miles, and he is unseasoned in the ministry, the picture is hardly bright for improvement. Even if the rural areas involve less problem counseling on the average, partly because of their lesser population density, there we did locate exceptional areas that involve a heavy load of counseling among farm people;[18] and we were reminded by frequent data of the need for preventive group work in these sections.

The Pastor and Community Resources

Because pastors reported they do not feel comfortable or competent to counsel about some problems involving neuroses and abnormal behavior, and since the interdisciplinary consultants had registered so definite an opinion that clergymen should refer to the psychiatrically oriented services when parishioners require therapy, it is useful to inquire what they do about community resources. The questionnaire had listed fifteen family serving agencies to be found in typical American metropolitan communities; and the respondent was asked to check which of these was to be found in his area. More than that, he had an opportunity to tell whether he had ever used these community resources for referral or had announced their program and availability to his congregation. The results indicate only a modest use of referral services in the pastoral ministry. Because research itself helps to alter attitudes, it could be surmised that this very exercise would have led some clergymen to turn anew to the assistance open to them in the locale.

TABLE 6 PERCENTAGE OF PASTORS USING COMMUNITY RESOURCES FOR REFERRAL

Community Resource	*Percentage of Pastors Referring*
1. Physicians	52%
2. Alcoholics Anonymous	47%
3. Private psychiatrists	30%
4. Family counselors	29%
5. Family service agency	26%
6. Agricultural extension parent classes	23%
7. Public health clinic	22%
8. Child guidance or psychiatric clinic	20%
9. Consulting psychologists	18%
10. Vocational counselors	18%
11. Lawyers specializing in family relations cases	13%
12. PTA parents' classes	12%
13. Planned Parenthood Associations	10%
14. YM or YWCA courses on marriage	9%
15. Church counseling center	6%

We had no way of determining through the questionnaire whether a pastor actually knew every family-serving agency in his community or whether he was merely checking off those which he had referred to, leaving unmentioned others that might be in the neighborhood but untouched in his ministry. There are some 487 national organizations working in the family-serving field; but no one area in the country would have branches of every one of these. One out of three pastors could not tell us whether the nearest high school offered any courses in family relations or preparation for marriage. Sometimes ministers whose sons and daughters were enrolled in that school could not answer, we learned in one pretest.

Physicians turn out to be the clear favorite of pastors for referral possibilities. In many parishes the minister and physician work hand in hand on the cases of disturbed persons; and their teamwork is frequently beneficial. Still even this, the most frequent of referral connections, is called upon by only half of the pastors.

The relationship between the pastor and his community resources is, to put it modestly, not a close one. This analysis of 1000 pastoral records simply confirms a number of observations from social workers themselves. In Charles F. Kemp's manual, *The Pastor and Community Resources,* he tells of the social worker who was disturbed at learning that most persons prefer to turn to their church in time of trouble because he feared the pastor would not know the resources that were available or might not make the effort to secure adequate help. Then the author adds:

> The pastor, for the good of his people, has the obligation to be informed about community resources. This may be a difficult task, especially in larger cities. There is a great variety of agencies, public and private, local, state, and national, all providing different services; nevertheless the very number increases the possibility of securing help. The pastor must know not only the agencies in general (such as are described in the textbooks in an introduction to social work); he must know also what particular resources are available in his own community. All communities differ. The services that are available in Chicago, Cleveland, or New York are quite different from the services that are available in a small town in Minnesota or a county-seat town in Wyoming, for example. He does need to know the over-all pattern of community resources as such. He also needs to know what exists in this town where his people live and work. He must know more than what agencies exist. He should know the people who operate them, what their effectiveness is, what are their attitudes and points of view, what they are prepared to do and what they can't do. There is no point in requesting a service that an agency is not prepared to give, or which may be forbidden by law. One of a pastor's first tasks is to become acquainted with these men and women who work in these other fields. Successful referral and interprofessional co-operation is a result of mutual acquaintance and understanding. It works most effectively when the pastor and the social worker, or doctor, or teacher, or whoever it may be, know

each other and understand the role or position the other expects to fill.[19]

There remains much room for improvement in the relationships between clergy and community services. Family Life Clinics, conducted under the National Council of Churches Department of Family Life, found that in more than a dozen American cities, clergymen and social workers were neither acquainted with each other nor inclined to be particularly friendly. Suspicion and misunderstanding can develop where no attempt is made to see how hands can be joined in a division of labor for mutual benefit and for the welfare of persons. Community agency personnel are able to guide the pastor at a number of points where he is unlikely to be competent himself. They are skilled at sociological analysis, in research and its interpretation, in diagnosis and treatment, and in counseling with deeper emotional problems.

From our research there emerges a strong plea on the part of the helping professions for churches and community agencies to pool their resources in helping families in need of counseling and relief. A family can become sick in somewhat the same way that a person can; and churches in any community will need to clear with each other and with social agencies their plans and progress in ministering to families. Churches and community agencies would do well to have a periodic inventory of local helping professions and resources in order to avoid duplication and to open the way to efficient service. Although this would hardly solve all problems, it just might solve one, namely, opening the way to communication between pastors and social workers. Misunderstandings between these two disciplines have prevented a comprehensive approach to their collective problems in a number of cities.

It would not be a bad idea, one social caseworker advanced in an interview with the authors, for a parish church to make an organizational contact with one particular agency (for example, a child guidance clinic), become thoroughly acquainted with its work, budget some funds for the agency, and consider their staff as part-time staff of the church. Such a plan, now unique in any church-agency co-operation, could go a long way toward opening the way for group approaches on local problems they share. It could even begin to effect a *rapprochement* with those agency workers who are now the most critical of church leadership. One such group of more than 500 social work consultants in New York City reveal that they have not made a referral to a church in the past ten years because "we never think of the church as a place where our people get help."[20]

If pastors are remiss in referring cases to the social workers, the social workers in turn seldom appeal to the advantages of the church for help in community affairs. But one agency executive, in an interview with the authors, expressed an envy of the church's genius and an appreciation of what it can do: "The church is not so rigidly specific as our agency. The church is usually able to do what needs to be done with less repair of machinery and less conflict of interest. Here is a community of faith that can influence people to achieve personal integrity, gain interpersonal competence, increase skills in relationships, and find new avenues of communication. And one of the readiest means of bridging the communication gulf is in the experience of family life. Everyone has some family orientation. To speak to that memory, or to use that experience is the privilege of any church in its religious education."

Referrals, it became apparent from close study of the data, depend upon several correlative situations. By and large, younger men in the ministry, newer graduates from seminaries, turn more readily to the other helping professions when in doubt than do their maturer brethren. The extent of counseling training likewise plays a part in such decisions; and, predictably, the men with more training make more use of referrals. Needless to say, the nearby availability of help makes a difference too, although realism compels us to note that numerous clergymen eschew professional relationships close at hand because they may be unaware of them, distrustful of them, or untrained in how to approach them. Quite evidently, the tendency to refer depends more on the relationship built up with these helping professions than on the seriousness of the counseling problem. To the extent that such contacts have been developed, they have proved valuable to clergymen, social caseworkers, and psychiatrists alike.

Premarital Interviewing

Premarital interviewing is by now an established part of the pastor's repertoire of shepherding skills. The majority of pastors now offer some planned premarital guidance; but the average pastor, we found, does not have many opportunities for this work. He officiates at only four or five weddings per year, on a median average. Eleven per cent of these pastors reported no weddings at all during the year preceding the survey; most of these were in smaller rural churches. (At the other extreme, some city pastors report they keep busy with more than 100 weddings annually.) It is difficult for the average pastor to develop his skills in this line without more experience in it. Frequent practice will not necessarily make perfect; but any criticism of pastoral abilities must consider this factor. A realistic review of this factor may compel a revision of some seminary courses to allow for more role playing in premarital interviewing and a revision of the literature to take into account the infrequency and the unfamiliarity of many pastors with the field.

For the pastor relies heavily upon literature in his premarital work. Three out of every four respondents of the questionnaire told that they give or lend books and pamphlets to those couples at whose weddings they officiate. Some three dozen different titles were listed by the pastors as useful for this purpose. We glean the impression from our data, however, that the pastors seldom discuss the content of these books with the couple. Apparently the printed page too often serves in lieu of a personal relationship, rather than as a means of enriching the interview.

The pastor's favorite interview guide is the marriage service itself. The majority (65 per cent) attempt to stimulate thought about the marriage relationship by reference to the very words of the service they use in the wedding. Seasoned pastors know what depth of insight can be found in the time-honored sentences of that liturgy. Point by point, as they discuss the inferences of the service, they find that most topics of importance to marriage are covered. It has the advantage of being an educational technique with a more-than-human reference. The worship element in the service emphasizes the God-given genius of the one-flesh relationship; but this is not all. With rare candor, the service mentions realistic expectations of marriage in its familiar pairs of richer or poorer, in sickness and in health, for better or for worse.

It was found that pastors differ widely in what topics they feel are appropriate for these sessions in premarital guidance.[21] Most men were willing to talk with couples about their religious responsibilities in the new home they were about to form, the religious backgrounds of the couples, the symbolism and meaning of the wedding service itself. At least two out of three pastors found no difficulty in these subjects; these corresponded to his conception of his role. But when it came to the more personal topics, a change can be detected. Just half would regularly bring up topics about interpersonal relationships of engagement and marriage. Only one out of four speak of planning for parenthood, housing plans, or in-law relationships. Family background information, anticipated economic arrangements, and sex attitudes were considered proper to the premarital interview by less than half of these pastors.[22]

Upon a cursory reading of the list one might be forgiven for wondering if the contemporary clergyman realizes what goes on in the minds of marrying young couples today. If he spends so much time on the "sacred" side of marriage and so little on the personal, is he veering off from his Reformation heritage with its strong insistence that false distinctions between sacred and secular be eradicated?[23] This may be the case, but there are other factors to be considered.

It should not be decided in advance that the "ideal" pastor systematically discusses all these topics with every couple he marries. For one thing, the nondirectively oriented pastor (unusual as he may be) might not wish to bring up specific topics for discussion but "having indicated his availability the pastor would then allow the couple to bring forward a problem or not as they wished."[24] Perceiving the pastor in his religious role, it is not unlikely that the couple would introduce religious topics. Still, this explanation must account for only a few of the cases in which the homiletical subjects predominated in premarital interviews.

More likely is the guess that pastors themselves are human enough to experience some anxieties about personal and sexual topics and often omit them for that very reason. The sociologist may have an insight for us too as he reminds us that community situations affect a person's status and role. (In support of this, our data clearly show that rural pastors were almost twice as likely to skirt around subjects of sexual relationship, and planned parenthood as the metropolitan pastors. They had also done far less with housing arrangements, in-law relationships, and family background of the couple in their premarital interview sessions. Rural community mores and close-knit relationships are doubtlessly related to these choices.) The sociological dimension cannot be ignored.

So many factors were shown by the survey to contribute to the variety of interviewing patterns among pastors that it would be all but impossible to come up with either a picture of what the average pastor (that fictional figure of statistics) or what the ideal premarital interview could be. The pastor's age, his use of specialized community resources, his background and training, locale, and parishioners make such a difference that it is obvious that educational assistance of several types are needed for the different situations that surround premarital interviewing. Pastors had indicated that they feel the need for new literature in this field, not just to hand to the couples but something for themselves so that they might be better prepared for this exacting ministry. One man included with his questionnaire a quite unsolicited note in which he made known his opinion:

It would be far better to publish a course with basic requirements for premarital counseling instead of leaving the entire educational task of preparing people for Christian marriage up to the individual pastor. The pastor is too much of a jack of all trades to do this job as well as a specialist could. Christ said, "Feed my sheep"; but we parsons are spread so thin we are treating people as guinea pigs.

Baptism and Counseling

For a group of pastors from the Reformed tradition, respondents in the questionnaire survey proved strangely unmotivated to counsel with parents about the sacrament of baptism for their children. Reformed churches provide for Christian baptism both for infants and for adults, but put special stress on admitting the young child into the church family through this rite. Historically, this has meant that a priceless opportunity is ready for the pastor to interpret to his people some tenets of their faith as well as some pertinent teachings about child rearing and family life. The way is open for a significant counseling opportunity at the developmental stage where parents bring their young children to the church for the sacrament. Seminary training and denominational tradition have laid stress on the desirability for pastors to hold conferences with parents at this step, to explain to them some of the major doctrines of the church as these relate to the acceptance of their child, and to help them to see clearly their task as Christian parents.

Yet with all this recognition that baptism provides an important contact between church and home, we have no compelling evidence that many pastors are adequately helping parents to enter into this relationship, either through counseling sessions or through the parents' classes that have been effectively organized in some parishes. Just half of the pastors replied that they hold any regular interviews with parents of children about to be baptized. Younger men, it turns out, are the most likely to be aware of the need for this practice and to follow it through. Without doubt, this has some connection with their recent classes in theological schools where they are trained to provide a more complete pastoral ministry.

A marked correlation is seen between the practice of baptism counseling and the general educational stance of a parish church. If the church makes rather complete use of denominational curriculum materials, if they are alive to the possibilities in Christian education for their parish, the likelihood is that they will not only attract larger crowds of children in their church school, but, our statistics show, they will also have more baptisms as well as more careful counseling about baptism.

The frequency of baptisms, of course, plays a part here; and the statistics are of interest. The average church in our survey reports a median of ten children baptized during a year. Six of every one hundred churches in the sample reported no baptism at all for the preceding year. The picture of adult baptism differs considerably. Here the significance is also somewhat different because the adult who comes for baptism is taking this step on his own volition and understanding rather than upon the commitment of parents. His is a preparatory step to uniting with the community of faith. On the average, churches in the sample had four such baptisms a year. Larger churches in urban and suburban areas, particularly those with a multiple staff of ministers, report substantially more than this average of four. It may be safely assumed that more counseling goes on with these adults than with the parents of children at time of baptism. Ministers traditionally discuss the meaning of church membership and the marks of the Christian faith with persons making their first profession of faith. This is an integral activity in evangelism.

That half of them neglect to explain the significance and implications of this sacrament to parents is not only strange. It is an omission that may complicate their pastoral work and cause them subsequent problems in the educational program. Given the importance of the sacrament of baptism to the theology and polity of a church in the Reformed tradition, one might reasonably expect that adequate counseling about it would be practically universal.

It could provide one of those opportunities for preventive and educational counseling that had been singled out by members of other helping professions as the church's unusual privilege. Evidently many pastors remain yet to be convinced.

Vocational Counseling

Research turns up its little surprises. The researchers seek one type of information, but sometimes uncover important items they had not expected to find significant at all. The wide interest in counseling about Christian vocation was such a finding. This phase of pastoral work proves to be on the increase. Some 42 per cent of the pastors reported that they regularly engage in conversations about their vocations with young people and adults; and of six types of counseling it ranked second in frequency only to the field of husband-wife relations.[25] In one question where pastors were given a chance to indicate how their ministerial plans are changing, they show that they are planning to step up this phase of their program substantially in church school, discussion groups, and interviewing. Parents of young people had stated their strong desire for the church to assist in this field, as do the young people themselves.

Recent conferences of public school guidance people and Protestant church representatives have concluded that the churches should not supplant the services offered by public agencies but rather supplement their services and enlist greater public support for them. Protestant denominations might well supply such centers with adequate information about church vocations. In addition to the self-assessment which the school guidance centers can provide Protestant young people, they need an opportunity to explore the relation of their faith to the job. To have helpful guidance at this point, particularly from a pastor who brings with him the Protestant understanding of Christian vocation, can be highly valuable. Seminary training is being stepped up in this field. A news release tells of a recent young adults conference where the consensus was that churches be urged to arrange group discussions on vocations, and afford opportunities for young people to interview Christians employed in various fields. "The conferees questioned whether the average pastor possesses the technical knowledge necessary for sound vocational counseling. They also asserted that many pastors do not know all their young people as individuals and do not have their full confidence."

Yet it is not only the young who have need for vocational guidance. Many an adult wrestles with problems of his vocational commitment, particularly if he is sensitive to the Christian values involved. The men's organizations in church life have in recent years sponsored a number of conferences on the inferences that Christianity has for their work. Groups of lawyers, of business men, of artists and other craftsmen have come together to ask searching questions about their own ministry on the job.

The emergence of occupation as a locus of values for the family has been pointed out previously. And these values are easily absorbed by the children partly because of the keen awareness the parents have of the problem. They want vocational guidance for their youth. But what here appears to be the parents' concern that their children choose aright may also reflect a desire to recover the meaning of vocation in today's world for themselves. These middle-age parents, our pastors discover, are stuck with their life's major decisions; they have few options left. Their own children have the opportunity to do what parents can no longer do; consequently parents are vicariously involved in the major decisions of their offspring. This observation is but one more bit of evidence that the pastor, and director of religious education, even in the area of vocational guidance must take the family as a whole into account.

The Growing Interest in Counseling

Strongly and clearly through many a study and from hundreds of schools and institutes for pastors comes the word that pastors have a growing interest in their work of counseling. We had found that ministers felt this feature of their pastoral care to be one of their two greatest contributions to family stability (the other being their ministry of preaching and worship). From it they revealed that they gain more sense of satisfaction and accomplishment than from any other ministry they perform. Nor is that all. They had been asked to rank ten functions in the order of those they would most like to improve through special training if given the opportunity and time. The list is instructive for what it reveals of their assessment of their own ministerial tasks and where abilities play a part. Counseling heads the list.

TABLE 7 PASTORAL PREFERENCES FOR ADDITIONAL IN-SERVICE TRAINING

1. Counseling
2. Leadership training and recruitment
3. Preaching and preparation of sermons
4. Prayer and devotional life
5. Methods of reading and study
6. Organizational strategy and program
7. Teaching and youth leadership
8. Worship, rites, and sacraments
9. Pastoral calling
10. Improving church efficiency through correspondence, records, committees

The earnestness of the ministers in granting this priority to counseling training can be judged by the type of training they would choose. They chose the hard way: more men favored a three-month clinical training course than any other possibility. Other and lesser votes went for a course in guided reading (which could be a far easier way to learn a few things), one- and two-day discussion seminars, ministers' study retreats, seminary courses, and six-session practice courses in that order.[26]

Scores of letters accompanied the questionnaires although there had been no request or encouragement for this practice. Many of the writers alluded to their counseling experience, or to this need for improving this demanding area of their ministry. One pastor of an inner-city church writes:

> *Family life here is in a high degree of disintegration. The nation-wide problems are magnified here because of a great many women working, low educational levels, lack of social agencies to deal with family problems, and general culture of the area. Values in family life are a long way from those of typical middle-class Protestants. It is the rule rather than the exception for women here to become pregnant before marriage. There is need for leaders of our church to understand industrial people, what their life is really like, and how they think.*

Whatever their situation, urban, suburban, or rural, pastors everywhere are seeking additional help in their counseling because these problems are growing more complicated and difficult as our culture grows more complex and unfathomable.

The majority of them would prefer to have had more help in pastoral psychology during their seminary education. No less than 78 per cent expressed the viewpoint that their seminaries failed to give them adequate preparation for this ministry to families. A write-in question offered respondents the chance to make up an ideal seminary course; and they leaned heavily toward the practical fields. If they had their theological courses to take over again and had the option to elect their own courses[27] throughout, these they said, would be their preferences in order: General Pastoral Psychology and Counseling, Family Counseling, Pastoral Theology, Dynamics and Sociology of the Family, Advanced Clinical Work, General Education, and Church Administration. One pastor pointed up the inadequacy of his seminary training for his present work with families in appending this note:

> *I am quite sure that the seminary I attended when I attended it, was not only of no help in this matter of the ministry to families but in all probability was of some harm in preparing me for the kind of work I find myself now expected to do, and wanting to do. We studied Hebrew for a year and a half, Greek for three years (including college) and for one semester, once a week, we had a "visiting dignitary" who gave us pastoral psychology.*

Neither the name of the man nor the name of his seminary accompanied the note. But the expression of resentment at a seminary deficiency is of interest. The reader cannot pass over that last verb "gave" without reflecting that it is probably an accurate description of how the course was taught. Impressive unanimity can be assembled from all our samplings from pastors, parents, social agency workers, psychologists, and educators that theological seminaries could materially improve their course offerings in the pastoral psychology fields.

The deep interest, indeed sometimes the vehemence, detectable in the tone of these questionnaires and additional letters underscores the strong emphasis that ministers now place in their counseling. It may be that the median average spend just five hours weekly in that which is designated as formal counseling; but if those five hours are devoted to a problem of illegitimacy, or of a breaking marriage, or concerning a retarded child, the poignancy of those hours would but cry for greater skills and for more training in competence. The rising interest in all aspects of pastoral care has attracted comment from many sources; and a variety of suggestions are advanced to explain it. The motives certainly are complicated; but we offer several accepted interpretations, together with our judgment about them.

1. Pastors can be drawn to the practice of counseling because they may be more interested in the work and the status of the psychiatrist than that of the minister of the gospel. While this is undoubtedly true of some few clergymen, those most closely connected with the training of pastors consider that only a minority are ever motivated by this tendency to see the grass so green on the other side of the professional fence. The extensive study by H. Richard Niebuhr, Daniel Day Williams, and James M. Gustafson corroborates this criticism in their observation that with the development of the behavioral sciences,

> . . . some men abandoned their ministry for medicine or social service, while other attempted to transform their traditional work into semiclinical or social service activity. The great mass of clergymen remained true to their primary calling, but they were puzzled. There was good reason for their perplexity, for the theological view of man is always bound up with natural and social views of man and what had happened was that old views of man and society had changed radically.[28]

2. It is also possible that pastors can be drawn, as we have noted, to counseling because of their own loneliness or because of their need to see the concrete effects of their ministry in the lives of parishioners. These motivations, too, are doubtless to be found at times in almost any pastor; and they are understandable. But many could satisfy these needs

in other ways within their parish or outside of it. On this matter of professional loneliness we have already commented. We do not see it, however, as an explanation that covers the major reason for all ministers to engage in counseling.

3. There is, we believe, a more plausible explanation, theological in emphasis. Pastors may be responding to the increased willingness to meet counseling needs of parish and community on the one hand, and on the other by their desire to express effectively in a distinctly theological framework, the traditional emphasis on the cure of souls. This involves our reconciliation to God as well as to man through a personal ministry. The new element in such work seems to consist of calling into service the aid of many other men and agencies able to help a person in need. Very frequently in interdisciplinary co-operation, unusual though we now know it to be, there develops a counseling of counselors. In their cure of souls, pastors may also be hoping to acquire through counseling experience and training the qualities generally needed for effective parish work as a whole. In one of his studies Samuel Blizzard's informants were asked to name the characteristics of ministers that they believe lead to effective parish work. Seventy-eight per cent of them mentioned reconciling items as being approachable, being empathetic, having a concern for the individual, or being a good listener. It is possible that all pastors now perceive counseling and the necessity of training for it, as the best means by which their general effectiveness as the ministers of the Word is enhanced.

Preaching and Corporate Worship

Research study is not needed to show that preaching and common worship are highly regarded by clergy and parishioners in American Protestantism today. Multiple Sunday services, at one time predominantly found in Roman Catholic churches, have taken firm hold in our churches. Newspaper coverage of sermons, the emphasis upon preaching in seminary, the numerous professional journals devoted to preaching, and books of collected sermons—all give evidence to the wide interest in the pulpit. Attendance at church worship, a renewed enthusiasm for the family pew, and a revived liturgical movement within Protestantism, all testify to the wholesome attention that the church service is again receiving.

Needed or not, such interest is confirmed in our research findings. The pastors in this sampling ranked ten phases of their ministry according to the time they spent on each in an average week. Preaching and sermon preparation tops the list in the composite order of rank for the pastor of the average church. The average pastor in this survey not only reports that he spends more time in preparation and preaching of sermons than on any other work, but also that his sense of accomplishment derived from his pulpit work ranks second only to counseling. And preaching is one of the three most popular topics in the line-up of subjects in which these men might like to do additional study. (The other two, it may be remembered, are counseling training and leadership education.)

Our data show listed preferences are often connected with the size of church in which a man ministers, his type of community and its population. The larger the church (particularly those over 600 in membership), the more likely it is that the administrative function will be most time consuming. (These churches represent less than 15 per cent of the parishes but over 50 per cent of the membership of the denominational group from which the survey was made.) Even in these parishes, preaching and sermon preparation is demonstrably one of the topmost tasks both in the time it takes and in the value the clergyman places upon it.

To us it seems premature to adopt the image of the "pastoral director" for the group we have analyzed. That term, popularized in the studies of H. Richard Niebuhr and others, would certainly apply to a number of leading clerics both in our survey and in others; but it leaves out a still larger number of ministers whose workday life is organized around homiletical studies and kindred tasks. Normatively the preacher's office is seen as his most important. Frequently he is known as the preacher; and this is the activity in which he is seen by the most people, and by which he is characterized by the man in the street. But his identification with such a role involves some conflict. As Samuel Blizzard has observed:

> Role ambiguity is inherent in the profession. He is expected to be a man of belief, a saint, but his rights to completely express ethical judgments based on his personal understanding of and commitment to the Christian faith are often challenged and jeopardized. He is expected to be a man of action, a practitioner, but he is also expected to be a scholar of religion, a contemplative role. The practitioner roles are both privately and publicly focused (pastor role vs. preacher role). They are oriented to a message or ideology as well as to helping people.[29]

Preaching Emphases

It is altogether conceivable that preaching topics not directly related to family life could nonetheless have some effect upon family living in a parish. The sermon on forgiveness need not mention husbands and wives in order for listeners to begin thinking of their spouses. But we had specifically asked in the questionnaire about sermons that treat family life themes. Almost three-quarters (71 per cent) of the pastors report that they preach on family life themes. The wording of the question allowed for wide interpretation; they could include topics, side references, or illustrations. Their list certainly reveals what a pastor considers appropriate to the context of a sermon; but it probably also gives us yet another clue as to what the clergy regard as important issues in family living. Their replies can best be seen in the composite rank order:

TABLE 8 INCIDENCE OF FAMILY PREACHING

References in Sermons	*By Percentage of Preachers*
1. Worship in the Home	88%
2. Christian Parenthood	80%
3. Discipline in Family	66%
4. Handling Conflicts in the Home	43%
5. Family Crises	37%
6. Protestant Meaning of Marriage	36%
7. Democracy in the Family	31%
8. Interfaith Marriage	26%
9. Divorce	25%
10. Sex Ethics	21%
11. Planned Parenthood	4%

The list is reminiscent of the topics treated by these pastors in premarital interviewing. As in that case, these descend from the more general and accepted subjects to the more personal ones that are relatively difficult to talk about. Yet the wide publicity given to such questions as divorce, sex ethics, and planned parenthood in press and conversation would indicate that the pulpit may be skirting warily around the very questions about which parishioners are quite ready to hear. It may be more serious than that. It may be that the Protestant pulpit is avoiding controversial topics on which we have an obligation to speak to help our confused churchmen understand something of the way the Christian faith informs these sensitive issues today.

Correlations rise to the surface in regard to this matter that we ought not to pass over. We found through cross tabulations of data that "Worship in the Home" was treated relatively more often in sermons by men who made personal use of the church's curriculum materials (and this concern is repeatedly treated in curriculum magazines that go into the homes). The same general group of men were likely also to preach on "Christian Parenthood." The minister in a multiple-staff church who is closely acquainted with these curriculum materials for parents and teachers (we deduce that he is frequently the minister of Christian education) will preach relatively often on "Handling Conflicts in the Home" and "Family Crises" when he does preach, which may not be regularly. Men in the Northeast urban areas were more likely to preach on the "Protestant Meaning of Marriage" and "Interfaith Marriage" than others; they live in an area, as we have already noted, heavily Roman Catholic where many mixed marriages take place. Younger men less often than others preach on "Democracy in the Family"; this could reflect the fact that their children, if any, are too young to yet demand a voice in the councils of the family; or it may reflect something of the stepped-up attention on biblical preaching in recent years at all major seminaries.

All in all, the selection of these topics, and the way that clergymen answered the question, may lay open the definition they have of Christian family living. Indeed, it had been observed that the meaning of the Christian family more often means the practice of certain rituals, and the acceptance of certain concepts than it does standards for interpersonal relations. It simply would not occur to many clergymen and church members that the Christian faith can inform family life at such points as their sexual behavior or their family planning. Although the Roman Catholic church is outspoken and specific on these questions, many a Protestant preacher contents himself in speaking of them only in reaction. If the press carries a release about a Roman bishop's statement on contraception, the minister may respond briefly in a subsequent sermon; but he seldom advances a positive position on his own initiative. Be it said to his defense that this is exactly the way some of his congregants want it. They may be explicit on the point that they want to hear what they narrowly define as the gospel, and not to be bothered by lectures that deal with what they would think of as personal or secular subjects "where the church has no business." But the conscientious preacher of biblical sermons can assist his flock to understand something of the way that their faith relates to life and its harder questions.

The Family Church Service

The church service in which parents and children share together in regular common worship is growing in popularity. As now interpreted, this is not simply a recapitulation of the time-honored family pew. A new dimension has enriched this old-time tradition; for such services are now planned and accommodated to the family constituency. By this is meant that the timing of these services (they are generally shorter, often running about 40 minutes), the teaching aspect (with special instruction on the meaning of worship), and the co-ordination of these services with the Christian education program of the church contrive to bring family members of all ages into a reverent and meaningful worship experience.

More than one-third (38 per cent) of our respondents report family corporate worship services in their churches and our data show the tendency to be growing. A large proportion of them are in smaller (100 to 300 member) churches whose pastors are younger men. In a number of cases such men tie into the church family services a continuing emphasis on worship in the homes. Each of these has a way of supporting the other; for families at worship are hardly different in home or in church. This practice of worship by families throughout the week and on the Sabbath has the advantage of dramatizing the concept of "the church in thy house." It was a heartening finding to learn that the number of family services is increasing.

The Teaching and Educational Ministry

In summarizing Samuel Blizzard's study of the pastor's various roles, David Ernsberger concludes that the primary or face-to-face group life of the church is minimized in favor of the ministry to individuals on the one hand, and to the entire congregation on the other.[30] Our data confirmed this conclusion. Yet while the average minister tends to neglect the importance of educational groups in the church, he nevertheless maintains some indirect relationship to them. (In contrast, the director of religious education spends most of her time with the church's primary group life.)

Pastors report that they spend a considerable amount of time in teaching classes, leading groups, and advising youth fellowships. This cluster of typical educational chores ranks fourth out of ten in a list of ministerial tasks. Teaching is more time consuming in the life of young assistant pastors and ministers of education in multiple-staff churches than in others; and they show an appreciably higher use of church curriculum materials than other ministers. As a whole they indicate that a greater proportion of their time and energies are spent in study than many men would claim. They also were more inclined than the average pastor to see the contribution the church school curriculum and its parent program might make to the stability of family life in the parish, a factor of which many of the respondents were seemingly oblivious.

But a minority of the ministers (perhaps one in four) in the sampling had what might be described as an "educational stance" in their ministry. They have an intellectual bent and enjoy the teaching and study life in ministry. They are able to see broad educational implications in parish life: through the church school, parents' classes, family night programs, couples' clubs, and classes in family living. These pastors tend to use every function of their office as a learning opportunity for the laity. Many of these men, of course, are staff specialists in Christian education although some are pastors who have an enthusiasm for the educational phase of the ministry.

Pastors as a whole in this sample had an opportunity to describe their favorite methods of conveying Christian family education through materials. To no one's surprise, they leaned heavily to easily read, light literature. But they also had an interest in audio-visual educational methods. The tabulation of their choices yielded this response according to preference: (1) leaflets dealing with family problems, (2) filmstrips, (3) articles for parents in curriculum magazines, (4) small books for parents' reading, (5) motion picture films on family subjects. Other choices, receiving rather scant support, also include long-playing recordings on family subjects, and tape recordings. It is a fair guess that the comparative low rating for audio tapes and records is connected with the fact that many churches still do not have the equipment to play these, and that they are relatively late entries into the church educational field. We were made aware, once again, of the dependence of our churches upon printed materials in the educational process.

Even a quick survey of the churches would show wide experience in family education of numerous types. The larger and metropolitan area parishes are likely to maintain a fairly constant program in family education of several sorts; smaller churches reflect an on-again off-again record as new ideas are tried and program plans are for the time being fulfilled (depending upon availability of membership and leadership in a given year). Progress is being made in interchurch programing in small communities; this, perhaps, is the only answer open to the smallest churches. A glance at the following table illustrates the variety of these educational approaches.

TABLE 9 GROUP EXPRESSIONS OF FAMILY LIFE EDUCATION IN THE CHURCHES

Type of Program	*Percentage of Pastors Reporting*
Married Couples' Clubs	53%
Young Adult Groups	34%
Parents' Discussion Groups	26%
Parent Co-operative Nursery Schools	11%
Parents' Study Courses	10%
Mothers' Clubs	6%

Most churches of over 300 members, we found, sponsored a *"couples' club"* for the younger (and often older) married people of the church. These groups bring people together for the express purpose of strengthening their Christian faith and living in the family. The majority of the groups follow no one pattern of organization and emphasis but derive their identity and program largely from the local situation and its leadership. Programs are infinitely varied, and there is little evidence of any movement in Protestantism to foster definite patterns for the couples' clubs or a family life movement (such as expressed for Roman Catholics in the Catholic Family Movement).[31] Parents testify to the helpfulness of such group fellowship but sometimes state their opinion that these groups are so "couple conscious" that total family events are overlooked.

One of every three churches in the sample had an organized *"young adult group,"* most of them in urban centers where young, single persons tend to concentrate. In general, our pastors see these groups as composed of unmarried persons, roughly from 21 to 35 years of age for the most part, who have started to assume adult responsibilities. As would be expected, the "developmental tasks" for this age level include the establishing of effective love and work relationships. And it is about these two foci that most church programs tend to cluster. A major temptation of these groups lies in what Gordon Allport has called "privatism": the overwhelming concern with the private life to the exclusion of civic responsibility and concern for wider cultural problems.[32] Imaginative leadership, interchurch planning and co-operation, and a varied program have often made these groups a major Christian education resource for the city young adult as he moves out on his own.[33]

It is apparent that fathers and mothers facing dilemmas in family living want not only expert advice but also a chance to talk together and share solutions. For this reason, *parents' discussion groups* are proliferating throughout the church. Younger men, fresh out of seminary, and often with beginning families of their own, are particularly aware of the need that these groups are designed to meet; and it is in churches they serve (even the smaller congregations) that the recent increase of such groups is recorded. The subject matter differs greatly from group to group, but most groups center their discussion on various aspects of parent-child relationships. Materials used for resource may include books, mental health pamphlets, *Parent's Magazine,* or denominational materials published especially for this purpose.

The helpfulness of parents' discussions, fathers and mothers were frank to say, depends heavily on the leadership of the group. It is not that they want a professional family educator to guide them constantly; a well-trained parent would do, some said.[34] But he must be the kind of person who can provide an atmosphere of safety in which Christian parents might be quite frank with one another about their problems. Sometimes a director or minister of religious education is able to serve effectively as a leader; and an increasing number are being trained for just such a function. The Protestant Council of New York City in co-operation with the Child Study Association of America has provided training in the leadership of parents' discussion groups for the past few years. Under the supervision of the Child Study Association Staff (notably A. D. Buchmueller, Aline Auerbach, and Gertrude Goller), clergymen, directors of religious education and other church leaders with graduate degrees are taught the techniques of group leadership, the content of parent problems, and the organization of parent groups in various settings. This kind of advanced education holds great promise for informal group work with parents in the church.

Contrary to much outdated church education philosophy in the area of parenthood, church leaders are beginning to discover that where deep feelings reach to the root of the self (as they do in parent-child relationships), a simple "telling" process will not do. But the problem, as in so many areas, is to find and train the kind of leadership which can "lead a man to the threshold of his own mind," to use a phrase from Kahlil Gibran.

Parent co-operative nursery schools, we were to discover, are a product of multiple-staff suburban churches with a few exceptions. The desire of suburbanites to get started early on their child's "social education" under Christian auspices is demonstrated in this new and growing opportunity for the church. (Regrettably often, we noted, there is no integrated relationship of the day nursery school with its general Christian education program.) In one sense these schools represent a new educational outlet for Protestants in providing for parents' co-operation, not only in the organization and business end of the school but, under trained guidance, in the education of the children.[35] In this process many parents report gains for the relationships in the home; joint participation gives the mother and child a new kind of comradeship. Participating in this educational venture, the mother can relieve her all-too-present role conflicts. She can learn to use special skills; she meets stimulating persons; and she provides a focus of activity for the family (including equipment repairs and crafts for the father). There is no doubt that parents confined to the home with small children often see without perceiving. Guided observation sponsored by the church, can be an eye-opener and an incentive for Christian family living.

Parents' study courses are definitely on the increase, according to our survey. Systematic study of the work of Christian parenthood is long overdue in the churches. Reuben Hill and Emily Mudd remind the clergyman and religious education director in no uncertain terms that

> Families are peculiarly unprepossessing groups to get the world's work done. Think for a moment of the composition of the average family of husband and wife and children as compared to other work groups. Peopled by only two adults, one of whom has traditionally played the role of the weak one in need of protection, plus a number of children for most of their lives relatively helpless dependents—such a group would be a poor athletic team, a weak combat team, and unproductive work team, and a weak planning committee. It is a puny, unwieldy group to bring into action on any problem. It requires advanced training and great persistence during the period of family formation. No new family can start off with the consensus and *modus vivendi* of the veteran parental families from which the newly-weds have just graduated. Here is a place where extrafamily educational agencies can make a significant contribution.[36]

Professional leaders in the church are discovering that in addition to material designed specifically to aid parenting, the inclusion of straight theological materials and Bible study often provides a perspective on human life generally which obliquely aids participants to become better parents as they learn to be real persons in a Christian sense.

Mothers' clubs and forums are a highly specialized venture designed to aid the child-rearing efforts of young mothers through a program of speakers, discussions, and guided reading. Found almost exclusively in large city and suburban churches, the trend toward a focused approach to young parents is catching on throughout the country, our data show.

The problem in programing is often to avoid a repetition of what these Protestant mothers receive in child guidance fare from PTA and other public group forums.[37]

There are, of course, other occasional events in parish life that are related to family life education; and their irregularity or infrequent offering bears no relationship to their effectiveness. *Family night suppers* with a variety of themes, are held now and then in two out of three churches; father-son and mother-daughter dinners, in one out of three churches.

Family camps and conferences are found in one church out of seven; but interest in this form of education is growing faster than leadership can be provided. The National Council of the Churches of Christ in America together with its constituent denominations is anticipating a great increase in family camping and to this end preparing guides for this kind of experience.[38] Requiring a wide range of leadership (much of which can be drawn from parents themselves), family camping allows whole families to worship, play, and live together as well as to study systematically according to age-levels. Families learn from each other in such a setting. Compared with the youth conference with which Protestantism is quite familiar, the learning promoted among a group of families living together for a week or a week end is more likely to carry over directly when they return home.[39]

Periodic *courses in marriage preparation and family relations* are held by one of ten of the sample churches. Such offerings are practically unknown in rural churches where few young people of marriage age congregate. A change in the attitude of the generations about marriage and sex is evidenced in the fact that pastors over 50 years of age working alone in their churches seldom report any educational effort in this area.

Registering a light rate statistically, though perhaps deeply effective in themselves, were *wedding anniversary reunions and family hobby or display nights*. Less than one in sixteen churches reported such activities.

The picture of family education in the church as a whole resembles a smattering of attempts of greatly differing quality rather than a comprehensive program of any systematic nature. Furthermore, church efforts in family education still suffer from an overdose of "inspiration" in the program. We mean by this the tendency to instill in parents a picture of "ideal" family life. (It is assumed that such an emphasis on what families *ought* to be will actually improve relations within the family; and this is a highly debatable proposition.) Two earmarks of this inspirational approach to family education are an idealization of family life and simplification of the problems involved. When it emphasizes parental responsibility, church literature (whether Protestant, Catholic, or Jewish) tends to repeat the same truisms, use the same general statements of "fact" as scare techniques, and give the same generalized answers to almost any family situation. Moralism runs rampant through church family literature. But our more perceptive parents in the interviews and our professional consultants ask, "Is not honest appraisal of human problems actually more inspiring than the so-called 'religious' approach which fosters denial and concealment in its oversimplified ideal of family life?" This question should make family educators among the clergy and directors of religious education ponder long and hard.

The Pastor and His Home Life

It was a healthy admission from the pastors who filled in the questionnaire when seven out of ten frankly reported that they had come to understand family life more through having a family of their own than in any kind of reading or study. Our questionnaire was not designed so that we could determine just what things ministers had learned from parsonage life that they could transfer into their ministry. But they are clear about the fact that this understanding has come out the hard way. The pastor has family problems too. Though it is true that his complaints could be misplaced and his motives as unconscious as those of anyone else, the list of family troubles in the parsonage is instructive. Presented in their order of frequency are nine problems that clergymen report from their family living:

1. First, and out in front by far, is the concern that there are too many demands which leave the pastor without sufficient time for his family. Some critical analysts might attribute such a complaint to the parson's overevaluation of work life, compounded by his guilt-ridden, Calvinistically trained conscience, but our data indicate that there are some situational determinants. Middle-age pastors, who logically would be most likely to have teen-age children, report this difficulty out of proportion to their number in the sample. And parents of teen-agers could guess why in a trice; this is a busy, hectic period of development. The comings and goings of such a household preclude any easy meeting of all family members at any one time. A busy professional man would somewhat naturally wonder what was happening to his time that so little of it ever found him at home when his family was also to be found there.

The minister's time pressures are connected with any number of household conflicts; some of them are completely justifiable and quite unavoidable. The pastor must shoulder a heavy schedule of parish duties, for which all the new wonders of automation can aid him but little. The tasks of worship, study, counseling, and calling require hard work and long hours. There are whole blocks of time when he has no choice but to be absent from the family while dealing with some parishioner's personal problems that he cannot even mention upon his return home. Yet there are pastors who have unrealistic reasons for being absent from family responsibility. Sometimes their absenteeism smacks of flight. Suffering from anxieties of various natures, they seek to handle their problems through busyness and attention to "administrivia." The pastor may have some difficulty that originates from within himself that he seeks to solve with activity outside himself. The complaint about time pressure is real enough in parsonage life. We do well, however, to note that the time problem may be mixed with other factors.

2. The second most frequent problem reported by these ministers is that they can find almost no one outside the family with whom a pastor can be himself openly and genuinely. The pastor, and perhaps his family also, often feels imprisoned within a stereotyped role and finds it almost impossible to escape. From a questionnaire we cannot tell the degree to which individual clergymen may be self-imprisoned by their own inner expectations and the extent to which community and parish pressures compel him to conform. This problem is often pronounced, we find, among younger men in the smaller churches of rural communities. It is seldom the problem of men who are employed in multiple staffs. They evidently have colleagues with whom they can be themselves. We have already commented on the essential loneliness of some aspects of the ministry in a previous discussion on counseling. There is no ready, honorable way out of this one; the ministry often requires that a man stand alone, that he forego some intimate friendships outside the family and accept as one price of his calling that he cannot always locate companionship in his work. Indeed, the arresting note in this plaint is that phrase "outside the family." If he can be himself within the intimacy of his home, this in itself could be enough. Many there are who have less.

3. And the third of these problems from the parsonage is that work tensions from the ministry spill over into relations with wife and children. Conflicts with the building committee may be kept on a polite and restrained plane; but then the tense cleric may explode at home over a trifling annoyance that on other occasions would have resulted in a joke. Men who serve on collegiate staffs again report relative freedom from

this problem. Here it can be surmised that in contrast with the pastor who works alone, there is generally an opportunity to talk things out when there is concern about aspects of the work and work performance.

4. It is the irregular work schedule that ranks next in this series of problems. And it is here that those men on church multiple staffs, so free from the previous two concerns, now come to the fore. Particularly the younger men, perhaps those whose status on the church staff is such that they have little choice in determining their time, are apt to cite this problem as needling them and their families. An irregular schedule prevents them from counting on any set time to be with their families. It sometimes necessitates a cancellation of long-anticipated plans for a family outing or celebration. In one mail questionnaire survey, it was found that ministers' wives complain less about the amount of time that their husbands are out of the home than about their inability to count on the time they had agreed upon. It does not take much imagination (or for family men, much recollection) to see how relationships would be affected by this undependability. We found that middle-age and older pastors are less likely to voice this particular complaint. It can be safely theorized that they can regulate their time on the job with more authority, and may also have become less bothered by the aspects of unaccountability in the minister's schedule.

5. Financial stress plagues some parsonage homes. Difficulty in making ends meet is more likely to be mentioned by pastors serving smaller churches where resources are scarcer, of course. And ministers in the 35 to 50 age range report this least; their income seemed more stable. But the younger clergyman just beginning his career, and the older man now past his peak earnings were among those who brought this item into fifth place. That it rises no higher is a result both of the national income which our nation now enjoys (imagine the reaction to this issue during Depression years) and of the relatively secure income of many of our sample whose presbyteries have set a minimum salary scale for their constituent churches.

6. It is when the pastor's family is expected to be different or even "perfect" that some clerical resentments rise; for this too has its reverberations in the family. Once again we witness the expectations of parish and community (and perhaps the pastor's perception of these) coming to the fore as a source of embarrassment. Younger men report this family tension far more often than others, to the rate of three times as many as would be expected statistically. Theirs are the younger chil-

dren whose behavior is less trained. Theirs are the less experienced parsonage wives who are adjusting to a new marriage and to a role that is like no other. The minister's wife is in a unique position of responsibility, honor, and conspicuousness that can be highly gratifying at times and notably vexing at others.[40] Could it be that this younger pastor is just too sensitive about being different or having his family seem different? In another cultural era, ministers of an earlier day took it for granted that their calling made them different and they expected to be so. In the suburbs we find the pastor comparatively free of this conflict; but the rural pastor confesses that he finds it real.

7. A closely related problem, one that in fact overlaps the previous conflict, is the complaint about lack of privacy and the feeling of living in "a glass house." The fact that these two are listed separately more reflects the differing expression of ministerial concern than any great distinction between them. The "goldfish bowl" complex would be expressed by responses of some men, we hypothesize, and the "perfection" image would express it for others. In either case, it is from their own words in pretest experiments that these categories are used. And contrary to any ordinary expectations, it was the city pastor, of all people, who responded that this goldfish bowl complex was for his family a problem. The very fact that men from different areas tend to rate these two overlapping categories higher than others supports the guess that the terms themselves make a difference in the reply.

8. Only a relatively small number of pastors say that their problem centers in religious practices at home becoming artificial. Even among this small group in what we have dubbed the wastebasket categories toward the end of the list, we find some differences. Men over 50, for instance, tend not to check this question; their children are grown and have mostly left home, and it could be that issues over family worship practices have simmered down with the lessening necessity for disciplinary measures. And pastors serving churches of over 600 members (they had told us that they are busy and their family contacts are too hurried) tend to cite this complaint which being among the less significant statistically, is yet one of the sadder findings on the list.

9. Into last place fall specific complaints against the pastor's wife. Not many men admitted to strained marital relations; but some of those who reported that their wives were too active in church either by their own choice or that of the parish or community added comments that were vehement. Though the statistics here ran low, feelings ran high.

Urban pastors reported this problem more than others. But as is the case in nearly all "wastebasket categories," the substance of this complaint may have been drained off in some of the previously reported problems. We noted, for instance, that those resentments about being expected to be different or perfect (item six) might also reflect the marital situation of pastors. In fact, there is no reported problem among all these nine that could not have its marriage connotations. It would be illogical therefore to assume that marriage concerns play no part other than in this bottom category of excessive expectations of the wife. Given the limitations of an anonymous questionnaire and the necessity of asking questions in only one way, this bare report of occasional marital infelicity in the manse is all the information our pastors offered.

Conflicting Roles and Goals

The professional life and the family life of the pastor are closely interwoven. How he ministers to families in the parish may be strongly influenced by his own home experience. The way that parishioners respond to him, to his preaching and his counseling, may be conditioned by what they know about his family life. Ever since the Reformation a strong tie has existed between the pastor's family life and his calling. As William Pauck writes,

> Nothing shaped the social status of the Protestant ministry as decisively as the fact that they were permitted and indeed encouraged to marry. . . . Ministerial households often exemplified the practical application of the Reformers' new understanding of the Christian religion, namely, that the faith in Christ must be practiced in mutual love and service in the natural, social setting of human life and in the ordinary secular pursuits. Thus the married ministry came to demonstrate that family life together with the manifold social activities it engenders can be a more effective vehicle for religion and the service of God than asceticism, celibacy, and other-worldliness.[41]

Conflicting goals confront the minister when he is expected to be both a professional man and an exemplary family man; but the long hours demanded of him may crowd out much of his family life. Community and ecclesiastical expectations force him to understand that the family education he accomplishes in his ministry must be by example as well as by instruction. Some denominational pronouncements remind clergymen of the heavy responsibility their families carry in serving as a laboratory of Christian living for the community. Not infrequently letters of reference of personnel information blanks will inquire about the pastor's family; and his placement opportunities can hinge upon the answer to these queries. But what seems to us more important than these men, 95 per cent of whom were married, credit their own family life with aiding them in understanding better their pastoral ministry and its contacts with homes of the congregation.

One pastor's wife, quoted by John G. Koehler from his survey of 150 American Baptist ministers' homes,[42] speaks appreciatively of their privileged relationship: "Ministers and their wives are peculiarly lucky in that they work as a team much more than any other couple, and for this reason, are closer to each other. In spite of being in demand I think ministers as a whole are with their families more than a great many men are. All executives, public figures and professional men have to spend much time outside their homes as do ministers, and the families have to understand and be proud that father is in demand."

Protestant tradition has come to expect that in order for a man to be an adequate pastor he should have achieved a satisfactory adjustment in life's most intimate relationship, the family. The expectation is both reasonable and sound; for not a little experience shows that parsonage family conflicts can precede church conflicts. Paul's salty word to Timothy is appropriate: "If a man does not know how to manage his own household, how can he care for God's church?" (I Timothy 3:5).

It is our contention that the clergyman himself needs the benefit of a concerted, well-integrated program of family education. Theological seminaries, recognizing that the clergy family is somewhat different from others in the neighborhood, dare not let three or four years of a man's preparation for the gospel ministry slip by without also helping to prepare him for marriage and family life. The very fact that many students now are married during seminary days makes this possibility the more attractive because of the readiness these couples would have for such help. Boards of education in the several denominations, or councils of churches, could aid mightily if they would offer short courses in child development and psychology for the clergy. Such a boon could be tripled: in helping them better to understand their family relations, in facilitating their understanding of parish children and church school pupils, and in assisting them to know more about human personality.

Clergymen, we have found, require encouragement to seek counseling help when they need it. Why should they, of all persons, fear that some stigma lies in seeking counsel when their family relations need repair work? The experience of some ministers in this very sampling can be cited to show that when they availed themselves of professional help, they gained much for themselves and their ministry as well as in the solution of the immediate problem.

The quest to find new dimensions for role and vocation in the ministry (now sorely needed as these problems in relationship and administration exhibit) will require more than the study of professors and researchers. It is a quest that should enlist the wisdom of pastors, the experience of their wives, and the insight of their frequently misunderstood children.

NOTES

1. See Samuel W. Blizzard, "The Minister's Dilemma," *The Christian Century,* April 25, 1956, pp. 508-509 and "The Protestant Minister's Integrating Roles," *Religious Education,* July-August, 1958, pp. 374-380; and H. Richard Niebuhr, Daniel Day Williams, and James M. Gustafson, *The Purpose of the Church and Its Ministry,* and *The Advancement of Theological Education.* Also H. Richard Niebuhr and Daniel Day Williams, eds., *The Ministry in Historical Perspectives.*
2. See Claude Welch's trenchant discussion of this point in his *The Reality of the Church,* Chapter 2.
3. See especially Hendrick Kraemer, *A Theology of the Laity,* and Arnold Come's *Agents of Reconciliation.*
4. Daniel Jenkins, *The Protestant Ministry,* p. 34.
5. Our research committee faced quite early both the advantages and limitations of such a procedure. Among the advantages are the possibilities of obtaining information from more people less expensively than by any other method; of providing a standardized procedure by which answers can be given without the direct influence of the investigator's personality; and of using structured questions which could be answered meaningfully by most of the respondents. Disadvantages of the questionnaire approach were also recognized. We regretted that in this procedure individual motives and responses were likely to be submerged in answering the questions. (However, almost 100 notes and letters accompanied the returned questionnaires, and these furnished us with much of the personal reaction to items we might have missed.) Of course, as in any structured questionnaire, we ran the risk of having questions and statements misinterpreted. This error we had tried to eliminate through pretesting. Naturally, too, there is always present the tendency of respondents in submitting a record to an official board of the church to give "respectable" answers—even though the questionnaires carried no information by which the respondent could be personally identified. It is also possible, we discovered in the pretest, that some persons respond in a negative way to all questionnaires as compared to their reaction to interviews. These were dangers inherent in the method. In spite of them, this research tool was adopted; and the decision paid off.

6. In the view of the authors, any Christian education content becomes education for family life when in the course of teaching, preaching, or counseling, the subject matter is definitely and consciously addressed to the family relationship. This is not to deny that subject matter not related to the family, may nevertheless affect it profoundly.
7. See Appendix.
8. It was decided that questionnaires should be sent only to churches served by full-time pastors. Since it was too expensive to make a complete census of all United Presbyterian full-time pastors (a total of 7381 ministers serving churches), it was decided to draw a fifty per cent sample composed of every other pastor serving a local congregation in the denomination. One hundred fifty names were eliminated; these were found to represent duplicates to multiple-staff churches, incorrect addresses, and deceased pastors. The adjusted total (3541 questionnaires) was sent to pastors with a cover letter by church executives with a prepaid business reply envelope for ease in returning.
9. The terms one chooses to give to these age-groupings depends, no doubt, upon the existential position of the reporters. We have called the men under 35 years of age, "younger pastors"; those men in the 35 to 49 range, "middle-age pastors"; and the men over 50, "older pastors." This classification, the middle-age authors hasten to assure, is no attempt to evaluate virility and mind-set, however.
10. Only 5.4 per cent of rural churches in the study claimed one or more professional persons in addition to the pastor on the staff full or part time. Among urban churches, the figure rises sharply to 41 per cent; and for suburban, 39 per cent.
11. The analysis was accomplished statistically through the use of IBM machines and the technical assistance of Dr. David Saunders of The Educational Testing Service, Princeton, New Jersey.
12. We were interested, of course, in knowing not only whether there was a difference percentagewise between the subgroups mentioned but also whether this difference could have occurred by chance. Statistical methods were used by our tabulation consultant to eliminate this chance factor. Differences among groups of pastors are cited only when they are of a magnitude that will occur less than 5 per cent (and more often only 2 to 3 per cent) of the time by chance. Having established the relationship between two items (for example, the relatively greater number of small churches in rural areas, to mention an obvious example) we are then freed to seek for the reason why this relationship exists. In the example given above, sparse population would be an obvious answer.
13. From Chapter 3, "Religion and the Home," *Sermons on Marriage and Family Life,* edited by J. C. Wynn, p. 38.
14. John S. Whale, *Christian Doctrine,* p. 134f. New York: Cambridge University Press, 1941.
15. These categories will add up to slightly over 100 per cent because the replies were not mutually exclusive ones and pastors occasionally entered several answers.
16. William H. Whyte, Jr., *Is Anybody Listening?*

17. Denominational groups with a higher than (Protestant) average of broken homes in their membership include the American Baptist, Church of the Nazarene, Church of God, Disciples of Christ, Evangelical United Brethren, and Presbyterian U.S.A., according to a 1958 mail survey of 325 churches conducted by the Bureau of Research and Survey, National Council of the Churches of Christ in the U.S.A.
18. One rural pastor reports by letter: *"My main work in this town of 3200 is in the area of family conflicts due to personality problems and tensions."* Then he lists a series of eleven pastoral "cases" that include the following: a young mother who is a victim of severe neurasthenia and hostile against parents and husband; the psychosomatic illness of a woman in an unhappy marriage; an alcoholic church officer trying to readjust his life; an older man attempting to regain social relationships after antagonizing everybody in town following his illness; an in-law conflict in one family over their several preferences in churches; a woman suffering from neurotic grief since the death of her mother; a schizophrenic parishioner referred to psychiatry but still in supportive contact with the pastor; a manic-depressive church member now hospitalized in another state and in regular contact by correspondence; a couple on the verge of divorce after numerous drinking bouts; a family whose father is jailed for his kleptomaniacal behavior; an unmarried teacher unable to readjust to life after her mother's death.
19. Charles F. Kemp, *The Pastor and Community Resources,* p. 22ff. St. Louis, Mo.: Bethany Press, 1960. Used by permission.
20. Gayraud S. Wilmore, Jr., "The Church as a Redemptive Fellowship," unpublished manuscript.
21. One pastor added this explanation: *"I have a program of premarital counseling that requires a minimum of three interviews. I use the 'Sex Knowledge Inventory' and the Bernreuter 'Personality Inventory' in all my premarital cases. I have one interview alone with the bride, another with the groom, and make it a rule not to marry those who refuse to participate in the premarital counseling program."*
22. *"I would never presume to counsel anybody about duties before, during, or after a marriage unless I were specifically asked to do so,"* a pastor writes. *"I do not believe that any minister or anyone else has any right to make it his business to mention sex relationships or any other matters that are certainly most assuredly their own intimate business."*
23. The Commission on Christian Marriage and Divorce of the United Church of Canada found in a survey of nearly 1,000 ministers that three-fourths of them deal with religion in the premarital consultations; and that six out of ten treat questions of personal relations including courtship and sex, a somewhat higher percentage than our sample showed in 44 per cent.
24. Carroll A. Wise, *Pastoral Counseling,* p. 176.
25. It is not to be assumed that the pastor ordinarily uses the particular skills and psychometric devices of the professional vocational guidance counselor. Generally, he deals more in the area of motivation than the assessment of abilities and job information.

26. A small percentage say they would choose to be on the receiving end of counseling in order to learn more about it. Seven per cent revealed that the greatest contribution to their understanding of family ministry had been the experience of being counseled themselves. One such respondent writes: *"The most important factor in my work in the ministry to families has been the necessity to solve a family problem in the manse. I have been working with the Family Service Agency myself. As I have become a more secure and whole person, I have become a better minister to families."*
27. We are not unaware that a questionnaire on family ministry would set respondents to thinking about the very courses that relate to the questions they were then answering. Yet it is significant that they were listed in such preponderance, and written into the sheet by respondents.
28. H. Richard Niebuhr, Daniel Day Williams, and James M. Gustafson, *The Purpose of the Church and Its Ministry,* p. 77. New York: Harper & Brothers, 1956.
29. Samuel Blizzard, "Role Conflicts of the Urban Protestant Parish Minister," *The Urban Church,* Vol. VII, No. 4, September, 1956, p. 14.

    In his research, however, Blizzard has findings at discrepancy with ours. His order of ministerial tasks from the most time consuming to the least is as follows: administrator, pastor, preacher and priest, organizer, and teacher. Though his classifications differ from ours by name and content, their definition is reasonably consistent enough to emphasize that the preaching function which turns out to require the most time in our sampling comes third in his—after administration and pastoral care. It may be that these variances arise from differences in the survey design. The two studies drew different samples. His was interdenominational, ours from the Presbyterian ministry. Our study also has a proportionately larger group of pastors from small, rural churches; and they are shown in the research data to be less involved in administrative duties than their metropolitan counterparts. Another, and not insignificant difference, was the way in which pastors were asked to report their time expenditure. Blizzard required a diary of actual time spent while we asked for a ranking of 10 items in a multiple-choice question. In such a multiple list, it is possible that a man would make a quick judgment based more upon the normative than the descriptive situation.
30. David J. Ernsberger, *A Philosophy of Adult Christian Education,* p. 23.
31. One exception to this trend is the presence in the United Presbyterian Church of National Presbyterian Mariners who follow a detailed "nautical" organization plan, specific purposes, and participate in regional events as constituent groups. This organization of couples' clubs is found almost exclusively in the larger-than-average churches of the Far West with some representation in the North Central region of the country. About one in six United Presbyterian churches is affiliated with this organization through the couples' groups.
32. According to church leaders, these young adult groups tend to draw an inordinate number of young single people with personality problems who are seeking to find adjustment within a permissive group.

33. See Robert S. Clemmons' book, *Young Adults in the Church,* for a survey of the most effective approaches to this group tried by Protestant denominations.
34. One survey of parents indicated the majority preferred a "lay leader" over a professional because they felt freer to talk and because the professional was often too technical. The minority which preferred the technically trained leader felt he could give more to the group and could better keep the discussion on the track.
35. See Katharine Whiteside Taylor's insightful book, *Parent Co-operative Nursery Schools.*
36. From *Memorandum on Strengthening Family Life in the United States,* a report to the Department of Health, Education, and Welfare of the Social Security Administration, by Emily H. Mudd and Reuben Hill.
37. See Phoebe Anderson's *Religious Living with Nursery Children* for some highly creative approaches to programing.
38. See the National Council of Churches publication on *Church Family Camping* by William Genné and the "Church Family Camping Issue" of *Adult Times* published by the United Presbyterian Board of Christian Education, for example.
39. The usual summer conference builds up an artificial "reference group" (as the sociologists would say) for a short period of time, but family camping involves natural groups which often learn interpersonal competence, a religious outlook, and devotional habits which can frequently be more easily maintained as the family returns to familiar ground.
40. Prof. William Douglas of Boston University School of Theology has been engaged in a research project designed to learn more about the relationships between the minister and his wife, the effects of the parish upon this marriage, and the nature of the wife's role. To the results of this study of a subject on which there has been altogether too little light, we look forward.
41. H. Richard Niebuhr, Daniel Day Williams, and James M. Gustafson, *The Ministry in Historical Perspectives,* p. 146. New York: Harper & Brothers, 1956.
42. See *Pastoral Psychology,* September, 1960, "The Minister as a Family Man," by John G. Koehler.

- **Communication of the Gospel**
- **To Church Families**
- **Within Church Families**
- **By Church Families**

8

Postscript

In a book that has decried the church's penchant for moralism, we shall not use our final pages to point some easy moral. Nor can a study that has repeatedly shown the wide diversity that exists among clergymen, their churches and communities, among households and parents, conclude in prescribing general recommendations as if they could cover a multitude of problems. Our work has been one of analysis and interpretation; it has not been intended for prognostication. Who would be equal to such a task? To lift out certain of our findings at the expense of others in order to forecast future developments of church and family is a cheap device, and also is a risk because one church's solution is another's problem. And the data that appear most insightful to some readers may turn out to be already familiar to others.

Communication of the Gospel

We began this survey of Protestant families and their theological heritage with the admission that it takes some temerity to conduct research into family life because this subject is so well known to everyone that we have experts without number. But now upon completion of these chapters we are more than ever convinced that new and continuing research is needed in this field. Our inquiries have taken us through a consideration of the changing American family and its crises, a review of biblical and historical theology, a perusal of what Christian parents are thinking, and a survey of the churches and their ministry to families. There are, of course, important family concerns which have yet to be explored deeply by Protestantism. Light might be shed by new research upon questions such as these:

1. How do children view the dilemmas which their parents confront in this changing world?
2. What are the crucial incidents in the lives of families which influence their relationship to the church?
3. What educational experiences in the church actually increase interpersonal competence in family living?
4. What can the church do to help parents enhance their ability to make decisions in the light of the Christian faith?
5. What (in the face of the sexual revolution of our time) represents a teachable Christian position with reference to sexual relationships outside of marriage?

Even tentative answers to these questions would set forward the church's educational ministry to families in our day.

Our study may well close with our own brief interpretation of the basic task to be accomplished by the community of faith: the proclamation of the gospel to families, within family life, and through families.

To Church Families

Contrary to the easy assumptions of the old-time Mother's Day sermon, it is not really any simpler to fulfill the kingdom of God at home than elsewhere. The family is a place where emotions run deep, where conflicts are common, and forgiveness is frequently necessary. To put it plainly, the home itself is a mission field; and the church must reach out to it evangelistically, instructing the family in its internal task of Christian nurture.

As traditionally understood in the covenant this nurture has come about through a chain of teaching: God's communicating through his church, then the church to parents, and the parents in turn to their children. There are common situations of family interaction, however, where the children are the real communicators of the gospel, and by their reconciling spirit have forged the link between family and faith.

As is the case in all human institutions, the family only has potential. The active forces of alienation and sin, we have seen, are active here too. And when destructive relationships pervade family life they can be more damaging to persons than in any other context unless relieved by forgiveness and reconciliation. And yet this peculiar group has also within its potentiality the blossoming of sacrificial love, of wholehearted acceptance and understanding. If these godlier characteristics are to be nurtured in home life, the gospel must be communicated *to* families vigorously and without stint. This is an aspect of the mission of the church to the world.

Within Church Families

There we cannot stop; for the gospel is also to be communicated *within* family life.

Emil Brunner would contend that where this is being done out of a full heart and prayerful motivation, in a family gathering together in their own worshiping community, there you will find the church. There also, it can be added, we find the ministry of Christian laymen carried forth into action. If we see our own families as a part of God's people in his covenant relationship, we witness to his gospel through our attempt to carry out his will in our homes, and as we look to him for guidance in our family life. Caught up into this commitment our parenthood becomes a calling, that is, a new vocation. The vocation of parenthood has the possibility of being at variance with our personal concern about individual success and advancement, and this is a risk Christians cannot ignore. But our major vocational concern within the family is to be *gospel bearers to one another*. It was John Calvin who exclaimed that parents receive an entirely new gift in their child through whom spiritual values can be introduced into a world that is not spiritual.

This may be a clue to the special purpose that God intended when first he created this relationship that is the family. The family's destiny could well be, in scriptural terms, "the making of a people." The family often is a stage where the drama of alienation and reconciliation is re-played in full vividness. Over and again the redemption of Christ can be seen within their interpersonal relationships. Here, normatively speaking, there is to be a full mutuality in loving trust (being subject to one another in Christ) where the lessons of love, of forgiveness, and of obedience are learned. In all these relationships the doctrine of justification by faith can save us from the hopeless perfectionism which enslaves countless families within the church—and motivates not a little of the heretical preaching and literature to which our families are exposed.

By Church Families

And the gospel, moreover, is to be carried *by* families to the world beyond their household walls. They are called to be witnesses and to testify to the power of God in Christ. As gospel bearers to the outside world, they witness corporately as well as individually to the culture in which they live. Their household of faith is summoned by the church and sent into the world as missioners themselves. This calls for active witness in the areas of work and of community life. It demands an active filtering of society's values through minds which are loyal above all to their Lord. The church never assumes that the gospel stops when it is understood and accepted; from that point, it must be carried on because its very essence requires it to be shared.

Yet the church dare not expect the gospel to be spread by families without sufficient preparation and training. It must be clear that the gospel can hardly be communicated within and through families unless it has been vividly conveyed to them by the church. But when the Word is truly preached and heard, the sacraments are rightly administered, and *koinonia* is experienced through a mutual ministry of believers, then young families with their children become potentially redemptive cells within the body of Christ, his church. Thus they are enabled to grow in grace, a demonstration of God's creativity and love. They, in their own family life, are a part of the whole family of God, a continuum of the church.

Appendices

APPENDIX I

The Committee on the Christian Home, United Presbyterian Board of Christian Education

Throughout the three-year period of our primary and secondary research studies at the Board of Christian Education, we enjoyed the counsel of a staff committee that met regularly for study and discussion of the emerging data. Each member represented a different unit within the staff, and was able to bring to these meetings something of the experience and viewpoint of his colleagues; conversely he was able to return to them with information about the research project and its relevance to their work. To them for their able advisory service, we are indebted: Walter L. Jenkins, chairman, Locke E. Bowman, Dorothy B. Fritz, Emily Gibbes, Ray J. Harmelink, George L. Hunt, Nevin E. Kendell, Norman F. Langford, Helen Link, Theron B. Maxson, William A. Morrison ex officio, Ralph N. Mould, Paul Calvin Payne ex officio, Richard E. Plummer, William B. Schram, H. Ben Sissel, W. H. Vernon Smith, Rachel Swann, Roland Tapp, Hamlin Tobey, Eli F. Wismer.

APPENDIX II

Research Consultants

From the very outset of the research study, it was of invaluable benefit to be able to turn to those in the field of family education and research who could advise on elements of research design, methods, and interpretation. From these persons we received counsel for which we are deeply indebted. Without the following experts and their guidance we should have lost both time in our work schedule and some of the significance of our findings:

Purnell Benson, Edgar F. Borgatta, Claude C. Bowman, James H. S. Bossard, Orville G. Brim, Jr., A. D. Buchmueller, Ernest W. Burgess, Robert

J. Cadigan, David Cole, Evelyn Millis Duvall, Gunnar Dybwad, Nelson E. Foote, Paul C. Glick, Armin Grams, Dale Harris, Richard N. Hey, Reuben Hill, Seward Hiltner, Ethel Kawin, Emily H. Mudd, James A. Peterson, Paul Pruyser, Carl R. Rogers, David Saunders, Robert Winch, Carroll A. Wise.

APPENDIX III
The Interviewers

Chapters 5 and 6 owe much to the skill and enthusiastic service of fifty-two interviewers who joined us in guided discussions with groups of parents across the nation. That process is described in Chapter 5; but their names are gratefully recorded here:

Mark W. Abernethy, Wesley C. Baker, William S. Baker, Mrs. Wayne Barron, Russell J. Becker, J. Lennert Cedarleaf, Dugald Chaffee, William E. Crane, C. M. Croughan, Fitzhugh J. Dodson, B. David Edens, Frank R. L. Egloff, James G. Emerson, George W. Ennis, Roy W. Fairchild, Robert G. Foulkes, Edward S. Golden, Richard Harsh, John B. Hawley, Marshall B. Hodge, Hugh S. Hostetler, John M. Humphreys, Gordon Jackson, LeRoy G. Kerney, Lester E. Kim, Elaine Jones Knutsen, Paul Koper, LeRoy Loats, William N. Lovell, Robert W. Lynn, Gordon A. MacInnes, Alfred B. McNair, Alfred W. Melton, John C. Narciso, Alfred E. Rath, E. Alan Richardson, Dale Robb, Roy H. Rodgers, William B. Rogers, Donald F. Schroeder, Luther E. Stein, John W. Stettner, John M. Stevens, Carl G. Stromee, Roland W. Tapp, Jean A. Thompson, Aaron J. Ungersma, Frank E. West, Glenn E. Whitlock, Robert E. Williams, Joseph S. Willis, Ray T. Woods, J. C. Wynn, H. Walter Yoder.

APPENDIX IV
Pastors Who Arranged Interviews

The pastors of those churches which played host to group interviews of parents aided materially in the gathering of data that enrich this entire study. Without the careful attention of the following pastors to a sampling procedure and their time-consuming, careful work on behalf of the research study, our findings would have lost much in meaning and scope:

The Reverend Messrs: Benjamin J. Anderson, Wesley C. Baker, Ulysses B. Blakeley, John R. Bodo, Calvin H. Buchanan, Robert C. Clapham, Lindley E. Cook, Joseph J. Copeland, R. W. Copeland, Virgil M. Cosby, Ben T. Cowles, John D. Craig, Paul E. Crane, Frederick Cropp, Robert M. Davidson, Robert N. Davis, James Emerson, Mitchell S. Epperson, Burton Erickson, Donald P. Evans, Robert R. Ferguson, Bert G. Fedor, Forster W. Freeman, Stanley K. Gambell, Robert K. Goodwin, Richard A. Geiger,

Julian R. Gresham, J. Robert Henderson, Roy E. Howes, David C. Jacobsen, Robert Kerr, Jr., Frank L. Kinsman, Donald C. Kuntz, Charles T. Leber, Jr., H. Ganse Little, Robert W. Lynn, Gordon W. Mattice, David H. McAlpin, Thomas J. McLaren, Robert W. McClellan, Hayward H. McCollough, Ronald W. McNeur, John O. Mellin, William S. Meyer, Arthur L. Miller, Dale K. Milligan, Alvin L. Morris, Hugh Mullings, Lester Nickless, Burney Overton, Robert E. Palmer, Donald J. Peterson, John E. Ranson, Arthur P. Rech, Kenneth E. Reeves, John L. Reimers, Edwin Roberts, Thomas R. Stone, Morris C. Robinson, J. V. Roth, John B. Rowland, William F. Rogan, Ralph C. Shanks, James A. Shiflett, Hans Sidon, Byron H. Sprague, Samuel L. Stuart, Warren G. Studer, George F. Telle, William Carl Thomas, John W. Voth, Charles W. Watt, Paul S. Wright, Donald W. Zimmerman. Also assisting in this phase were: Mrs. Archie B. Freeman, Miss Mildred A. Neumeister, and Miss Billie Smith.

APPENDIX V
The Interdisciplinary Consultants

In a series of fruitful interviews, the authors met with the members, listed below, of various helping professions who share in many aspects of family education in church and community. Because of their clear and objective view of churches and families, they aided us in seeing numerous places where church and community agency can work co-operatively in family education through an interdisciplinary approach.

Mark Abernethy, Mrs. James E. Barbee, Dorothy E. Bradbury, Ralph P. Bridgman, Muriel W. Brown, Marian M. Crane, Orville W. Crays, Lincoln Daniels, Roy E. Dickerson, Evelyn M. Duvall, Sylvanus M. Duvall, W. Clark Ellzey, Armin Grams, Dale B. Harris, Reuben Hill, Alan Ingleby, Freda H. Kehm, Paul Pruyser, Sheldon L. Rahn, Carl F. Ruess, Annie Lee Sandusky, James H. Scull, Mark Shedron, Jean A. Thompson, David B. Treat, Helen L. Witmer.

APPENDIX VI
The Theological Conference

In order to open the way to relevant theological inquiry, a conference of theologians and staff members of the United Presbyterian Board was held over a three-day period in October, 1957. Their discussions centered on the contributions of biblical and historical theology to the subject of family life. The papers they presented and the recorded discussions proved immensely profitable to the entire project.

Those who participated in the consultative conference were Markus

Barth, Dora P. Chaplin, William Graham Cole, Arnold B. Come, Fred J. Denbeaux, Joseph Fletcher, William H. Genné, Harry G. Goodykoontz, Joseph Haroutunian, William E. Hulme, Gordon E. Jackson, Robert Clyde Johnson, Robert W. Lynn, Randolph Crump Miller, Richard V. McCann, Otto A. Piper, Mrs. Ben Russell, R. Paul Ramsey, Walter E. Wiest, Gibson Winter.

The conference plan included the reading of a set of three previously circulated papers: "Marriage and Family in Christian Thought" by Gibson Winter, "Can There Be a Protestant Theology of the Family?" by Robert Clyde Johnson and Walter E. Wiest, and "Fifty Church Families and Their Role Expectations" by Robert W. Lynn.

APPENDIX VII

The Pastors' Questionnaire on Ministry to Families

QUESTIONNAIRE ON MINISTRY TO FAMILIES

DO NOT SIGN OR IDENTIFY THIS QUESTIONNAIRE. EVERY RESPONDENT REMAINS ANONYMOUS.
IF MORE THAN ONE PASTOR IS ON A CHURCH STAFF, ONLY ONE OF THEM IS REQUESTED TO ANSWER THE QUESTIONNAIRE. **IF YOU SERVE MORE THAN ONE CHURCH,** CHOOSE THE CHURCH WHICH IS BEST ORGANIZED AND IN WHICH CAN BE FOUND THE MOST COMPLETE MEMBERSHIP RECORDS AND FILL IN THE ENTIRE QUESTIONNAIRE WITH THAT ONE CHURCH IN MIND.

ABOUT THE CHURCH AND COMMUNITY

What is the population of the community in which the church you serve is located? **(Check one)**

1
1 ☐ One family to 1,000 persons
2 ☐ 1,000 to 5,000
3 ☐ 5,000 to 10,000
4 ☐ 10,000 to 25,000
5 ☐ 25,000 to 50,000
6 ☐ 50,000 to 100,000
7 ☐ 100,000 to 250,000
8 ☐ 250,000 and over

What is the name of the **county** in which your church is located?

2 County name:____________

How would you describe the **community** in which the church you serve is located? **(Check one)**

3
1 ☐ Rural
2 ☐ Urban
3 ☐ Suburban

Approximately what percentage of the employed members of your congregation work within your immediate community?

4[2] _________%

In what kind of neighborhood is your church located? **(Check one)**

5
1 ☐ Chiefly residential
2 ☐ Chiefly commercial
3 ☐ Chiefly industrial
4 ☐ Mixed
5 ☐ Farm or open country

How many members are there in the church you serve? **(Check one)**

6
1 ☐ 1 to 99
2 ☐ 100 to 299
3 ☐ 300 to 599
4 ☐ 600 to 1,199
5 ☐ 1,200 and over

How many pupils (including adults) are enrolled in your church school? **(Check one)**

7
1 ☐ 1 to 99
2 ☐ 100 to 299
3 ☐ 300 to 599
4 ☐ 600 to 1,199
5 ☐ 1,200 and over

What percentage of church school enrollment is composed of children and youth, rather than adults?

8[2] ________%

Is there any other professional person on your staff full or part time, not counting secretarial or custodial help?

9
1 ☐ Yes
2 ☐ No

ABOUT YOURSELF

Do you serve as a pastor full time? (If you are a seminary student serving weekends only, answer "No")

10
1 ☐ Yes
2 ☐ No

What is your age? **(Check one)**

11
1 ☐ Under 35
2 ☐ 35 to 49
3 ☐ 50 or over

What is your marital status? **(Check one)**

12[2]
1 ☐ Single
2 ☐ Married
3 ☐ Widowed
4 ☐ Divorced

If you are a parent, how hold is your **oldest** child?

13[m] ________years

Since leaving seminary, what experiences have contributed **most** to your ability to understand and minister to families? **(Check three)**

14[m]
1 ☐ None in particular
2 ☐ Having a family of your own
3 ☐ Frequent personal contact with families
4 ☐ Having to counsel about family crises in the parish and community
5 ☐ Working with Sunday church school and/or youth program
6 ☐ Premarital, prebaptismal or other preparatory counseling
7 ☐ Personal experience as a counselee
8 ☐ Experience as a military chaplain
9 ☐ Reading and study
0 ☐ Other (Please specify)
____
____

Please list two features of **your** ministry that have seemed most effective in contributing to family stability. **(List each feature on a new line)**

15
1 ☐ ________________
2 ☐ ________________

Has your experience ministering to families made you feel the need for more thorough preparation in any area of the seminary curriculum?

16[m] **1** ☐ Yes
2 ☐ No

If so, what courses, whether or not they are now part of the regular seminary curriculum, do you feel would provide you with a more thorough preparation? **(List each course on a new line)**

17 **1** ☐ ____________
2 ☐ ____________

YOUR OPINIONS

What is your reaction to the following statement: **"The parents are the chief educators of their children in religious faith and the church school can at best only supplement their efforts." (Check the one that best expresses your views)**

18 **1** ☐ Yes, home influences are stronger than any others
2 ☐ Yes, especially if the parents are also active in the church
3 ☐ Perhaps, but community standards influence the parents' views strongly
4 ☐ True in theory, but in fact the church school does the main job
5 ☐ In this day we may have to rely upon children to educate their parents religiously
0 ☐ Other (Please explain) ____________

____

What is your reaction to the following statement: **"A church program for teaching a CHRISTIAN INTERPRETATION of sex to youth and adults is called for at this time." (Check one)**

19 **1** ☐ No, this is the privilege and main responsibility of the home alone
2 ☐ No, the schools are doing a good job at this
3 ☐ The church should help parents to do this
4 ☐ Yes, but we must not magnify this out of proportion to the total program
5 ☐ This is important enough to pursue vigorously in the church now—no one else can or will
0 ☐ Other (Please explain) ____________

____

What do you feel are the first, second, and third most important obstacles **in your community** to building Christian family life? **(Use numbers 1, 2, and 3 to show order of importance)**

20 **1** _____ Indifference and sin
2 _____ Ignorance of the meaning and practice of Christian family life
3 _____ Families divided in their religious loyalties
4 _____ Competition from too many outside activities tending to separate the family
5 _____ In many homes both parents working for wages
6 _____ Tensions created at work expressed at home
7 _____ Unchristian standards set by the neighbors
8 _____ Alcohol too easy to obtain and use
9 _____ Family altars and dining rooms disappearing
0 _____ Other (Please explain) ____________

____

Among the **Presbyterian churches** with which you are acquainted, what do you feel are the first, second, and third most important obstacles to building Christian family life? **(Use numbers 1, 2, and 3 to show order of importance)**

21

1 _____ There is no serious obstacle

2 _____ Church members are unconcerned and lacking in zealous spirit

3 _____ Teachers are too busy to work with families

4 _____ Ministers are inexperienced in working with family problems

5 _____ There is too much pressure to achieve goals irrelevant to Christian faith

6 _____ Churches are too large and impersonal

7 _____ Present programs promote separate age group activities

8 _____ They have no clear guidance for building family life

9 _____ There is no standard as to what constitutes Christian family life

0 _____ Other (Please specify) ___________

____

As you observe the home life of Presbyterian ministers, what would you say are the first, second, third, and fourth most frequently encountered problems in such families? **(Use numbers 1, 2, 3 and 4 to show the order of occurrence)**

22

1 _____ No apparent problems

2 _____ Irregular work schedule

3 _____ Too many demands on pastor that leave him without time for family

4 _____ Wife too active in church by own choice or expectation of congregation

5 _____ Pastor's work tensions that spill over into his relations with wife and children

6 _____ Family members expected to be different, even "perfect"

7 _____ Misunderstandings among family members

8 _____ Almost no one outside family with whom pastor (or a family member) can be himself and "let down his hair"

9 _____ Lack of privacy; living in a "glass house"

X _____ Religion in family becomes artificial

Y _____ Difficulty in making ends meet financially

0 _____ Other (Please specify) ___________

____

What, in your experience, do parents expect of the church?

23 ___________

____

What does the church expect of Christian families?

24 ___________

____

Which **three** of the following areas of family life education do you feel are most needed by the congregation you serve? **(Use numbers 1, 2, and and 3 to show order of importance)**

25[3]

1 ______ Adolescent boy-girl relationships
2 ______ Child Development
3 ______ Parent-child relations
4 ______ Husband-wife relations
5 ______ Preparation for marriage
6 ______ Sex and reproduction education
7 ______ Old age and retirement
8 ______ Christian interpretation of vocation
0 ______ Other (Please specify) ____________

____

ABOUT YOUR MINISTRY

Which of the following Christian family life themes did you adopt as subjects, references, or illustrations in your sermons in 1957? **(Check all that apply)**

26

1 ☐ Worship in the home
2 ☐ Sex ethics
3 ☐ Interfaith marriage
4 ☐ Christian parenthood
5 ☐ Discipline
6 ☐ Democracy in the family
7 ☐ Protestant meaning of marriage
8 ☐ Divorce
9 ☐ Handling conflict in the home
X ☐ Family crises
Y ☐ Planned parenthood
0 ☐ Other (Please specify)

____

____

Does your church use the **Christian Faith and Life** curriculum in any departments?

27[2]

1 ☐ Yes
2 ☐ No

What percentage of families with children receive the parent-teacher magazines regularly?

28[2]

____________%

Of families who receive them, what percentage, in your estimation, regularly read these magazines?

29

____________%

With which **one** of the following parent-teacher magazines are you most familiar? **(Check one)**

30

1 ☐ **Growing** (for Nursery and Kindergarten)
2 ☐ **Opening Doors** (for Primary)
3 ☐ **Discovery** (for Juniors)
4 ☐ **Counsel** (for Junior Highs)
5 ☐ **This Generation** (for Youth)
6 ☐ **Crossroads** (for Adults)
X ☐ None of them

How extensively do you read the magazine checked just above? **(Check one)**

31[m]

1 ☐ Have not looked into it during the last 3 months
2 ☐ I browse through it occasionally
3 ☐ I browse through it regularly
4 ☐ I regularly read one or two articles
5 ☐ I regularly read most or all of it

During the **last three months,** which of the following uses have you had occasion to make of **any** of the curriculum magazines listed above? **(Check all that apply)**

32[f]

1 ☐ Used it as a guide in own teaching
2 ☐ Preached on topic suggested by reading
3 ☐ Recommended an article personally or from the pulpit
4 ☐ Distributed to parent when calling
5 ☐ Read and discussed in own family
6 ☐ Used it as a worship guide in own family
0 ☐ Other (Please specify) ____________________

____

If you had your way, what **one or two** things would you change about the curriculum magazines which would increase their acceptability in the families of your congregation? **(Check one or two)**

33[m]

1 ☐ Add more Bible content
2 ☐ Use less fine print and less crowded layouts
3 ☐ Use more good cartoons and pictures
4 ☐ Simplify the vocabulary and idea level
5 ☐ Try the material out on typical parents before publication
6 ☐ Separate the material for teachers and parents into different magazines
7 ☐ Reduce the number of magazines; there is too much material
8 ☐ Use part of each issue to **sell** families who are reading for the first time
9 ☐ Satisfied with magazines as they are
X ☐ Would be unwilling to see any change
0 ☐ Other (Please describe) ____________________

____

____

In the Christian family education materials provided for churches, which **three** devices for conveying it do you feel are **most practical** in your situation at this time? **(Use numbers 1, 2, and 3 to show the order of usefulness)**

34

1 ______ Movies
2 ______ Pamphlets
3 ______ Filmstrips
4 ______ Tape recordings
5 ______ 33⅓ LP recordings
6 ______ Small books for parents
7 ______ Leaflets dealing with family problems
8 ______ Parent articles and discussion guides in curriculum magazines
0 ______ Other (Please specify) ____________

____

Below is a list of items that might be a part of your church's program. Please check in the left column if you **used** this in 1957. Please check in the right column if you **plan to use** this in 1958.

35[a]

1957	1958	
☐	☐	Preaching on family life themes
☐	☐	Adult Bible classes
☐	☐	Sunday morning **family** worship
☐	☐	Family night suppers
☐	☐	Married couples club (not Mariners)
☐	☐	Mariners
☐	☐	Mother-daughter, father-son suppers
☐	☐	Young adult group
☐	☐	Family hobby or display night
☐	☐	Premarital or family counseling
☐	☐	Parents of youth group members used as hosts or sponsors

☐ ☐ Husband-wife teaching teams
☐ ☐ Parents' discussion group using **Crossroads**
☐ ☐ Parents' study course
☐ ☐ Mothers' club
☐ ☐ Co-operative nursery school
☐ ☐ Courses on family relations
☐ ☐ Courses on preparation for marriage
☐ ☐ Family camps and retreats
☐ ☐ Prebaptismal counseling
☐ ☐ Prebaptismal class
☐ ☐ Wedding anniversary reunions
☐ ☐ Counseling about vocations

58[a] ☐ ☐ Other (Please specify) ____________
1 2

About how many hours do you spend in an average week in pastoral counseling, i.e., in discussion of personal problems presented to you in your office or in calling?

59 ________hours

Indicate first, second, third, and fourth largest categories of **problems** presented to you in pastoral counseling. **(Use numbers 1, 2, 3, and 4 to show the frequency of problems)**

60[2] _____ Husband-wife relationships
_____ Parents-child relationships
_____ Adolescent boy-girl relationships
_____ Problems involved with courtship and preparation for marriage
_____ Counseling about vocations

65[2] _____ Other counseling problems

If the problems listed below were brought to you as a pastor, on which of them would you generally feel the need for referral to, or collaboration with, a counseling specialist? **(Check all that apply)**

66[m]
1 ☐ Sexual inversion, e.g., homosexuality
2 ☐ Parent-child and disciplinary problems
3 ☐ Drinking patterns and family strife
4 ☐ Unmarried parents
5 ☐ Counseling someone you know intimately
6 ☐ Instructing couples planning marriage about sex relations
7 ☐ Persons whose marital or family problems are connected with deep neuroses
8 ☐ Family conflicts that include physical violence
0 ☐ Other (Please specify) ____________________
____

The activities listed below represent some of the phases of a minister's work. On the line next to each, rank **all** the items according to the **proportion of time you spend** on each phase in an **average week.** Use number 1 for the most time-consuming task, number 2 for the next, and so on through to number 10.

67[10]
1 _____ Counseling with people about decisions and personal problems
2 _____ Preparing and preaching sermons
3 _____ Visiting members of congregation and others in community

4 _____ Teaching classes, leading groups, and advising youth groups
5 _____ Recruiting, training and assisting lay leaders and teachers
6 _____ Following a schedule of reading and study
7 _____ Improving efficiency of church through correspondence, records, and committees
8 _____ Leading worship, administering sacraments, and officiating at weddings and funerals
9 _____ Supplying ideas and organizing people for over-all church strategy and program
10 _____ Maintaining a discipline of prayer and devotion

Now, looking over the list above, place on the line below the **number** of the activity which gives you the most personal enjoyment and sense of accomplishment.

68 __________

Again referring to the list, place on the line below the **number** of the activity which, **at the present time,** you would most want to **improve through special training** if the opportunity and time were available.

69 __________

If you would like more training in counseling, please indicate below what **kind** of counseling training you would prefer to receive **(Check one)**

70
1 □ Guided reading
2 □ Seminary course
3 □ Informal case discussion with other pastors
4 □ One- or two-day discussion seminar
5 □ Six-session practice course
6 □ One course in a minister's study retreat
7 □ Three-month clinical training
0 □ Other (Please specify) __________________
____

Do you give or lend books or pamphlets in counseling couples before their marriage?

71
1 □ Yes
2 □ No

If yes, which ones? **(List below)**
Author __________________
Title __________________
Author __________________
Title __________________

Which, if any, tests or interview guides do you use in premarital counseling? **(Check all that apply)**

72
1 □ None
2 □ The Wedding Service itself
3 □ Sex Knowledge Inventory
4 □ Something you have developed yourself
0 □ Other (Please describe and specify source) ___
____
____

Pastors differ in what they regard as appropriate in a premarital interview. Which topics are included in your counseling of couples before marriage? **(Check appropriate box for each item)**

	Always	Sometimes	Never	
73 1	☐	☐	☐	Symbolism or meaning of ceremony
2	☐	☐	☐	Religious responsibilities of new family
3	☐	☐	☐	In-law relationships
4	☐	☐	☐	Housing plans
5	☐	☐	☐	Sex attitudes or information
6	☐	☐	☐	Planned parenthood
7	☐	☐	☐	Economic arrangements
8	☐	☐	☐	Interpersonal relations between partners after marriage
9	☐	☐	☐	Religious backgrounds of couple
X	☐	☐	☐	Family backgrounds of couple
	1	2	3	

Does the high school nearest your church offer at least one course in family relations or preparation for marriage?

74 1 ☐ Yes
2 ☐ No
3 ☐ Not sure

Below is a list of resources for improving family life. Please check in **Column A** for each one that is present in your community or in one nearby. Check **Column B** also if you have ever announced this resource or used it for referral.

75[a]

A	B	
☐	☐	Public health clinic
☐	☐	Planned Parenthood Association
☐	☐	Private psychiatrists
☐	☐	Family counselors
☐	☐	Agricultural extension parent classes
☐	☐	P.T.A. parents' classes
☐	☐	Family Service Agency
☐	☐	Consulting psychologists
☐	☐	Child guidance or psychiatric clinic
☐	☐	Vocational counselors
☐	☐	Physicians
☐	☐	Alcoholics Anonymous
☐	☐	Lawyers specializing in family relations cases
☐	☐	Church counseling center
☐	☐	YM-YWCA courses on marriage
☐	☐	Other (Please specify)
1	2	________________
		________________

90[a]

FROM YOUR RECORDS

At how many weddings did the minister(s) officiate in 1957?

91[3] ________

How many persons did the minister(s) baptize in 1957?

92[3] ________children

93[3] ________adults

Approximately how many **households** are there in the membership of the church?

94[4] ________

Approximately what **percentage** of your church families move each year into a different community?

95[4] ________%

Approximately what percentage of your church families are "interfaith" families, i.e., where one or more members of the immediate family is not an adherent of a Protestant faith?

96[4] ______%

Indicate the first, second, and third largest occupational groups in the congregation. **(Use the numbers 1, 2, and 3 to show occupations)**

97[2] — Unskilled workers, farm labor, and domestic workers

98[2] — Semiskilled and service workers

99[2] — Skilled workers and foremen

100[2] — Clerks and office workers; sales

101[2] — Minor professionals and managers, small business and farm owners, sales representatives

102[2] — Major professionals, owners, and managers of large businesses and farms

Below is a list of kinds of family specialists you may have **in your congregation.** For each of them, check **Column A** if you have **one or more** such persons.
Check **Column B** also if you have ever used these persons **in their professional capacity** in your family ministry.

103[a] A B

☐ ☐ Social workers

☐ ☐ Lawyers specializing in family relations cases

☐ ☐ Nursery school teachers

☐ ☐ Physicians, general practice

☐ ☐ Physicians, obstetricians, and those working with sexual problems

☐ ☐ Psychiatrists

☐ ☐ Consulting or clinical psychologists

☐ ☐ Family counselors

☐ ☐ Hospital or prison chaplains

☐ ☐ Teaching nurses

☐ ☐ Writers in childhood education and family relations

☐ ☐ College teachers

☐ ☐ Adult education leaders

☐ ☐ YM and YWCA secretaries

☐ ☐ Public-school teachers

☐ ☐ Vocational counselors

☐ ☐ Personnel managers

120[a] ☐ ☐ Others (Please specify)

1 2 ____________________

____

Please use a blank sheet to record any further comments you would like to share, either to clarify or expand your previous answers, or to contribute ideas to this study. Enclose this with questionnaire and send to Dr. D. R. Saunders, Educational Testing Service, 20 Nassau St., Princeton, N.J.

APPENDIX VIII

The Parents' Questionnaire

Do not sign your name to the questionnaire. You will be helping churches in the U.S.A. to do a better job of family education and counseling if you will answer the following questions *frankly* and with your real feelings and experiences. There are no right or wrong answers. Check your answers in the boxes provided—i.e. (*X*). Thank you.

1. How many children do you have?

None	(__)
1	(__)
2	(__)
3	(__)
4 or more	(__)

2. What age is your *oldest* child?

Under 2½ years	(__)
2½ to 6 years	(__)
6 years to 13 years	(__)
13 years to 20 years	(__)
Over 20 years	(__)

3. What is your sex?

Male	(__)
Female	(__)

4. What is your marital status?

Married and living with original husband or wife	(__)
Divorced and remarried	(__)
Divorced and not now married	(__)
Widowed and not now married	(__)
Widowed and remarried	(__)
Currently separated	(__)

5. Where did you grow up (where you spent most of your childhood), and where do you live now?

	Grew Up	*Now*
On a farm	(__)	(__)
Village of less than 2,500	(__)	(__)
Town of 2,500 to 10,000	(__)	(__)
Town of 10,000 to 100,000	(__)	(__)
Large city of 100,000 or more	(__)	(__)
Suburb of a metropolitan city	(__)	(__)

6. How old are you? (check correct range)

Under 20	(__)
20–24	(__)
25–34	(__)
35–44	(__)
45–54	(__)
55–64	(__)
65 or over	(__)

7. How much education have you had?

Grade school or less	(__)
Some high school	(__)
Graduated high school	(__)
Some college	(__)
Graduated college	(__)

Graduate work beyond college .... (__)
Other (write in) .... (__)

8. Have you taught a Sunday school class during the last year?
Yes, regularly .... (__)
Yes, but not regularly .... (__)
No .... (__)

9. How often do you attend Sunday worship services? (check according to your usual practice)
At least three times a month .... (__)
About twice a month .... (__)
About once every three months .... (__)
About once or twice a year .... (__)
Less than once a year .... (__)

10. At your family meals does anyone say grace or give thanks to God at mealtime daily?
Yes .... (__)
No .... (__)

11. Does your family worship at home as a group using prayer and Bible or devotional readings?
Never .... (__)
Once a year or less .... (__)
At selected holidays only .... (__)
At least monthly but not every week .... (__)
At least weekly but not every day .... (__)
Every day .... (__)

12. *Taking your personal family situation into account* and the age of your children, would your family be likely to begin family worship at home (or worship there more often) if good materials and guidance in using them were provided for the parents?
Would not .... (__)
Probably would not .... (__)
Probably would .... (__)
Definitely would .... (__)

13. Do you read *Presbyterian Life* magazine?
Yes .... (__)
No .... (__)

14. Do you think the churches should provide more help than they do now in interpreting sex and reproduction from a Christian standpoint?
Yes .... (__)
No .... (__)
Not sure .... (__)

15. Our family receives the following parent-teacher magazines from the church: (check which)
    Growing (for Nursery and Kindergarten) .... (__)
    Opening Doors (for Primary) .... (__)
    Discovery (for Juniors) .... (__)
    Counsel (for Junior Highs) .... (__)
    This Generation (for Youth) .... (__)
    Crossroads (for Adults) .... (__)
    None of them, as far as I know .... (__)

16. Do you read this curriculum magazine (or these magazines if you receive more than one)? Check *one.*
    Regularly most or all of it .... (__)
    Regularly one or two articles .... (__)
    Occasionally .... (__)
    Not in the last three months .... (__)
    Never .... (__)

17. Check any items below which express your *personal opinions* about the magazines listed above.
    I'm not well enough acquainted with any of them to have any reaction .... (__)
    I think the magazines are good as they stand .... (__)
    I don't know how I am expected to use these magazines as a parent .... (__)
    I don't have time to read any of the magazines ...... (__)
    They are interesting to me and not too difficult to understand .... (__)
    There are too many curriculum magazines to read or too much material to cover .... (__)
    They are too technically religious; we need something simpler .... (__)
    I'm not really interested in the content of the magazines I've seen .... (__)
    I usually try to find out from the magazines what my child is being taught in Sunday school on a given Sunday .... (__)
    I think the magazines should be distributed to parents in a better way in our church .... (__)
    The magazine articles have helped me over some rough spots in my own family living .... (__)
    The magazines carry too many psychology articles .... (__)
    I would be more likely to read the articles if they were to be discussed in a parents' group .... (__)
    My husband or wife knows the magazines better than I do .... (__)
    Other (write in)
    ____ (__)

18. With which of the following three opinions are you in *closest* agreement? (*check one only*)

"It is the church school which should do the major job of Christian education of children; parents are a minor influence in this process." .... (__)
"It is the parents who are the chief educators of their children in religious faith and the church school can at best only supplement their efforts." .... (__)
"Parents and church school are both influential in the Christian education of the child, but parents need as much help (through adult education in the church) as children in understanding Christian faith." .... (__)

19. How much help in understanding yourself in your family relations have you received from the following *church experiences?* (check in one column for each item)

	None	*Some*	*Much*
Sermons and congregational worship ..	(__)	(__)	(__)
Church classes or groups with other parents	(__)	(__)	(__)
Talking with the pastor or other church worker	(__)	(__)	(__)
Parents' curriculum magazines	(__)	(__)	(__)
Presbyterian Life magazine	(__)	(__)	(__)
Personal friendships within the congregation	(__)	(__)	(__)
Books and pamphlets on family living	(__)	(__)	(__)
Teaching Sunday school or working with youth groups	(__)	(__)	(__)
Other (please write in) ______________________________	(__)	(__)	(__)

20. What is the occupation of the *head of the household?* (write in and be as specific as possible)

21. Most parents know of some things about life in their family which disturbed them, things needing improvement. Remembering this questionnaire is anonymous, will you please check those items which you saw as a problem needing solution during the past year.
TV and radio listening habits .... (__)
Health of family members .... (__)
Lack of closeness between brothers and sisters ...... (__)
Your recreation and leisure time, including visiting .. (__)
Too little time spent together as a family .... (__)
Your community as a place to live .... (__)
Your children's achievement .... (__)
Conflict of religious views in family .... (__)
Family's housing and furniture .... (__)
How children are disciplined .... (__)
Husband's job and its demands .... (__)
Drinking by family members .... (__)

Tenseness and low morale in family .... (__)
Amount of income .... (__)
Lack of closeness between husband and wife .... (__)
Religious life and church participation of family ...... (__)
Who does what among family responsibilities ...... (__)
How income is spent .... (__)
Your family's community activity .... (__)
Wife's work at home or outside home .... (__)
Your family's action for community and world betterment .... (__)
Sex relations with mate .... (__)
Behavior of children .... (__)
Friendships of family members .... (__)
Other (please be specific)
____ (__)

22. Which of the following areas of family life education do you feel your local church ought to stress at this time? (check two which seem most needed as you view the families of the congregation and community)
Adolescent boy-girl relations .... (__)
Child development .... (__)
Parent-child relations .... (__)
Husband-wife relations .... (__)
Preparation for marriage .... (__)
Christian sex and reproduction education .... (__)
Old age and retirement .... (__)
Christian interpretation of vocation .... (__)
Other (please write in)
____ (__)

23. What would you hope for your children in their experience in the church?

24. What kinds of things do you want your children to remember about your family life when they grow up?

25. In what ways would you change your church's present program to make it more helpful to families?

THANK YOU FOR YOUR ASSISTANCE

LIST OF SOURCES

Books

ADAMS, CLIFFORD, *Preparing for Marriage.* New York: E. P. Dutton & Co., 1952.

ALLPORT, GORDON, *The Individual and His Religion.* New York: The Macmillan Company, 1950.

ANDERSON, PHOEBE, *Religious Living with Nursery Children.* Boston: Pilgrim Press, 1956.

BABER, RAY E., *Marriage and the Family.* New York: McGraw-Hill Book Co., Inc., 1953.

BAILEY, DERRICK SHERWIN, *Sexual Relation in Christian Thought.* New York: Harper & Brothers, 1959.

———, *The Mystery of Love and Marriage.* New York: Harper & Brothers, 1952.

BAINTON, ROLAND H., *The Reformation of the Sixteenth Century.* Boston: Beacon Press, 1952.

———, *What Christianity Says About Sex, Love, and Marriage.* New York: Association Press, 1957.

BARCLAY, WILLIAM, *Train Up a Child.* Philadelphia: The Westminster Press, 1959.

BARTH, MARKUS, *The Broken Wall.* Philadelphia: Judson Press, 1959.

BECKER, HOWARD, and HILL, REUBEN, eds., *Family, Marriage, and Parenthood.* Boston: D. C. Heath and Co., 1955.

BERDYAEV, NICOLAS, *Slavery and Freedom.* New York: Charles Scribner's Sons, 1944.

BERGLER, EDMUND, *Divorce Won't Help.* New York: Harper & Brothers, 1948.

BERNARD, JESSIE, *Remarriage: A Study of Marriage.* New York: The Dryden Press, 1956.

BOISEN, ANTON T., *Religion in Crisis and Custom: A Sociological and Psychological Study.* New York: Harper & Brothers, 1955.

BONHOEFFER, DIETRICH, *Ethics*. New York: The Macmillan Company, 1955.

BOSSARD, JAMES H. S., *Parent and Child*. Philadelphia: University of Pennsylvania Press, 1953.

———, and BOLL, ELEANOR S., *Ritual in Family Living*. Philadelphia: University of Pennsylvania Press, 1950.

———, and BOLL, ELEANOR S., *The Sociology of Child Development*. New York: Harper & Brothers, 1948.

BOWMAN, HENRY A., *Marriage for Moderns*. New York: McGraw-Hill Book Co., Inc., 1954.

———, *A Christian Interpretation of Marriage*. Philadelphia: The Westminster Press, 1959.

BRIM, ORVILLE G., JR., *Education for Child Rearing*. New York: Russell Sage Foundation, 1959.

BRUNNER, EMIL, *The Divine Imperative*. Philadelphia: The Westminster Press, 1957.

———, *Man in Revolt*. New York: Charles Scribner's Sons, 1939.

BUELL, BRADLEY, BEISSER, PAUL T., *et al., Classification of Disorganized Families for Use in Family Oriented Diagnosis and Treatment*. New York: Community Research Associates, 1954.

BULTMANN, RUDOLF, *The Theology of the New Testament*, Vol. II. New York: Charles Scribner's Sons, 1951.

BURGESS, ERNEST W., and WALLIN, PAUL, *Engagement and Marriage*. Philadelphia: J. B. Lippincott Co., 1953.

———, and LOCKE, HARVEY J., *The Family: From Institution to Companionship*. American Book Company, 1953.

BURROWS, MILLAR, *An Outline of Biblical Theology*. Philadelphia: The Westminster Press, 1946.

BUSHNELL, HORACE, *Christian Nurture*. New York: Charles Scribner, 1888.

CALHOUN, ARTHUR W., *Social History of the American Family*, Vol. II. Worcester, Mass.: Clark University Press, 1917.

CANTRIL, HADLEY, *The Psychology of Social Movements*. New York: John Wiley & Sons, Inc., 1941.

CASTEEL, JOHN, *Spiritual Renewal Through Personal Groups*. New York: Association Press, 1957.

CAVAN, RUTH S., *The American Family*. New York: Thomas Y. Crowell, 1955.

CLARK, ELMER T., *The Small Sects in America*. Nashville, Tenn.: Abingdon-Cokesbury Press, 1949.

CLEMMONS, ROBERT S., *Young Adults in the Church*. Nashville, Tenn.: Abingdon Press, 1959.

COLE, WILLIAM GRAHAM, *Sex and Love in the Bible*. New York: Association Press, 1959.

———, *Sex in Christianity and Psychoanalysis*. New York: Oxford University Press, Inc., 1955.

COME, ARNOLD, *Agents of Reconciliation*. Philadelphia: The Westminster Press, 1960.

DE DIETRICH, SUZANNE, *The Witnessing Community*. Philadelphia: The Westminster Press, 1958.

DILLENBERGER, JOHN, and WELCH, CLAUDE, *Protestant Christianity: Interpreted Through Its Development*. New York: Charles Scribner's Sons, 1958.

DILLISTONE, FREDERICK W., *The Structure of the Divine Society*. Philadelphia: The Westminster Press, 1951.

DONIGER, SIMON, ed., *Sex and Religion Today*. New York: Association Press, 1954.

DUVALL, EVELYN M., *Family Development*. Philadelphia: J. B. Lippincott Co., 1957.

———, and HILL, REUBEN, *When You Marry*. Boston: D. C. Heath and Co., 1953.

———, and DUVALL, SYLVANUS, eds., *Sex Ways in Fact and Faith*. New York: Association Press, 1961.

ELMSLIE, W. A. L., *How Came Our Faith*. New York: Cambridge University Press, 1948.

EMERSON, JAMES G., *Divorce, The Church, and Remarriage*. Philadelphia: The Westminster Press, 1961.

ERNSBERGER, DAVID J., *A Philosophy of Adult Christian Education*. Philadelphia: The Westminster Press, 1959.

FAGLEY, RICHARD M., *The Population Explosion and Christian Responsibility*. New York: Oxford University Press, Inc., 1960.

Family Today, The, Lambeth Conference 1958. The National Council, Episcopal Church.

FEUCHT, OSCAR E., *et al., Engagement and Marriage*. St. Louis, Mo.: Concordia Publishing House, 1959.

———, *et al., Helping Families Through the Church*. St. Louis, Mo.: Concordia Publishing House, 1957.

———, *et al., The Church and Sex Attitudes*. St. Louis, Mo.: Concordia Publishing House, 1957.

FREEDMAN, RONALD, WHELPTON, P. K., and CAMPBELL, ARTHUR, *Family Planning, Sterility, and Population Growth*. New York: McGraw-Hill Book Co., Inc., 1959.

FOOTE, NELSON N., and COTTRELL, LEONARD S., JR., *Identity and Interpersonal Competence*. Chicago: University of Chicago Press, 1955.

FROMM, ERICH, *The Art of Loving*. New York: Harper & Brothers, 1956.

———, *The Sane Society*. New York: Rinehart & Co., Inc., 1955.

GLICK, PAUL C., *The American Family, A Factual Background*. U.S. Government Printing Office, 1949.

GOODE, WILLIAM J., *After Divorce*. Chicago: Free Press, 1956.

GUILLAMONT, A., *et al.,* ed. and trans., *The Gospel According to Thomas*. New York: Harper & Brothers, 1959.

GURIN, GERALD, VEROFF, JOSEPH, and FELD, SHEILA, *Americans View Their Mental Health*. New York: Basic Books, Inc., 1960.

HALVERSON, MARVIN, ed., *A Handbook of Christian Theology*. New York: Meridian Books, 1958.

HATT, P. K., and REISS, A. J., JR., eds., *Reader in Urban Sociology*. Chicago: Free Press, 1951.

HAZLITT, WILLIAM, ed. and trans., *The Table Talk of Martin Luther*. London: George Bell, 1895.

HERBERG, WILL, *Protestant-Catholic-Jew.* New York: Doubleday & Company, Inc., 1956.

HESS, ROBERT D., and HANDEL, GERALD, *Family Worlds: A Psychosocial Approach to Family Life.* Chicago: University of Chicago Press, 1959.

HILL, REUBEN, *Families Under Stress: Adjustment to the Crisis of War Separation and Reunion.* New York: Harper & Brothers, 1949.

HILTNER, SEWARD, *Sex and the Christian Life.* New York: Association Press, 1957.

———, *Sex Ethics and the Kinsey Report.* New York: Association Press, 1953.

HORDERN, WILLIAM, *A Layman's Guide to Protestant Theology.* New York: The Macmillan Company, 1955.

HOWE, REUEL L., *The Creative Years.* Greenwich, Conn.: Seabury Press, Inc., 1959.

JACOBI, JOLANDE, ed., *Psychological Reflections—An Anthology from the Writings of C. G. Jung.* New York: Pantheon Books, Inc., 1953.

JACOBS, C. M., *et al.*, trans., *The Works of Martin Luther,* III. Philadelphia: A. J. Holman Co., 1930.

JENKINS, DANIEL, *The Protestant Ministry.* New York: Doubleday & Company, Inc., 1958.

———, *Tradition, Freedom, and the Spirit.* Philadelphia: The Westminster Press, 1951.

JOHNSON, ROBERT CLYDE, *Authority in Protestant Theology.* Philadelphia: The Westminster Press, 1959.

KEMP, CHARLES F., *The Pastor and Community Resources.* St. Louis, Mo.: Bethany Press, 1960.

KINSEY, ALFRED C., POMEROY, WARDELL B., and MARTIN, CLYDE E., *Sexual Behavior in the Human Male.* Philadelphia: W. B. Saunders Co., 1948.

———, *Sexual Behavior in the Human Female.* Philadelphia: W. B. Saunders Co., 1953.

KIRKPATRICK, CLIFFORD, *The Family: As Process and Institution.* New York: The Ronald Press Co., 1955.

KOMAROVSKY, MIRRA, *Women in the Modern World: Their Education and Their Dilemmas.* Boston: Little, Brown and Co., 1953.

KOOS, EARL L., *Families in Trouble.* New York: Kings Crown Press, 1946.

KRAEMER, HENDRICK, *A Theology of the Laity.* Philadelphia: The Westminster Press, 1958.

KUHN, ANNE L., *The Mother's Role in Childhood Education: New England Concepts 1830–1860.* New Haven, Conn.: Yale University Press, 1947.

LANDIS, JUDSON T., and LANDIS, MARY G., *Building a Successful Marriage.* Englewood Cliffs, N.J.: Prentice-Hall, Inc., 1953.

MACE, DAVID, *Whom God Hath Joined.* Philadelphia: The Westminster Press, 1953.

MARTY, MARTIN E., *The New Shape of American Religion.* New York: Harper & Brothers, 1959.

MEAD, MARGARET, *Male and Female.* New York: William Morrow and Co., Inc., 1949.

MILLER, DANIEL R., and SWANSON, GUY E., *The Changing American Parent*. New York: John Wiley & Sons, Inc., 1958.

MINEAR, PAUL S., *Jesus and His People*. New York: Association Press, 1956.

NICHOLS, JAMES HASTINGS, *Primer for Protestants*. New York: Association Press, 1947.

NIEBUHR, H. RICHARD, *Christ and Culture*. New York: Harper & Brothers, 1951.

———, *The Social Sources of Denominationalism*. New York: Henry Holt and Co., Inc., 1929. Hamden, Conn.: Shoe String Press, 1954.

———, and WILLIAMS, DANIEL DAY, eds., *The Ministry in Historical Perspective*. New York: Harper & Brothers, 1956.

———, WILLIAMS, DANIEL DAY, and GUSTAFSON, JAMES F., *The Advancement of Theological Education*. New York: Harper & Brothers, 1957.

———, WILLIAMS, DANIEL DAY, and GUSTAFSON, JAMES F., *The Purpose of the Church and Its Ministry*. New York: Harper & Brothers, 1956.

NILES, D. T., *The Preacher's Task and the Stone of Stumbling*. New York: Harper & Brothers, 1958.

NISBET, ROBERT A., *The Quest for Community*. New York: Oxford University Press, Inc., 1953.

OGBURN, W. F., and NIMKOFF, M. F., *Technology and the Changing Family*. Boston: Houghton Mifflin Co., 1955.

PATAI, RAPHAEL, *Sex and Family in the Bible and the Middle East*. New York: Doubleday & Co., Inc., 1959.

PAUCK, WILHELM, *The Heritage of the Reformation*. Chicago: Free Press, 1950.

PIPER, OTTO A., *The Christian Interpretation of Sex*. New York: Charles Scribner's Sons, 1941.

PEDERSEN, JOHANNES, *Israel: Its Life and Culture*. New York: Oxford University Press, Inc., 1940.

PETERSON, JAMES, *Education for Marriage*. New York: Charles Scribner's Sons, 1956.

PLOSCOWE, MORRIS, *The Truth About Divorce*. New York: Hawthorn Books, Inc., 1954.

QUEENER, LLEWELYN, *Introduction to Social Psychology*. New York: William Sloane Associates, 1951.

RICHARDSON, ALAN, ed., *A Theological Wordbook of the Bible*. New York: The Macmillan Company, 1955.

RIESMAN, DAVID, GLAZER, NATHAN, and DENNY, REUEL, *The Lonely Crowd*. New Haven, Conn.: Yale University Press, 1950.

ROSSI, PETER H., *Why Families Move*. Chicago: Free Press, 1956.

RUESCH, JURGEN, and BATESON, GREGORY, *Communication: The Social Matrix of Psychiatry*. New York: W. W. Norton & Co., Inc., 1951.

SEELEY, JOHN R., SIM, R. ALEXANDER, and LOOSLEY, E. W., *Crestwood Heights: A Study of the Culture of Suburban Life*. New York: Basic Books, Inc., 1956.

SHERRILL, LEWIS J., *Family and Church*. Nashville, Tenn.: Abingdon-Cokesbury Press, 1937.

———, *The Gift of Power*. New York: The Macmillan Company, 1955.
SIRJAMAKI, JOHN, *The American Family in the Twentieth Century*. Cambridge, Mass.: Harvard University Press, 1953.
SMART, JAMES D., *The Teaching Ministry of the Church*. Philadelphia: The Westminster Press, 1954.
TAYLOR, KATHARINE W., *Parent-Cooperative Nursery Schools*. New York: Teachers College, Columbia University, 1954.
TERMAN, LEWIS M., *Psychological Factors in Marital Happiness*. New York: McGraw-Hill Book Co., Inc., 1938.
THOMAS, JOHN L., S. J., *The American Catholic Family*. Englewood, N.J.: Prentice-Hall, Inc., 1956.
TILLICH, PAUL, *The New Being*. New York: Charles Scribner's Sons, 1955.
TOURNIER, PAUL, *The Meaning of Persons*. New York: Harper & Brothers, 1957.
UNDERWOOD, KENNETH, *Protestant and Catholic*. Boston: Beacon Press, 1957.
WALLER, WILLARD, and HILL, REUBEN, *The Family: A Dynamic Interpretation*. New York: The Dryden Press, Inc., 1951.
WARNER, W. LLOYD, *et al., Social Classes in America*. New York: Science Research Associates, 1959.
———, *et al., Who Shall Be Educated?* New York: Harper & Brothers, 1944.
———, and WARNER, M. H., *What You Should Know About Social Class*. New York: Science Research Associates, 1953.
WEATHERHEAD, LESLIE, *The Mastery of Sex Through Psychology and Religion*. New York: The Macmillan Company, 1932.
WELCH, CLAUDE, *The Reality of the Church*. New York: Charles Scribner's Sons, 1958.
WHALE, JOHN S., *Christian Doctrine*. New York: Cambridge University Press, 1941.
WHYTE, WILLIAM H., JR., *Is Anybody Listening?* New York: Simon and Schuster, Inc., 1952.
———, *The Organization Man*. New York: Doubleday & Co., Inc., 1957.
WINCH, ROBERT F., *The Modern Family*. New York: Henry Holt and Co., Inc., 1952.
WINTER, GIBSON, *Love and Conflict*. New York: Doubleday & Co., Inc., 1957.
WISE, CARROLL A., *Pastoral Counseling*. New York: Harper & Brothers, 1951.
WYLIE, WILLIAM P., *Human Nature and Christian Marriage*. New York: Association Press, 1958.
WYNN, J. C., *How Christian Parents Face Family Problems*. Philadelphia: The Westminster Press, 1955.
———, ed., *Sermons on Marriage and Family Life*. Nashville, Tenn.: Abingdon Press, 1956.
———, *Pastoral Ministry to Families*. Philadelphia: The Westminster Press, 1957.

Articles and Periodicals

Aberle, D. F., and Naegele, Kaspar E., "Middle Class Father's Occupational Role and Attitudes Toward Children," *The American Journal of Orthopsychiatry,* Vol. 22, 1952.

Allport, Gordon W., Gillespie, J. M., and Young, J., "The Religion of the Post-War College Student," *Journal of Psychology,* Vol. 25, 1948.

American Catholic Hierarchy, "The Christian Family," *The Catholic Mind,* Vol. 43, February, 1950.

Anders, Sarah Frances, "Religious Behavior of Church Families," *Marriage and Family Living,* February, 1955.

Axelrod, M., "Urban Structure and Social Participation," *American Sociological Review,* Vol. 21, February, 1956.

Benson, Purnell, "Familism and Marital Success," *Social Forces,* Vol. 33, March, 1955.

Blizzard, Samuel W., "Role Conflicts of the Urban Protestant Parish Minister," *The Urban Church,* Vol. VII, No. 4, September, 1956.

———, "The Minister's Dilemma," *The Christian Century,* April 25, 1956.

———, "The Protestant Minister's Integrating Roles," *Religious Education,* July–August, 1958.

Bossard, James H. S., "Family Life: Conversation Is the Key," *Presbyterian Life,* January 25, 1958.

———, and Boll, Eleanor S., "Marital Unhappiness in the Life Cycle," *Marriage and Family Living,* February, 1958.

———, and Boll, Eleanor S., "Some Neglected Areas of Family Life Study," *Annals of the American Academy of Political and Social Science,* November, 1950.

———, and Letts, Harold C., "Mixed Marriages Involving Lutherans—A Research Report," *Marriage and Family Living,* November, 1956.

Braden, Charles S., "Churches of the Dispossessed," *The Christian Century,* January 26, 1944.

Brown, James Stephen, "Social Class, Intermarriage, and Church Membership in a Kentucky Community," *American Journal of Sociology,* Vol. 57, November, 1951.

Christensen, Harold T., and Meissner, Hanna H., "Studies in Child Spacing III. Premarital Pregnancy as a Factor in Divorce," *American Sociological Review,* Vol. 19, December, 1953.

Dinkel, R. M., "Attitudes of Children Toward Supporting Aged Parents," *American Sociological Review,* Vol. 9, 1944.

Douglass, Truman B., "The Job the Protestants Shirk," *Harper's Magazine,* November, 1958.

Duvall, Evelyn M., "Implications of Different Conceptions of Motherhood, Fatherhood, and Childhood," *Human Development Bulletin,* January, 1950.

Fairchild, Roy W., "The Church Faces a Changing Family," *Social Progress,* May, 1957.

———, "Variety in Premarital Counseling," *Pastoral Psychology,* December, 1959.

———, and WYNN, J. C., "As the Family Sees the Church," *Presbyterian Life,* October 15, 1959.
———, and WYNN, J. C., "The Dilemmas of Parents," *Presbyterian Life,* November 1, 1959.
FOOTE, NELSON N., "Changes in American Marriage Patterns," *Eugenics Quarterly,* Vol. I, No. 4, December, 1954.
———, "Family Living as Play," *Marriage and Family Living,* Vol. XVII, No. 4, November, 1955.
———, "The Appraisal of Family Research," *Marriage and Family Living,* Vol. XIX, No. 1, February, 1957.
FRANCIS, ROY G., RAMSEY, CHARLES E., and TOEWS, JACOB A., "The Church in the Rural Fringe," *Minnesota Farm and Home Science,* February, 1955.
GILL, THEODORE A., C.B.S. "Church of the Air," Seminary Sunday Sermon, January 11, 1959.
GLICK, PAUL C., "The Life Cycle of the Family," *Marriage and Family Living,* February, 1955.
GOLDSCHMIDT, WALTER, "Class Denominationalism in Rural California Churches," *American Journal of Sociology,* Vol. 49, January, 1944.
HARRIS, DALE B., "Stand Up and Choose," *Presbyterian Life,* May 17, 1958.
HORDERN, WILLIAM, "America's Religious Revival," *Advance,* June 28, 1957.
Information Service, "Birth Control and International Development," "Social Class and the Churches," Bureau of Research and Survey, National Council of the Churches of Christ in the U.S.A., Vol. XXXVII, No. 12, June 14, 1958.
JACOBSEN, ALVER H., "Conflict of Attitudes Toward the Roles of the Husband and Wife in Marriage," *American Sociological Review,* Vol. 19, April, 1954.
KLUCKHOHN, F., "What's Wrong with the American Family?" *Journal of Social Hygiene,* June, 1950.
KOEHLER, JOHN G., "The Minister as a Family Man," *Pastoral Psychology,* September, 1960.
LERNER, MAX, "The Ordeal of American Women," *The Saturday Review,* October 12, 1957.
LE MASTERS, E. E., "Parenthood as Crisis," *Marriage and Family Living,* November, 1957.
LEW, EDWARD A., *Profile of the American Family,* Metropolitan Life Insurance Co., 1956.
MARTY, MARTIN E., "The New Establishment," *The Christian Century,* October 15, 1958.
MEAD, MARGARET, "American Man in a Woman's World," *The New York Times Magazine,* February 10, 1957.
Metropolitan Life Insurance Company, "The Marriage Rate and the Business Cycle," *Statistical Bulletin,* Vol. XIX, No. 7.
New York Times, April 24, 1957, for article on study made by home economists of the Department of Agriculture on changes in recreational habits.
OGBURN, W. F., "Implications of the Rising Standard of Living in the

United States," *American Journal of Sociology,* Vol. LX, No. 6, May, 1955.

ORT, ROBERT, "A Study of Role-Conflicts as Related to Happiness in Marriage," *Journal of Abnormal and Social Psychology,* Vol. XLV, No. 4, October, 1950.

REISSMAN, LEONARD, "Levels of Aspiration and Social Class," *American Sociological Review,* Vol. XVIII, June, 1953.

SIRJAMAKI, JOHN, "Culture Configurations in the American Family," *American Journal of Sociology,* Vol. LIII, No. 1, July, 1947.

SITTLER, JOSEPH, "The Maceration of the Minister," *The Christian Century,* June 10, 1959.

SOCIAL PROGRESS, "United Presbyterians Speak—1959," July, 1959.

STENDLER, C. N., "Social Class Differences in Parental Attitude Toward School at Grade I Level," *Child Development,* Vol. XXII, No. 1, March, 1951.

WEEKS, H. ASHLEY, "Differential Divorce Rates by Occupations," *Social Forces,* Vol. 21, 1953.

WHELPTON, P. K., and KISER, C. V., "Social and Psychological Factors Affecting Fertility," *The Milbank Memorial Fund Quarterly,* Vol. XXI, No. 3, July, 1943.

WHITMAN, HOWARD, "Keeping Our Sanity—VII," *The Philadelphia Evening Bulletin,* April 8, 1957.

"Why Church Family Camping?" *Adult Times,* Vol. II, No. 3, Winter, 1958–1959, United Presbyterian Board of Christian Education.

WHYTE, WILLIAM H., JR., "Budgetism: Opiate of the Middle Class," *Fortune,* May, 1956.

———, "The Wife Problem," *Life,* January 7, 1952.

WYNN, J. C., "What Is TV Doing to Children?" *Presbyterian Life,* January 19, 1957.

Unpublished Material

BUERKLE, JOHN V., and BADGLEY, ROBIN F., "A Study of Marital Interaction" (mimeographed).

GREER, SCOTT, "Individual Participation in Mass Society" (mimeographed). Prepared for Conference on the Study of the Community, Northwestern University, March 15–17, 1956.

JOHNSON, ROBERT CLYDE, and WIEST, WALTER E., "Can There Be a Protestant Theology of the Family?" (mimeographed). Presented to Consultative Conference on Theology and Family, Atlantic City, October 17–20, 1957.

LYNN, ROBERT W., "Fifty Church Families and Their Role Expectations" (mimeographed). Presented to Consultative Conference on Theology and Family, Atlantic City, October 17–20, 1957.

MUDD, EMILY H., and HILL, REUBEN, "Memorandum on Strengthening Family Life in the United States" (mimeographed). A report to the Department of Health, Education, and Welfare of the Social Security Administration, 1956.

RAINWATER, LEE, "The Family Relationships of the Working Class Housewife" (mimeographed), July, 1958.

SPAULDING, HELEN F., and WILL, DAVID W., "A Study of the Church Relationships of Parents and Children in the Elementary Division of the Church School" (mimeographed). Bureau of Research and Survey, National Council of the Churches of Christ in the U.S.A., 1958.

STROMMEN, MERTON *et al., Lutheran Youth Research* (mimeographed), 6 volumes, 1960.

WHITMAN, LAURIS B., SPAULDING, HELEN F., and DIMOCK, ALICE, "A Study of the Summertime Activities of Children in Relation to the Summer Program of the Churches" (mimeographed). Bureau of Research and Survey, National Council of the Churches of Christ in the U.S.A., 1959.

WINTER, GIBSON, "Marriage and Family in Christian Thought" (mimeographed). Presented to Consultative Conference on Theology and Family, Atlantic City, October 17–20, 1957.

WILLIAMSON, ROBERT, "Economic Factors in Marital Adjustment," Unpublished Doctoral Dissertation, University of Southern California Library, Los Angeles, California, June, 1951.

WILMORE, GAYRAUD, "The Church as a Redemptive Fellowship" (mimeographed), 1959.

INDEX

Index

L

M

N

O

S

T

U

V

W

Y